Qualitative Research Design for Software Users

Qualitative Research Design for Software Users

Silvana di Gregorio and Judith Davidson

Open University Press

Open University Press
McGraw-Hill Education
McGraw-Hill House
Shoppenhangers Road
Maidenhead
Berkshire
England
SL6 2QL

email: enquiries@openup.co.uk
world wide web: www.openup.co.uk

and Two Penn Plaza, New York, NY 10121-2289, USA

First published 2008

A catalogue record of this book is available from the British Library

ISBN-13: 978 0 335 225217 (pb)
ISBN-13: 978 0 335 225200 (hb)

Library of Congress Cataloging-in-Publication Data
CIP data applied for

Typeset by RefineCatch Limited, Bungay, Suffolk
Printed in the UK by Bell and Bain Ltd., Glasgow

Fictitious names of companies, products, people, characters and/or data that may be used herein (in case studies or in examples) are not intended to represent any real individual, company, product or event.

*The **McGraw·Hill** Companies*

Contents

Figures

Tables

Project researchers

We would like to thank these researchers for allowing us to make their projects transparent in order to illustrate features of our design framework.

Chapter 6

Laura Richards-Gray

Laura Richards-Gray worked as a Research Manager for the Audit Commission until September 2006. She worked on a number of large-scale research projects relating to local and regional government, and consultation projects relating to Comprehensive Performance Assessments for local councils. Since then she has been a Senior Policy Officer for the Liberal Democrats, working across a number of policy areas. Most recently Laura joined Ipsos MORI as a Research Manager specializing in local and regional government.

She is an experienced interviewer and has commissioned and managed numerous quantitative and qualitative research projects, as well as conducting analysis in house.

Laura is also a local Councillor in the Borough of Hertsmere.

Chapter 7

Jessica Vince
Associate Director
Ipsos MORI
79–81 Borough Road
London, SE1 1FY
United Kingdom

jessica.vince@ipsos-mori.com

Jessica Vince is an Associate Director and Head of Ipsos MORI's Regeneration and Planning Research Unit. As well as leading on best practice and coordinating work within this sector, Jessica has extensive experience working with government and public sector clients. She has specialized in large-scale social surveys, including the New Deal for Communities national evaluation and the Local Areas element for Communities and Local Government's Citizenship Survey. Jessica is an experienced qualitative researcher and is a core member of the Ipsos MORI Participation Unit which looks at innovative ways to meaningfully engage people in the decision-making process.

Sara Butler
Associate Director
Ipsos MORI
79–81 Borough Road
London, SE1 1FY
United Kingdom

sara.butler@ipsos-mori.com

Sara Butler is an Associate Director in Ipsos MORI's Hothouse. Her fields of expertise include researching hard-to-reach and vulnerable groups in the areas of crime, health and housing, as well as designing and directing large-scale policy-driven consultations for a number of government departments. She has been instrumental in helping the team develop innovative methodologies, in particular video-based ethnographic research. Sara also leads on qualitative training, both within the organization and for external clients.

Chapter 8

Markella B. Rutherford
Assistant Professor of Sociology
Wellesley College
106 Central Street
Wellesley, MA 02481
United States

mrutherf@wellesley.edu

Markella Rutherford is Assistant Professor of Sociology at Wellesley College, in Wellesley, Massachusetts, where she teaches courses on social theory, culture and social inequality. She is currently preparing a book manuscript entitled *In Choice We Trust: Contemporary American Rites of Passage and the Sacredness of Individual Autonomy*. The book provides a tour of the key transitions that make up the family life cycle in contemporary US culture, including graduation, marriage, birth and childrearing, drawing attention to the ways that each of these contemporary transitions ritualizes individual autonomy and reflects the growing autonomy of women since the 1970s.

Selina Gallo-Cruz
PhD candidate
Emory University
Sociology Department
1555 Dickey Drive
Atlanta, GA. 30322
United States

scruzch@emory.edu

Selina Gallo-Cruz is a PhD candidate in Sociology at Emory University. She currrently studies social movements with a focus on social movement tactics.

Chapter 9

Carolyn Siccama
EdD, RD, Distance Learning Faculty Coordinator
University of Massachusetts Lowell
One University Avenue
Continuing Studies and Corporate Education
Lowell, MA 01854
United States

Carolyn_Siccama@uml.edu

Carolyn Siccama is the Distance Learning Faculty Coordinator at the University of Massachusetts Lowell Continuing Studies and Corporate Education. Siccama has a strong interest in how qualitative research software, such as NVivo, can be used to enhance the validity of qualitative research. Siccama is also interested in finding new techniques on how to blend narrative descriptions and visual representations as a way to share the process and outcomes of data analysis. Dr Siccama is a member of the University of Massachusetts Lowell Qualitative Research Network and is also a member of the team who assisted in the development of the *Qualitative Research and Design Using NVivo* training course offered by UMass Lowell Continuing Studies and Corporate Education and the UMass Lowell Qualitative Research Network.

Chapter 10

Stacy L. Penna
EdD, Business Development Manager
QSR International
QSR International Pty Ltd
225-R Concord Avenue
Cambridge, MA 02138
United States

s.penna@qsrinternational.com

Stacy completed her doctoral degree in the Leadership in Education Program at the University of Massachusetts Lowell, graduating in June of 2007. She previously had experience and training in international relations (she earned a BA in International Relations in 1990 from Connecticut College), business (she worked for two corporate companies, Pitney Bowes and Maynard Plastics as a sales representative), and education (she earned her MA in Teaching in 1994 from Simmons College, worked as a middle school social studies teacher at Amesbury Middle School, and served as a local school board member).

After finishing her doctorate in which she used NVivo 7, she was snapped up by QSR International to work as Business Development Manager responsible for working with the academic market to further knowledge of NVivo and XSight. Penna brings a rich background to this position as she continues to use the knowledge from her dissertation research and methods with other qualitative researchers interested in using software tools.

Chapter 11

Leslie A. Mandel
PhD, Program Evaluator/Policy Analyst
Self-employed
164 Bishops Forest Drive
Waltham, MA 02452
United States

Lednam39@aol.com

Dr Mandel completed her doctoral work in 2007 at Brandeis University with a concentration in Children, Youth and Families. She came to Brandeis in 1999 with over 15 years' experience working with or on behalf of children and youth as a manager, researcher and advocate. Dr Mandel was trained in health care management and spent much of her career working in academic medical settings overseeing programmes for urban youth who are disproportionately affected by health disparities and lack access to health services. Simultaneous with her doctoral studies, Dr Mandel taught classes pertaining to children's issues, social policy, health management and organizational behaviour as a teaching assistant and/or adjunct faculty member at several Boston-area universities. She currently works as a consultant for several Massachusetts non-profit organizations conducting programme evaluation and policy analysis on school-based health centres. She is also actively involved in national level associations dedicated to promoting school-based health care.

Chapter 12

Doris Hamner
Research Associate
Institute for Community Inclusion
PO Box 750005
Arlington, MA 02475
United States

hamner.doris@gmail.com

Doris Hamner is currently a Research Associate at the Institute for Community Inclusion, University of Massachusetts, Boston. She was the co-principal investigator on the NIDRR Emerging Disabilities Project and led the qualitative longitudinal research study of job seekers with diabetes and other related disabilities. Doris also worked on the AED Case Studies project that focuses on coordinated services for people with disabilities and the One Stop Career Centres in six national sites. She was a lead researcher on the Rehabilitation Research and Training Center, a project that focused on the success stories of individuals who used state systems, including the Workforce Development System. Doris combines her six years of experience at ICI with 10 years of research and teaching as a professor to design and conduct several longitudinal studies, and has presented and published findings related to these ongoing projects. Her experience, training and research has made her a versatile user of qualitative analytic methods including focus groups, interviews and participant observation.

Chapter 13

Catherine Montgomery
Research Fellow
Health Policy Unit
London School of Hygiene & Tropical Medicine
Keppel Street
London, WC1E 7HT
United Kingdom

catherine.montgomery@lshtm.ac.uk

Catherine Montgomery is a Research Fellow at the London School of Hygiene & Tropical Medicine. After completing a degree in Modern Languages & History of Art at the University of Cambridge, she spent a year volunteering as a peer educator on an adolescent sexual health programme in rural Tanzania. In 2004 Catherine completed an MSc in Reproductive & Sexual Health Research at the London School of Hygiene & Tropical Medicine. Since then she has been working on social science research projects in the fields of HIV/AIDS and Malaria in East and Southern Africa. Her research interests focus on gender and discourse in the design of prevention research and the delivery/acceptability of health interventions. She currently coordinates the social science component of a Phase III microbicide trial across six sites in Africa.

Robert Pool
Research Professor
Barcelona Centre for International Health Research (CRESIB)
CRESIB
Rosselló 132, 4a planta
08036 Barcelona
Spain

robert.pool@cresib.cat

Robert Pool studied cultural anthropology at the University of Amsterdam, where he received a PhD in 1989. He has carried out ethnographic research on food taboos in India, local explanations of illness in Cameroon, and euthanasia decisions in the Netherlands. After spending eight years in Tanzania and Uganda doing social scientific research relating to various aspects of HIV/AIDS, he moved to the London School of Hygiene & Tropical Medicine where he coordinated the medical anthropology course for five years and, as a member of the Gates Malaria Partnership, carried out research on the socio-cultural aspects of malaria in various African countries. He is currently Research Professor at the Barcelona Centre for International Health Research (CRESIB) where he heads the anthropology department and coordinates social science projects linked to medical research on HIV (mainly relating to vaginal microbicides) and malaria (mainly IPTi and malaria in pregnancy).

Acknowledgements

We would like to thank all the many students and researchers without whose questions and experiences about using and implementing Qualitative Data Analysis Software (QDAS) would not have challenged us to develop our thinking about methodological practice using QDAS. In particular, we would like to thank all the researchers who allowed us to use their QDAS experiences in the case chapters in this book. Their biographical details can be found on page xi. We also want to thank Derek Layder, Visiting Professor, Department of Sociology, University of Leicester, who read some of the chapters in this book and offered encouragement and excellent advice although we bear the responsibility for the final decisions made. We want to thank Christine Bishop, Heller School for Social Policy and Management, for reading Mandel's chapter and updating us on the current support for QDAS at Brandeis University. We would also like to thank Stuart Reid and Mark Wardman from the Audit Commission for reading through the Audit Commission study (Chapter 6) for accuracy. We want to thank Elaine Major, Director of Institutional Compliance at the University of Massachusetts Lowell, for her comments on the sections of the book that looks at IRB issues. Also at the University of Massachusetts Lowell, we would like to thank: Former Provost John Wooding for his support for the Qualitative Research Network (QRN) that made possible Davidson's learning in this area; the faculty, staff, and student members of QRN; and, the many UML doctoral students who have shared their QDAS journeys with us.

In addition, we want to thank Chris Cudmore, Jack Fray and the other Open University Press staff for their support and the anonymous reviewers for their comments and ideas about the book's structure.

We also want to thank the small community of QDAS scholars who over the years have enhanced our thinking. In particular, we want to thank Pat Bazeley, Linda Gilbert, Kristi Jackson, Lynn Johnston, Daniel Kaczinski, Ann Lewins, Lydia Martens, Christina Silver, Clare Tagg and Chris Thorn. We also want to thank the developers of these packages – Thomas Muhr (ATLAS.ti), Udo and Anne Kuckartz (MAXqda), and Lyn and Tom Richards and the team at QSR (NVivo and XSight).

Finally, but most importantly, we want to thank our families for their support. We both experienced some pressing personal issues during the writing of this book. di Gregorio's husband, Mick Gardiner, suffered a stroke the summer before we were due to submit our manuscript. di Gregorio would like to thank Davidson for stepping into the brink and looking after 15-year-old Laura Gardiner and her friend for three weeks on Cape Cod. Mick fortunately made a speedy recovery and continued to offer support by cooking great meals as well as offering stress-reducing excursions. Laura had to continue to suffer her mother's preoccupation while preparing for her GCSE exams. However, she still found time with her brother Tom to cook Thai curries. Davidson's husband, Bob Sweet also experienced his share of medical problems, including a knee replacement as we headed into the last stages of the book. Despite the pain, he offered good cheer and encouragement. Thanks to all our family members – human and animal – for what has been an experience of many years, across a few continents, and through many stages of learning.

Introduction: Starting points

We live in an age of new and constantly evolving technologies. Qualitative research, like all areas of endeavour, faces changes and adaptations in light of these dynamic circumstances. For qualitative researchers, some of this change may be welcome and some may bring on sighs of dismay, acts of denial, and outright anger. This book was written in the hope of providing qualitative researchers with better strategies for facing the new technological challenges of their field.

What is Qualitative Data Analysis Software?

Qualitative Data Analysis Software (QDAS) is software designed to assist qualitative researchers in the various stages of a research undertaking from design, data collection, and management to analysis and representation. Sometimes described as tools for non-numerical data analysis, it is also referred to as Computer Assisted Qualitative Data Analysis Software (CAQDAS) or as we refer to it in this book – QDAS. It has been with us for a couple of decades, but it is only very recently that it has begun to emerge as an important and necessary component of robust qualitative research work (Fielding and Lee 2007). Typically, such software provides researchers with capacities for storing textual or visual documents in reference to a coding system tagging or indexing parts of those documents. It is a complex database system that makes use of a computer's hyperlink capacity to shuffle these tags or index titles in varying relationships to each other and on instructions from the user. Contrary to popular misconception, QDAS does not make decisions about data – that is left to the researcher who must code and develop interpretations. QDAS, however, makes those processes far more easy and efficient, that is, if the research design is effectively represented in the software.

There has been strong debate, particularly in the early years of QDAS development, about the impact developers' assumptions might have on the capacity to use the software within different methodological traditions. As we discuss later, qualitative research software, like all technologies, has built in affordances and challenges. In QDAS, as in non-QDAS, qualitative research work, the researcher exercises intellectual control to ensure philosophical and methodological fit between the software and the design.

As is often the case in software development, in the early years of the technology's emergence there were multiple design attempts and individual entrepreneurs were the norm not the exception. This multiplicity still exists to some degree. For instance, in November 2007, the University of Surrey's web page devoted to QDAS issues, which hosts one of the world's most extensive online collections of qualitative research software links (www.caqdas.soc.surrey.ac.uk/links1.htm), had links to 13 freeware packages and 24 commercial packages. These packages provide researchers with tools for analysing textual and/or non-textual (audio and visual) data.

Despite the well-established presence of QDAS, leading qualitative research methodologists have been slow to take up the use of these tools. Whereas in quantitative research, software packages are essential for methodological training and for the conduct of a good study, in qualitative research within academia, it is the younger faculty and graduate students who are most likely to take up the use of these tools and often without adequate preparation in the use of the tool. This is problematic in that it means that those with the broadest and most comprehensive understanding of research design have separated themselves from the skills and tools used by the emerging generation of qualitative researchers. Moreover, given that these tools were developed by academics (or ex-academics) primarily for the purposes of academic research, their powerful potential commercial applications have been slow to be recognized (di Gregorio 2005a; Ereaut 2002).

Why is there a need for this book – who is it for?

QDAS is an emergent technology within qualitative research. As a technology it will need to be integrated within a dense cluster of practices that are informed by rich methodological literature, sophisticated theoretical discussions, and multiple exemplars of fieldwork. The majority of practising qualitative researchers were not trained in QDAS-based qualitative research methods. Already possessing a deep understanding of fieldwork practice and tools, they dislike having to start over again from what feels like ground zero. Many have made a good faith effort to try QDAS but lacking individual and/or institutional support were forced to abandon projects part-way through. The road to QDAS integration is littered with the carcasses of these aborted projects – it is ugly, but true.

Lacking a critical mass of users and adequate paths of knowledge distribution, users are often isolated within organizations or fields: graduate students from faculty; new faculty from older faculty; users from non-users; academia from commercial and public sectors. The limited number of places where people can go to share information about the good use of these tools has raised a barrier to the building of knowledge about these tools and hindered dissemination in significant ways. One of the most important venues for learning about QDAS has been the CAQDAS Networking Project in the UK which grew out of the Advances in Qualitative Computing Conference, and was held in the UK in 1989. The CAQDAS Networking Project has played an important role in bringing together users and developers to consider the development and impact of these tools as well as training in these tools (Fielding and Lee 2007). There is no equivalent of the CAQDAS Networking Project elsewhere. In addition to the CAQDAS project, a series of user conferences, but limited to the QSR software brands, organized initially at the Institute of Education, London and latterly at the University of Durham had been held between 1999–2006. Although small in scale these proved very useful in users learning from each other about using the software tools more effectively and raising awareness about issues that need to be considered when using QDAS (archives of these conferences can be found at www.qual-strategies.org).

Because of the newness of the area there has also been a lack of materials for users. There are how-to manuals available, but these focus on one tool and quickly become obsolete as software versions change (see, for example, Bazeley 2007; Bazeley and Richards 2000; Gibbs 2002). While there has been attention to the ways that these tools 'fit' the various methodological traditions (see, for example, Morse and Richards 2002), these texts may not have the capacity to adequately address technical issues. Several texts have been directed primarily at the novice and take an emergent perspective on research design (Gibbs 2002; Richards 1999). These texts are very helpful, but fail to address the needs of the experienced researcher who will approach software use with a more elaborated framework of understanding than the novice. Lewins and Silver (2007) is the first book which compares different QDAS brands and offers guidance and support for using three of the most popular packages. For most intents and purposes, however, the available texts have addressed the single package – NVivo, and, thus, fail to provide a meaningful meta-brand perspective. Finally, there has even been an effort to address those novice users outside of the academic community with an overall eye to the incorporation of software in their work (Lyn Richards 2005). All of the perspectives described above start from the software and work towards research design … or, as in Lyn Richards (2005) and Gibbs (2002), try to take standard qualitative research design and apply it to software use – neither approach is adequate. Moreover, there will always be new technologies or software packages emerging – and we need a view of research design that can work across multiple packages. What we lack is an integrated model of research design – one that creates a new starting point for thinking about qualitative research in the context of QDAS. It was difficult to do this without substantial experience with QDAS, but we now have that experience. Moreover, there has been a lack of templates or descriptions of how the sophisticated QDAS user undertakes research design. We are now at the place where a sophisticated approach to qualitative research design in software can also be described.

The aim of this book is to fill this critical gap in the qualitative research methodological literature through providing a model for understanding qualitative research design in the context of QDAS.

What can you expect from this book?

In this book, we aim to:

1 develop a theoretical foundation that will ground the use of qualitative research in a software enriched environment;
2 present a model for good research design in QDAS;
3 offer case-based examples of how to apply this model to qualitative research projects of diverse types, from multiple disciplines; and, from academic and non-academic settings;
4 provide discussion of the implications of QDAS for communities of researchers, organizations, and professions.

Who will benefit from reading this book?

1   Those who are already qualitative researchers – QDAS users and non-users:

   • Experienced qualitative researchers will be able to think with this text in a way that builds upon the rich stores of knowledge and experience they already possess.

2   Those who are learning to become qualitative researchers:

   • This text will provide beginners with a research design perspective that lets them 'see into' design from the mature perspective, rather than leaving them to work out their own model without benefit of experience.

3   Instructors of qualitative research:

   • This text provides a useable model for bridging the gap between the vast body of qualitative research methodological literature and traditions and the use of QDAS. It can assist students to better integrate these two worlds and acquire sophisticated design concepts with greater ease. In this book we share our hard-earned knowledge of how one teaches with QDAS.

4   Those working in diverse disciplines:

   • Readers will be able to see how qualitative research is used in a broad range of disciplines. Our experience and our case examples are drawn from diverse fields.

5   Non-academics and those working in non-academic settings:

   • Not all qualitative research is undertaken within academic settings. Increasingly it is used by evaluators and researchers in commercial settings and the public sector. In this book we demonstrate how this model works inside and outside academia.

6   Information technology (IT) directors and others with responsibility for system-wide technology use:

   • Our discussions of implications provide experience-based information on issues related to organizational-wide technology concerns, in particular the issue of scaling-up QDAS for broad organizational use.

7   Software developers:

   • The research design approach provides developers with tools to think broadly across design issues from the user's point of view.

Who are we, and why are we qualified to undertake this work?

We, the authors of this text – Silvana di Gregorio and Judy Davidson – were qualitative researchers before we were qualitative researchers using QDAS. We were also teachers of qualitative research before we were QDAS users. We have been working for several years now in the field of QDAS, using these tools in diverse settings.

Silvana di Gregorio

Silvana di Gregorio is a sociologist who has worked in a variety of applied social science settings – always involving qualitative research – since the mid-1970s. She has worked as a researcher in a health services research unit as a lecturer in Social Policy, and her last academic job was as Director of Graduate Research Training at Cranfield School of Management, UK, where she supervised many qualitative PhD theses. She developed the Management School's research training programme during the 1990s and it was during this period that she became interested in qualitative software programs as she started to introduce them to the doctoral students at Cranfield. She became so interested in the methodological implications of these new qualitative software tools that she resigned from her job at the end of 1996 to set up SdG Associates which specialize in training and consultancy in a range of qualitative software packages. She runs courses and consults from her two bases – in London, UK and Boston, USA. Her work has taken her to many locations in Europe and as far afield as South Africa. The packages she supports include ATLAS.ti, Decision Explorer, MAXqda, QSR NVivo, QSR N6 (formerly NUD*IST) and QSR XSight. She also has knowledge of The Ethnograph, HyperRESEARCH, Qualrus and Transana. She has worked with academics, public sector researchers, market researchers and commercial organizations. She has presented many papers at conferences on the use of qualitative software packages.

Judith Davidson

Judy Davidson is an Associate Professor in the Graduate School of Education at University of Massachusetts Lowell where she teaches qualitative research methodology at the master and doctoral level. She was first introduced to NUD*IST software in 1998, while engaged in a multi-year study of networked technology integration in K-12 schools (Davidson and Olson 2003). Since coming to University of Masachusetts Lowell in 1999, she has worked to embed qualitative research software into the range of courses she teaches, as well as supporting use of qualitative research software in the doctoral dissertation process. As Facilitator for the University of Massachusetts Lowell cross-campus Qualitative Research Network (2005–2007), she has vast experience in issues related to integrating qualitative research software use across an institution. Her research interests focus on the arena of creativity support tools for qualitative research.

Looking to the future

Learning about QDAS has taken us to many new places, literally and figuratively, introducing us to researchers around the globe and research projects in many different disciplines. We have been challenged, puzzled, and perplexed at times, but always excited and intrigued by the possibilities. In this book we share a part of that journey and introduce you to some of our fellow travelers. We view this work as the beginning of a conversation we hope will extend to many new participants in academic and non-academic settings, widening the invitation to use these tools and deepening the ways we understand our uses of them.

Structure of this book

In Part I we introduce our perspective for research design within QDAS. Chapter 1 presents our ideas about the Electronic Project or E-Project as a new genre that transcends software brands and has implications for the development of research within QDAS. Chapter 2 presents our framework for research design within QDAS. Chapter 3 discusses more general implications for research design an E-Project raises. Chapter 4 looks at the various contexts where E-Projects can be conducted and the implications for each.

Part II presents the case exemplars of real research projects conducted in QDAS. We have written them to illustrate our points about research design in QDAS. Chapter 5 gives an overview of the cases. They are organized from simpler research designs to the most complex research designs. Table 1 lists the case exemplars in this section.

Table 1 Table of case chapters, titles and researcher(s)

Chapter	Title	Researcher(s)
Chapter 6	The Framework for Comprehensive Performance Assessment of District Councils from 2006: an analysis of a consultation	Audit Commission
Chapter 7	Views of New Deal for Communities (NDC): focus group study	Ipsos MORI
Chapter 8	Buying birth: consumption and the ideal of natural birth	Rutherford and Gallo-Cruz
Chapter 9	Faculty support staff in online programs	Siccama
Chapter 10	Beyond planning a field trip	Penna
Chapter 11	Doing what it takes	Mandel
Chapter 12	Follow-along study	Hamner
Chapter 13	Microbicides Development Programme (MDP) case study	Pool and Montgomery

Part III concludes with more practical issues. Chapter 14 addresses the issue of scaling-up QDAS use in organizations. Appendix 1 is a guide to getting started with QDAS while Appendices 2 and 3 offer checklists and worksheets for representing the research design in the specific packages discussed in the book (Appendix 2) and for working in teams (Appendix 3). Appendix 4 provides a glossary of methodological and QDAS specific terms.

PART I
Principles of qualitative design

New foundations for qualitative research design

QDAS is a vital tool for modern qualitative research. Once we, as qualitative researchers, begin to use QDAS, it becomes the place where we can develop, modify, examine and represent our research designs. QDAS has been around long enough now (several decades) that we can approach it as more than a mere technology, where our focus is on the technical features of the tool. This book takes the discussion of QDAS to a new level, moving the conversation beyond specific software to the larger issue of: What is QDAS? How do we represent our research designs with it? What are the implications of using QDAS? In this chapter we examine these key assumptions underlying this book.

With the advent of QDAS, qualitative research moves into a new era. The shift from traditional methods (prior to QDAS) and QDAS-based methods raised significant tensions for researchers engaged in using the new tools. Lacking a meta-theory for understanding the implementation of QDAS, users were locked into brand-specific arguments that worked against the development of richer methodological perspectives.

This book, we believe, takes significant steps towards resolving that tension through presenting a notion of research design in qualitative research software that steps outside the old confines in which QDAS discussions were locked. Two ideas are key to this resolution: 1) the concept of the E-Project; and 2) the understanding of the E-Project as genre. These are the foundations for the presentation of our framework for representing qualitative research design in the E-Project.

The Electronic Project

For those who may be new to QDAS, 'the project' (or some such term depending on the software) is the basic organizational unit. It generally corresponds to our notion of a study, although some studies will be broken down into multiple projects because of their size, complexity, or other compelling issue. Each project within the qualitative research software contains all the documents generated by the project: (raw data, interpretive memos; or even final papers) as well as artefacts (which can be represented in the software by notes and, if they are in an electronic from, by hyperlinks to the source). In conjunction with the documents, the project also contains the entire interpretive or analytic system (codes, nodes, or other similar title) required to access those materials in different ways. Thus, one Electronic Project contains all the materials that were once part of several file cabinets, many notebooks and other full-scale materials. Some would say, 'well what's so special about that – doesn't a computer do basically the same thing?' A computer can store all the documents electronically, but without special programs it will not possess the indexes (researcher-created) or the search tools (software-provided) to allow one to get at various pieces of text with ease, nor the tools to build thoughtful interpretations through closely linked analysis of that data. These are the central differences between word-processing software and QDAS, and the reasons that use of word-processing software alone is insufficient for the purposes of conducting robust qualitative research.

With the advent of these new electronic containers, for the first time really, the work of qualitative researchers becomes portable, and, simultaneously, transparent. Graduate students can email the entire contents of their dissertation research to an adviser, and research teams can carry their data back and forth for group consultations. This new freedom can make one giddy. Like all technological transformations, however, it also brings new responsibilities that raise powerful implications for research design. We believe that approaching the Electronic Project as a genre provides researchers with a framework for addressing the issues of research design raised by qualitative research software.

For the purposes of our discussion, from this point on we refer to these electronic containers as the E-Project.

The E-Project as genre

It is our contention that the E-Project is a new research genre, and, as such, we must attend to it as a genre, meaning we must understand its structure and defining parameters, its functions, and the audiences who use it. Viewing the E-Project as a genre provides us with insight into how we might best structure the standards for broad use of these tools (Davidson 2005a, 2005b, 2005c). Our view of genre has much in common with the definition provided by Swales (1990: 58).

> A genre comprises a class of communicative events, the members of which share some set of communicative purposes. The purposes are recognized by the expert members of the parent discourse community, and thereby constitute the rationale for the genre. This rationale shapes the schematic structure of the discourse and influences and constrains choice of content and style. Communicative purpose is both a privileged criterion and one that operates to keep the scope of a genre as here conceived narrowly focused on comparable rhetorical action. In addition to purpose, exemplars of a genre exhibit various patterns of similarity in terms of structure, style, content and intended audience. If all high probability expectations are realized, the exemplar will be viewed as prototypical by the parent discourse community. The genre names inherited and produced by the discourse communities and imported by others constitute valuable ethnographic communication, but typically need further validation.

The notion of the E-Project as genre transcends specific software brands, allowing us to think more openly about the functions of QDAS and its relationship to methodological concerns.

The E-Project is a communicative vehicle for researchers

The E-Project both contains all components of a project, meaning the descriptive, interpretive and theoretical materials gathered or developed by the researcher during the course of the study and is, simultaneously, the vehicle by which these materials and the meaning assigned to them by the researcher can be communicated with others. These capacities offer radical possibilities.

Once we begin to make use of the E-Project in this way, however, we must pay attention to ways to make it 'readable' by others. Authorship of the E-Project must take into account the needs of potential readers for roadmaps, signals, flags and signs that will help the reader get to where the author would like them to go.

In this book we attend carefully to the ways that researchers build E-Projects to be able to communicate effectively with others about their work and their findings.

Researchers must learn to read and author in this genre

The E-Project is a complex genre. It could be compared to the form of the novel with the density of plot, settings, characters and the various techniques by which the author unfolds the story. Learning to appreciate the complexity of the E-Project as a reader and to produce an acceptable product as a writer is a developmental process that knits together many kinds of knowledge.

Not surprisingly, the E-Projects of novice users looks significantly different than that of skilled users. Novices are inelegant in their solutions, often redundant in their strategies, and may fail to understand the importance of documenting their process. E-Projects crafted by skilled users take the reader immediately to the heart of the project and its learning through the efficient organization of the documents, thoughtful interpretive system, and use of communicative markers for readers.

This book was developed around the premise that an essential tool for developing skill in the reading and writing of the E-Project is: knowledge of refined design principles for the E-Project and acceptable standards for its use; access to good models; and, information on the practices of skilled authors of the E-Project. In this way novices can learn from good practice, rather than no practice or bad practice.

Skilled use is evaluated within the community of users, based on ever evolving standards of the genre

As QDAS becomes more broadly acceptable in qualitative research circles, its use moves from the margins to the centre of our understanding of qualitative research. As this happens the need for standardization within the E-Project becomes a necessity, so that readers will not waste time trying to decipher the study in its electronic form and so an acceptable quality can be maintained among research products.

As standards emerge and are accepted by the community of research practitioners, they are 'fixed' through new nomenclature. The *E-Project* is an example of the development of these new terms, which did not exist before QDAS. These terms provide us with tools by which to build the new methodology of this era.

This book takes the first steps towards defining qualities or standards for the E-Project. We introduce terms to define qualitative research work that is embedded in an electronic environment.

The E-Project is the site where qualitative research design is represented

Qualitative research design and the technologies of tradition

In recent years, a plethora of qualitative research methodological texts have been published, and the notion of research design is central to each of these texts (see, for example, Blaikie 2000; Bogdan and Biklen 2007; Glesne 2006; Goetz and LeCompte 1984; Marshall and Rossman 1989; Miles and Huberman 1994). By research design we refer to the thoughtful planning of a research undertaking in order that the outcome of the study will yield useful or meaningful information about a topic or concern. Topics typically examined in texts on qualitative research design include:

- identifying a question for inquiry;
- formulating the research questions and objectives;
- choosing a research strategy – the logic for answering the research questions;
- integrating concepts, theoretical framework, models (dependent on the research strategy);
- identifying the site and participants for a study and/or data sources;
- determining what kinds of data can be collected and creating a blueprint for how this will be accomplished, as well as creation of any needed data collection instruments;
- working through the potential ethical questions of the study from initial access to withdrawal from the site;
- determining how the data will be organized, managed and analysed;
- considering how the research plan supports validity;
- locating oneself as a researcher (both philosophically and practically in the study).

Qualitative research design is influenced, in addition, by issues of: 1) philosophical foundations (the roots that connect qualitative research to discussions that are central to social science regarding what counts as knowledge); and linked to this 2) methodological traditions (the diverse paths qualitative researchers follow in how research should proceed, from grounded theory and ethno-biography to case studies and phenomenology, critical theory and feminist approaches, to name just a few).

Before the era of QDAS, qualitative research design relied heavily on the technologies of notebooks, pens, files and file folders, and, more recently, the similar kinds of device that the computer offers. These materials had become naturalized in their familiarity, and for that reason they were often not considered worthy of notice in project descriptions (di Gregorio 2005a, 2006b, 2007; Kuhn and Davidson 2007). In arguing against the use of qualitative research software what many qualitative researchers forget is that: 1) qualitative research has always been deeply imbued with technology – it did not start with QDAS; and 2) we have, are, and always will have to 'work around' the rough edges of technologies, that is, those places where the tool does not quite fit what we had in mind. Indeed, many 'work arounds' become standard features in subsequent versions of a software.

As we make the shift from traditional methods of qualitative research to QDAS-based methods, we are in need of new frameworks that will help us to understand how to represent research design in these new tools.

A framework for representing research design in the E-Project

This book presents a three-part framework for representing research design in QDAS. Like the notion of the E-Project, this framework is not specific to a particular brand of software; rather it provides a new way for the user to think about qualitative research in an electronic environment. The three parts of the framework include:

1 creation of a software shell in which the researcher develops a descriptive foundation for the study;
2 development of an interpretive system through disaggregation and re-contextualization of the data;
3 reliance on an iterative practice that sustains dialogue between technology and methodology.

We present this research design framework in Chapter 2. The eight cases in this book offer multiple lens through which to view the framework as it is reflected in the E-Project.

QDAS moves centre stage in qualitative research practice

Because the E-Project is at the heart of qualitative research design, QDAS becomes central then to a web of complex practices that include philosophical and methodological perspectives, institutional policy, disciplinary concerns and professional standards. This raises the necessity of revisiting all methodological topics in light of QDAS.

We have begun the process of addressing the implications of QDAS on standard qualitative research methodological topics in Chapter 3 through examination of issues related to ethics, validity and representation. Moreover, every case provides multiple perspectives on methodological issues that are touched upon by the use of QDAS as a tool for research design.

Scaling up the use of QDAS

The future of qualitative research lies in our ability to scale-up use of these technologies across multiple communities of research practice: organizations, institutions and professions. A critical question is: How do we use these tools with others? Genre implies communication and a community of practice. Where will these tools be used and what will users need to know to use them effectively with other researchers? How do organizations develop and leverage mass in regard to QDAS use, and why is this valuable in supporting the robust practice of qualitative research?

Chapter 4 provides in-depth discussion of QDAS use in various contexts, particularly the academic and commercial worlds. In each case there is also discussion about the ways the context of use impact research design. Chapter 14 takes a close look at concerns regarding implementation and 'scaling up' QDAS use within an organization.

QDAS: a vital tool for qualitative research

Qualitative researchers can no longer afford to ignore or stave off the advent of QDAS. It is here and it will be with us as long as computers are part of our lives. While the thought of changing our basic work practices is daunting, QDAS offers new methodological possibilities. The current divide between QDAS users and non-QDAS users (often the most experienced analysts) means that our most significant commentators on methodological issues are failing to engage in the discussion of the new affordances and also pitfalls that QDAS offers. QDAS should not be seen as something that can be added on in a chapter on qualitative methodology. It needs to be integrated in the whole discussion on methodological practice. Failure to grapple with the significant challenges QDAS raises for the practice of qualitative research could lead to QDAS practice being dominated by the inexperienced and the consequent misuse of QDAS leading to bad practice.

QDAS represents a unique methodological development in the course of qualitative research history. There are challenges, but there are many possibilities to be explored here. This is a moment of great significance in the course of qualitative research. We hope that our work provides a foundation from which new users can join that exploration.

Up until now the lack of information about research design in QDAS has made it difficult for experienced and not-so-experienced qualitative researchers to make the leap into the use of QDAS and/or to use QDAS in a robust manner. We hope our work will fill in that gap, presenting the users and non-users with an important means of entering the world of QDAS-based qualitative research.

Designing and conducting qualitative research in a software environment

Design in qualitative research

Many books have been written on qualitative research design (Blaikie 2000; Chadwick et al. 1984; Creswell 2003; Creswell 2007; Flick 1998; Hesse-Biber and Leavy 2007; Janesick 2000; Layder 1998; Mason 2002; Maxwell 1996; Morse and Richards 2002; Lyn Richards 2005) and while there are variations among authors all agree that while design in qualitative research should constantly be reviewed and developed throughout the course of a research study, it is important to begin a study with a research design. Authors vary in how much they see qualitative research design as being distinct from quantitative research design. Blaikie (2000) argues that the quantitative/qualitative distinction is relevant only 'for classifying *methods* and *data*, for *researchers* who use these methods and data, and for *research* in which they are used' (p. 272). It is not relevant for classifying research paradigms or strategies. Blaikie (2000) identifies eight core research design elements which are relevant to both qualitative and quantitative approaches. Creswell (2007) sees qualitative research design within the scientific research process with some variations in several aspects. Maxwell (1996) identifies five key design components of qualitative research which he claims are also relevant to quantitative designs with some modifications. Janesick (2000), on the other hand, uses the metaphor of choreography to characterize qualitative research design. While she too agrees that there are key principles of design which all newcomers to the field must learn; once mastered, researchers should be able to 'expand and embroider' these principles. She divides the research design process into *warm up* – design decisions at the beginning of a study; *work in progress* decisions; and *end of study* decisions. The other researchers quoted all identify key design decisions which should be addressed at the beginning of a study but revisited during the course of the study. Janesick takes a different approach in dividing up key decisions during different stages of a study – a strategy she sees as unique to qualitative research.

Despite such differences, all authors agree about the core design decisions – they may vary in how they elaborate them or break them down. This explains the variations, for example, in that Mason (2002) discusses 12 core areas, Blaikie (2000) 8 core areas, and Maxwell (1996) 5 key areas. However, they all cover the same essential issues. This is regardless of the paradigmatic stance or research tradition.

Leslie Mandel's PhD dissertation, which is one of the cases in this book (Chapter 11), will be used to illustrate some of the features of the core issues of research design discussed below.

Core issue: the research topic

First of all there needs to be a statement of the *research topic* or *problem* (see Figure 2.1). In identifying the topic, researchers need to examine their motivations or purpose for exploring the topic, including personal, political, intellectual and practical reasons for the choice behind the subject area. Layder (1998) emphasizes the role of theory when considering the research topic. He rejects the limited role often given to theory as either tightly formulated hypotheses to be tested or as an end-product of the research process. Instead, he advocates a flexible process of asking questions about key words or concepts when thinking about the topic area before even looking at the literature. All writers emphasize the need for *reflexivity* right at the initial stage of deciding what to research as well as throughout the whole research design process.

Mandel chose to look at School Based Health Centers (SBHC) (doctor's offices inside schools) that are inter-agency partnerships between school departments, schools and community health systems. Her reasons for doing so were partly personal – she had worked as a Health Services manager for SBHCs and was also involved in several advocacy groups working on behalf of SBHCs. She had developed an interest in them and was curious to understand why some were successful and others were not so successful. Her reasons were also partly practical. She had contacts in the state where she had worked and thought they would help her to gain entry to SBHCs. (In fact, gaining permission to study SBHCs was a very long-winded process involving several IRBs which is discussed later in this chapter.) She also was aware of previous research on SBHCs which focused on financing, ideological opposition and politics. However, from her personal experience she felt there was a gap in the literature regarding the basic organizational differences between health and education which poses challenges for successful collaboration in SBHCs. This became the topic of her research.

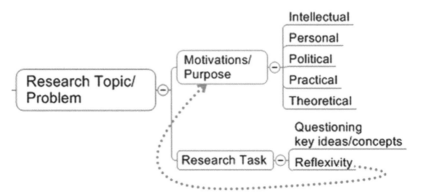

Figure 2.1 Core issue: the research topic

Core issue: the research question(s)

Having identified the topic and the purpose and motivations behind the chosen area, the researcher needs to decide on the *research questions* they wish to explore. This involves considering the literature in the topic area including existing theory and research as well as any experiential knowledge the researcher might have of the area. The kinds of question they want to explore – the what, the why or the how – will influence the paradigm or the approach to social enquiry. Hesse-Biber and Leavy (2006) describe the relationship among epistemology, theory and method as the 'research nexus'. Epistemology is a theory of knowledge; that is, what counts as knowledge, what is possible to know, what criteria that knowledge must satisfy in order to be considered knowledge (Blaikie 1993). Qualitative research is often mistakenly contrasted with quantitative research – meaning positivist research. However, positivist approaches may involve the use of qualitative data. Qualitative data is not just the preserve of social constructionists. The researcher needs to be clear about why they are using qualitative data and what methodological approach they are taking. The decisions made within the 'research nexus' should inform the research strategy, the types of data selected, the approach to sampling, and the type of analysis adopted. Morse and Richards (2002) refer to this idea as 'methodological congrurence'. Each component of the research design should be linked to the others. The researcher's purpose, research questions, data collection and analysis must fit together. Maxwell (1996: 25) emphasizes that the conceptual context of a study 'the system of concepts, assumptions, expectations, beliefs and theories that supports and informs your research' is an essential part of the design. This context informs the rest of the design. Charmaz (2006) argues that even grounded theorists use their disciplinary perspectives and what Blumer (1969) calls 'sensitizing concepts' as points of departure for asking certain types of questions about their research topics (see Figure 2.2).

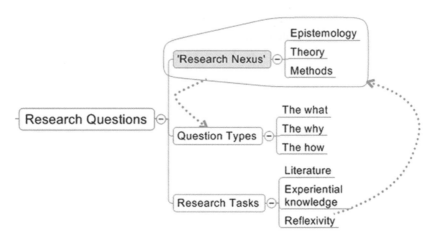

Figure 2.2 Core issue: the research questions

While theory did not inform Mandel's choice of research topic, it did inform the development of her research questions. She was influenced by three theoretical perspectives – domain theory (Kouzes and Mico 1979), the congruence model of organizational behaviour (Nadler et al. 1997) and social network theory. Social network theory, not attributable to any one discipline or researcher, draws from sociology, social psychology, math and anthropology (Wasserman and Faust 1999). Mandel's main research question in her study was:

• How do organizational issues of health systems and school systems make a difference in how SBHCs in Massachusetts achieve success as measured by a state rating system?

In addressing the above question Mandel looked to domain theory and the congruence model. Each of these theories offers a way to examine organizational operations and serves as a diagnostic tool through which organizational health can be assessed. Domain theory identifies factors that can reduce conflict and enhance cohesion between domains in human service organizations – in this case, policy, management and service. Domain theory also links the effectiveness of a system to the extent that domains can develop shared purposes and from those shared purposes can develop functional collaborative systems. The congruence model emphasizes the need for a state of balance and fit between organizational structure and organizational culture. Managers find the best way to configure elements in an organization so an organization can operate effectively. To this end, managers need to take account of the needs and characteristics of the workforce. The expectations and perceptions of stakeholders need to be addressed. In addition, formal structures such as job descriptions and reporting relationships are import-ant. Adaptability is a key factor in both domain theory and the congruence model. Leaders play a pivotal role in helping organizations to adapt and managers need to be flexible.

Mandel developed two secondary questions:

• Does the manner in which SBHC partnerships between schools and health systems were developed and maintained make a difference in how SBHCs achieve success?
• Are there variations in the ways that particular SBHCs and their sponsoring agencies align key organizational elements, manage conflict and promote understanding and cooperation across institutional boundaries?

In addressing the first of these secondary questions, Mandel looked at the history of the partnerships drawing on the congruence model's emphasis on identifying key inputs that feed into an organization in order to understand it.

In addressing the second of these questions, Mandel drew from social network theory which looks at social relationships based on the informal networks not found on formal organizational charts. Examining social communication networks helps determine the extent to which certain people are central to the effective or ineffective functioning of an organization.

Differences in these networks could contribute to understanding why some SBHCs are more successful than others.

It is not possible to do justice to the development of Mandel's ideas in this chapter. Suffice it to say that she began with a deductive approach and developed a series of

hypotheses which were derived both from the literature and her experiential knowledge in order to address her research questions. However, this initial deductive
approach was modified during several periods of reflexivity as she learned more
about research methodology. In the end, she used the theoretical framework she
devised more as a guide to uncover themes and patterns.

Core issue: data collection

The choice of *data sources* flows from the consideration of research questions,
theory and approach to enquiry (see Figure 2.3). Decisions need to be made as
to what kind of data – primary, secondary or tertiary – whether quantitative as
well as qualitative data – will be relevant to answer the research questions.
Primary data refers to new data that the researcher collects specifically for
the study; secondary data refers to data that had been collected for other purposes, such as agency records or data collected for a previous study – this data
has been generated by someone else; tertiary data refers to data that has
been analysed by another researcher, such as published reports of research,
and official statistics that have summarized or categorized the raw data (Blaikie
2000). The researcher has the most control over the primary data collected
in terms of quality control and relevance to the research questions. The
researcher has least control over tertiary data whose quality cannot be checked
and its relevance to the research questions may be tangential as it was collected
and analysed for a different purpose. However, for certain questions the
information they contain may be illuminating. In addition, the research
setting needs to be decided. If field research is appropriate, should respondents
be interviewed in their own location, for example their home, their office, and
so on or at a special location selected by the researcher? Is this special location
in the researcher's territory, for example university setting or in a neutral setting, for example community meeting room. If observations are relevant to
the research strategy, which locations would be the best suited to gather the
data required?

Linked to the choice on types of data sources required for the research are the
decisions the researcher needs to make on how to *sample* them. The sampling
strategy should be informed by the decisions made within the 'research nexus'.
The relationship between the epistemological and theoretical orientations will
inform whether, for example, a probability sampling strategy or a theoretical
sampling approach is appropriate. A probablity sampling strategy is appropriate when the researcher wants to generalize from the data about the population
under study. When adopting mixed methods combining quantitative and
qualitative data, this approach may be appropriate. Theoretical sampling is
used when the purpose of the research is more exploratory, often in areas that
are not well conceptualized, in order to develop conceptual categories and theory. When deciding on a sampling strategy, researchers also need to consider
what the *time orientation* of their sample should be. That is to say, whether
they need to look at a *snapshot* in time or need to sample at different time
points – either prospectively and/or retrospectively in time. Some studies

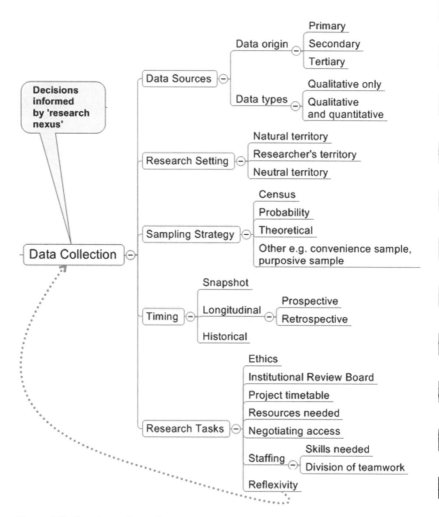

Figure 2.3 Core issue: data collection

require continuous observation over a period of time; other studies are purely historical.

These data collection decisions have to be tempered by what is possible. Access to documents, respondents, sites and so on has to be negotiated. Resources in funding, time and skills will restrict what the researcher is able to do. In larger projects, important decisions about how the teamwork will be divided and managed need to be made. In making these decisions, the researcher needs to be attentive to *ethical* considerations and requirements set by *Institutional Review Boards* (IRBs), which are discussed in more detail in Chapter 3. Researchers also need to reflect on the impact of these decisions on the *validity* of the data they will collect. The research design will need to be revisited when unexpected obstacles arise.

Mandel adopted a case study approach for her research. She looked at four SBHCs – two classified as successful and two classified as not so successful. However, she needed to satisfy not only her university's IRB but satisfy the IRB or gain formal permission to do the study (where no IRB existed) for both the school system and health agency in all four of her sites. The whole process took several months. In addition, the requirements of various IRBs had an impact on her research design. Originally, Mandel planned to interview students involved in SBHCs. The school boards, in particular, were not happy about this and Mandel altered her research design so as not to include students.

Core issue: data handling and analysis

Researchers also need to think ahead of how they will *handle and analyse the data*. In the Preface to her book *Handling qualitative data* (2005), Lyn Richards comments on how little the literature discusses what you do with data once you have collected it. This is the hidden side of practice. However, researchers also need to think ahead to how they will *organize* their data. What may appear to be mundane decisions on how to develop *filing systems* (electronic or other-wise) which allow for *cross-referencing* are key to the researcher's future ability to conduct a rigorous analysis of the large amount of information a qualitative study usually generates. Lofland (1971) is one of the few texts which discuss the practicalities of organizing and retrieving qualitative data. The first edition of their classic text (which pre-dates any QDA software package) describes in detail the process of keeping *housekeeping files* – to keep track of the factual information on the people, organizations and settings in a study; *analytic files* which involve duplicating transcripts and cutting out relevant pieces of text, each piece of paper cross-referenced and filed by theme; and *fieldwork files* or the 'ethnographer's path' which record the researcher's process including mundane records of sites visited and interviews conducted as well as reflections on the research while in the field.

In addition, the researcher should think ahead of what analysis strategy is appropriate for the study. Two basic strategies are *disaggregating data* and *contextualizing data*. *Disaggregating* data means *coding* or *indexing* the data – that is breaking up the data into categories which enables comparisons within and between these categories that leads to the development of theoretical concepts (Maxwell 1996). Contextualizing data is a more holistic approach to analysis. The data are not broken up. The focus is on identifying links or relationships within the data, which is done in certain forms of narrative or discourse analysis. Focusing the analysis case by case as opposed to looking for comparisons across cases is another form of contextualizing strategy (see Figure 2.4). Which strategy is appropriate to your study (and it is possible to combine the two strategies) will have implications on the best way the data should be organized in order to be able to retrieve and see what you need for the analysis. This link between analysis strategy and organizing the data is rarely mentioned in the literature although Maxwell (1996: 80) gives a good example of a study where

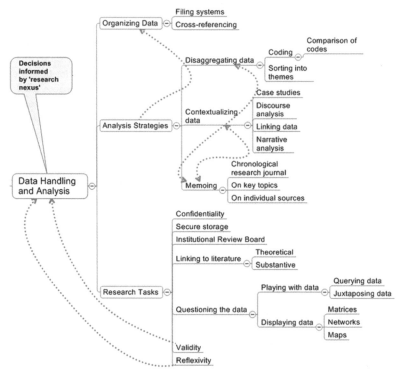

Figure 2.4 Data handling and analysis

the researchers did not organize the data for the analysis strategy required by the research questions.[1]

Memoing is a tool which is used in combination with both disaggregating and contextualizing strategies. It is a way to synthesize the data; to put it back together in order to elaborate on the relationships and patterns that you find in the data. Lofland and Lofland describe the development of initial 'elemental' memos from reflecting on particular codings.

> . . . to compose elemental memos many fieldworkers . . . lay out the piles of detailed codings on a table . . . This makes it easier to pore over the coded data – arranging and rearranging, labelling and re-labelling them . . . In poring over . . . such piles, analysts pose questions . . . to themselves . . . Is this idea clear? Does it have a logical order? Which of these examples best illustrates this point? Is there some small scheme that would fit these piles of materials better? Should I recode these materials? . . . is it possible this topic is not relevant at all and ought to be thrown out? . . .
>
> Lofland and Lofland (1995: 194)

Researchers will create a number of elemental memos. Sorting memos are composed when the researcher starts reflecting on the various elemental memos they have created. The elemental memos themselves become an object of analysis. By reviewing the issues and patterns recorded in the elemental memos, as well as any additional codings, researchers can achieve a higher level of abstraction. This is where researchers jump from the concrete to abstractions and/or generalizations.

Finally, integrating memos are where researchers explain the connections between the sorting memos. It is in these memos that the report of the research starts to take shape.

Lofland and Lofland (1995) are careful to stress that there is no single way of analysing qualitative data. But their approach stresses the importance of organizing research material so it can aid reflection and analysis. It is an example of good practice in conducting qualitative analysis. Their emphasis is on filing and categorizing material and then shuffling them around to aid the analysis process. Recording insights in memos go hand in hand with filing.

The way a researcher organizes the data affects how they can 'play' with the data. How they can contrast data, ask questions of the data, cut the data in different ways – using matrices to see patterns; networks and/or models to see relationships. How the data will be organized is a key component of research design.

> Mandel conducted both a within case and an across case analysis – using both disaggregating and contextualizing strategies. She began with a few a priori codes derived from her theoretical framework. During the analysis process, these codes were refined and others emerged. She used ATLAS.ti 5 to manage her data – details of how she did this are in Chapter 11. She developed an extensive system of memos including memos on methods (12), key themes (21), policy (5) and recommendations (3). These were all developed and stored within ATLAS.ti 5.

Summary on core design issues

There is a consensus about the four core design issues discussed above irrespective of paradigmatic stance or research tradition. Arts-based approaches and social science approaches – from grounded theory to classical ethnography – end up talking about these same core issues. There is also agreement that reflexivity and reviewing decisions made about these core issues are a constant activity throughout the research process. The importance of 'methodological congruence' (Morse and Richards 2002: 32–34) – that all the core areas must fit together – is a constant theme. However, the relationship between analysis strategy and the organization of data has been de-emphasized in recent literature but its importance pre-dates the introduction of QDAS (Lofland 1971; Mills 1959) and the implications of inappropriate data organization are not lost on more recent writers (Agar 1991; Maxwell 1996).

The next section looks at what QDAS offers to qualitative research design.

QDAS and qualitative research design

While a lot has been written about qualitative research design and a consensus has emerged, as discussed above, about the core elements of a qualitative research design, hardly anything has been written about the implications the introduction of QDAS has and could have on qualitative research design. Morse and Richards (2002) touch on the contribution of QDAS at the design phase of a qualitative research project. They focus on the organizational capacities of software as a place to store drafts of the design and proposed timetables for the various stages of the work. The code and retrieve functions of the software could be used to identify key issues in the design and as aids to inform and shape the design. Lyn Richards (2005) encourages the introduction of QDAS early on in a project and sees the software as a container that holds early design ideas and a place to log changes in the development of those ideas.

We, however, see QDAS as having a much larger role in research design. The E-Project *should reflect* the research design. QDAS is not a mere container of the design materials; the design is made visible in the way each project is set up in a software package. In the following discussion, we discuss the key features of research design that need to be considered by QDAS users.

Organization of research

As mentioned earlier, the organization of research materials is something that faces every qualitative researcher but there is little guidance in the literature on how to go about this task (with the notable exceptions mentioned earlier in this chapter). In designing QDAS, developers could not ignore the issue of how to organize research. As a result, all QDAS have developed structures that manage the organization of project materials and products. However, many QDAS users are not aware of the organizational tools available to them. The software is seen mainly as a coding tool. Adoption of QDAS tools requires the analyst to put the organization of the research as a top priority. It becomes a core issue in research design – not subsumed under more general discussions about data handling and analysis. Some researchers may be wary of doing this, fearing that they may be imposing a premature structure on the research. Yet they are ignoring the fact that whether they use a software tool or not, they will be required to manage the materials they are collecting and their ideas – in one way or another. As discussed earlier in this chapter, the way researchers organize their research materials and their ideas has an impact on how they are able to 'see' their data and on what they are able to pull out of their data. Organization is not a trivial occupation – it is core as an aid to analysis. QDAS packages have been designed specifically so that research project organization can be changed as the analysis develops. Unlike packages which have not been specifically designed for qualitative analysis – such as Excel, Access and Word (which some analysts have attempted to use as an alternative to a QDAS package) – researchers are not stuck with a predetermined rigid structure that would be very difficult to alter. QDAS developers realized that the nature of qualitative research had the dual requirement of the need to manage the vast amounts of materials such research generates at the same time as allowing for flexibility so structures can be revisited and altered.

This core feature of research design when using QDAS is illustrated in Figure 2.5. Two broad elements of research products need to be organized – the research materials themselves and the researcher's ideas – the tools and products of

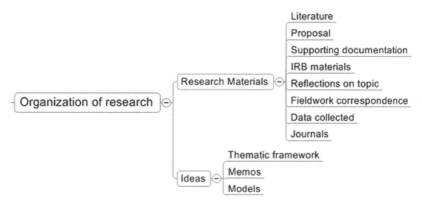

Figure 2.5 Organization of research

analysis. The range of research materials illustrated in Figure 2.5 is not exhaustive. They are indicative of the kinds of material that could be organized in a QDAS project. This is related to our notion that the E-Project is a container that holds all the information that relates to a particular piece of research (see Chapter 1). These materials may include notes on initial reflections on the topic, on literature in the area, on drafts of the research proposal, the final proposal itself as well as notes on ethical considerations and submissions to ethical committees or IRBs. di Gregorio has seen a project where the researcher organized all her fieldwork correspondence in the E-Project. The point is that the E-Project can hold more than the primary data which is the subject of analysis. It can be used to develop the research proposal, as advocated by Lyn Richards (2005). Once developed, it can be stored in the project so that the researcher has ready access to the proposal for reference.

QDAS packages can be used to analyse the literature relevant to the research. di Gregorio (2000) has written on how to do a literature review in NVivo 2. The principles are the same across any software package. Again, it allows for ready access to information that may be needed when analysing the data.

In addition to the research materials themselves, the researcher's ideas – the products of analysis – should be organized in the E-Project. Miles and Huberman (1994) emphasize the importance of *display* in qualitative data analysis. Their axiom is 'You know what you display' (p. 91). A precursor to displaying ideas is the organization of ideas. (It should be noted also that organizing ideas in a QDAS package is the first cut at displaying them.) QDAS provides the tools for the effective organization of ideas but it is down to the analyst to use them well. It is still possible for an analyst to create a poorly structured list of codes in a QDAS package. However, packages offer the flexibility to reorganize codes, merge or expand them and catalogue them, whether by using a hierarchical catalogue structure (NVivo and MAXqda) or grouping them in families (ATLAS.ti). They make it much easier to make the codes themselves an object of analysis. In addition, reflections, working ideas about the analysis can be organized and grouped together, whether as written memos or as visual models. Working memos and models themselves can more easily become the object of analysis. Organized and displayed in the E-Project, they become easier to 'see' and manipulate, regroup and organize.

Design structure visible in software

QDAS not only enables the organization and display of research materials and ideas; it also enables the whole design of the research to be visible. This fact may not be obvious to many qualitative researchers – even those who have been using QDAS. However, to use the full capability of this kind of software, the elements of the research design need to be represented in the software. Once represented in the software, they are visible and can be the subject of reflection and reworking. It is this capability to make visible the research design of a piece of research that makes possible what we have been calling the E-Project.

Figure 2.6 illustrates both the design elements that are visible in QDAS and the implications of this visibility. We have already discussed how the ideas about the research including the thematic framework are represented in the software. In addition, all QDAS have structures to represent the unit(s) of analysis and observation in a research design. However, these features of a research design are often implicit in the research question(s) and decisions on data sources and sampling. When using QDAS, researchers need to make these decisions explicit in the software. Otherwise, there is a danger that the software will be misapplied – a danger referred to earlier in this chapter (see endnote 1). The case examples in the second half of this book illustrate how seemingly straightforward qualitative studies are in reality quite complex – many are making comparisons at different levels in the data. It is not unusual for studies to make comparisons at both the individual level and at the group or organizational level. For example, Mandel (Chapter 11) sometimes made comparisons between the partnerships that were successful and those that were not successful. At other times she looked at differences between school boards and health agencies. Other times she looked at differences between managers, policy-makers and service providers. If these levels of analysis are not represented in the software package, such comparisons cannot be made. In addition,

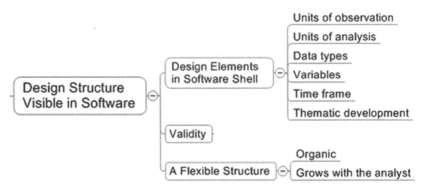

Figure 2.6 Visible design structure

variables relevant to the research, such as demographic information about the respondents and/or key characteristics of the organizations studied, and so on, need to be represented in the software. Again, such variables may be implicit in sampling decisions. In addition, if more than one type of data source is used, this needs to be made explicit in the software package in order to restrict analysis to one type of source material or allow comparisons across several types. Likewise, if a study is longitudinal, the various time points when data was collected need to be represented.

These design elements need to be represented in a QDAS package in order to use the software tools to support analysis. A by-product of this representation is that the research design is made visible and in being visible can be an object of analysis. In effect, the research project in the software reveals the research design. Issues such as methodological congruence and validity can be more easily checked. In addition, as QDAS software is designed to be flexible, the design can be altered in the software if needed during the course of the research.

Iterative process tracking

This flexible nature of QDAS supports the iterative, reflexive nature inherent in qualitative analysis. We have just discussed how the research design should be represented in the E-Project by the way it is set up in the software package. Once represented in the software package, it is visible. Once visible it is easily subject to review and alteration. Figure 2.7 shows some of the techniques used in an iterative way to develop analysis.

The thematic framework is one area that is under constant development throughout the life of a research project. Codes can be reviewed, merged together or further refined. So, while it is possible to create a tentative framework at the beginning of a project, QDAS allows for that framework to be constantly reworked. In fact, if a study is completely exploratory an initial

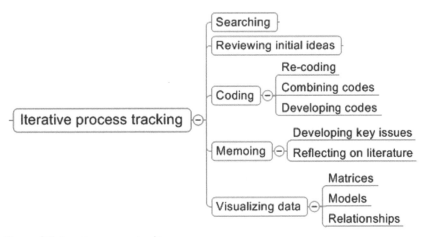

Figure 2.7 Iterative process tracking

coding framework is not necessary. In all packages it is easy to experiment with codes, refine them and/or discard them as necessary. Memoing features in all the packages allow for journaling in order to keep track of the conceptual development of a project. The QDAS tools for searching and reflecting on codes can reveal new patterns during the analysis that could lead to further data collection and changes in the overall design. New units of observations could be added or others can be abandoned as not fruitful and such changes can be made to the design of the E-Project. Existing data can be visualized by modelling ideas, displaying networks of codes or producing matrix tables to visualize possible patterns. This visualization could lead to new ways of working with the data. At the same time, given that the design of the project is visible in the software, researchers can easily check whether they are addressing the questions they posed or whether those questions and the design of the project need to be reworked. The E-Project in QDAS holds in harmony the need for organization and structure with the need for experimentation and flexibility.

Introducing the design framework for QDAS users

This chapter began by describing the current consensus as to the core issues of qualitative research design. We then discussed how the use of QDAS requires that the research design is represented in the software and in order to do this all aspects of the design must be made explicit. Certain aspects of research design – such as units of analysis and observation, variables, data types – which conventionally have been implicit or embedded within the core research issues – take a more prominent role. Novice qualitative researchers often have to rely on supervisors who are well versed in manual methods of qualitative analysis but have little understanding of how to approach an analysis in a QDAS package. This final section gives a general guide of how to approach working in a QDAS package. In Chapter 4 we refine this guide according to the research context in which you are working. Below is a checklist of issues you need to consider when starting such a project. The main rule is to consider the design of your project first when creating an E-Project in QDAS.

Step 1 Design first: review the research protocol

It is worth mentioning again that the research protocol can be developed in the qualitative software package itself. All the packages have memoing features so it is possible to write up the protocol in the package as a memo. In addition, the model function in some packages can be used to flesh out ideas about the design before writing the protocol. If the protocol has already been written, it can be imported into the project as a document so the analyst can have ready access to it while setting up the project and later, when analysing the data.

The research protocol specifies the design of the study. In the methods section is the information on the *structure* of the research which you will need to review when setting up a project in a software package. The elements of the structure of the research include:

- the unit(s) of analysis (individual, pairs, organizations, programs etc.);
- the unit(s) of observation;
- the attribute variables (the characteristics of the unit of analysis);
- the conceptual framework;
- the types of data collected;
- the sequence of data collection;
- the time frame (snap shot vs. longitudinal).

Step 2 The unit of analysis, the unit of observation and attribute variables

As we have been arguing, the unit of analysis and unit of observation are the key factors around which you should be setting up your research design in a software package. The units of analysis can be:

- individuals;
- groupings of individuals;
- organizations;
- departments within organizations;
- programmes;
- events.

Units of observation are the components that make up a unit of analysis. In simple designs the unit of observation is the same as the unit of analysis. For example, if you are looking at individuals and the information you are collecting is about individuals then the unit of analysis and unit of observation are one and the same. However, if your unit of analysis is a programme, your units of observation could be the individuals who run the programme, those who participate in the programme as well as any field notes you have written up based on your observations of the programme as well as documentation.

Attribute variables can be associated with units of analysis and/or units of observation. Attribute variables can be:

- demographic information about individuals;
- characteristics of organizations;
- responses to survey data;
- time period for longitudinal studies.

Step 3 The types of data collected

QDAS supports a variety of types of data. Data can be primary data (data which the researcher collects themselves), secondary data (data which comes from other sources) or tertiary (data which has been generated and analysed by others). Data can be textual or non-textual. All information relevant to a piece of research or a project can be stored in the E-Project.

Textual data includes:

1 Primary data

- Interview transcripts
- Responses to open-ended survey questions
- Focus group transcripts
- Observation/field notes
- Diaries

2 Secondary data

- Newspaper/magazine articles
- Professional records; for example GP records, solicitors' case notes
- Company annual reports
- Minutes of meetings
- The literature on a subject
- Correspondence, for example letters, emails
- Government reports

3 Tertiary data

- Published research reports
- Summarized tables of data (e.g. some official statistic reports)
- Any data that has already been manipulated in some way

Researchers need to decide whether they will work with the full transcript/the original document or summaries of the text. Either form can be used in QDAS. When relying on manual methods researchers often summarize interviews rather than work with full transcripts. Summaries are easier to manage when not working with a QDAS package. However, software packages make it easier to manage unstructured information so it is possible to work with full transcripts. This enables transparency when checking for the veracity of an interpretation.

Textual material can be completely structured (such as structured interview schedules or sections in a report), completely unstructured (such as in-depth interviews) or somewhere in between. Sometimes the structure is not immediately obvious. For example, when analysing an email discussion forum, instead of having numerous small documents each representing one email, a document could be a thread and the document would be divided up or structured by the different respondents who contributed to the thread.

Whether or not a textual document is structured is important because most QDAS have tools to enable you to automatically code for the structure of a document. So, for example, if you are analysing a structured interview schedule where all the questions are exactly the same for each respondent, you can prepare the transcript in a certain way so that the software can automatically code for each question when imported. If professional records or field notes are structured, they can automatically be coded for that structure in the same way. So structure in documents is something you should be aware of when using a package so the documents can be prepared to take advantage of the power of the software. However, if a document is leaning more towards the unstructured end of the structured–unstructured continuum, you may find that you are spending more time in Word trying to impose a structure. In that case, it is best to leave the document as an unstructured document and code it within the software.

QDAS packages are developing their capabilities to support the analysis of non-textual material, such as graphics, audio and video. ATLAS.ti 5 and HyperResearch 2.6 allow for direct coding of graphics, audio and video clips. However, currently, actual coded video or audio clips are not available in generated reports. They are currently only available from within the software. NVivo 8, which came out at the beginning of 2008, supports direct coding of graphics, audio and video clips. Transcripts can be synchronized with their associated audio or video file but audio and video files can be analysed without any associated text. Reports are generated as html files with the relevant extracts of audio, video or graphics that have been coded. With audio and video files, researchers need to consider whether they can be analysed unsupported with text, whether they need full transcripts or notes linked to relevant parts of the audio or video file.

Step 4 Setting up the analytical files (or codes)

So far we have focused on the design of your project and reflecting that design in a QDAS package. The analytical files (or codes) in a qualitative study usually but not always develop in an emergent way over the life of the project. Often it is not possible to set up the analytical files beforehand. There are exceptions. Studies which are based on earlier work can simply import the analytical filing system that was used before, with or without modifications. A study may be very structured so that the major analytical categories are already known. In these cases, the initial analytical framework can be set up in the software.

Different packages have different ways of organizing the analytical files. NVivo and MAXqda have a hierarchical filing system structure. Their system is a *catalogue* of codes. Search tools are used to pull out the combination of codes that is needed. ATLAS.ti has a flat list of files; however, these can be organized as families or sets which is a way of fulfilling the same purpose of a hierarchical filing system – grouping together similar files.

Design framework

Table 2.1 and Figure 2.8 illustrate the critical components of design that need to be considered when planning on using a QDAS package to support the analysis of qualitative data. We divide the type of design into three types: 1) simple designs, where there is only one unit of analysis and only textual data; 2) complex designs, where there can be more than one unit of analysis and some non-textual data; and 3) compound complex design where there is a longitudinal design.

The design framework should be used at the initial stages of a piece of research to help clarify the design and ensure that the design is represented in the software tool. While the issues in our design framework are relevant for any

Table 2.1 Critical components of design

	Unit of analysis	Attributes	Time frame	Data: textual (primary or secondary forms of data)	Data: non-textual (primary or secondary forms of data)	Thematic framework
Simple	One unit of analysis	Only one level; linked to unit	Snapshot	No more than two kinds of textual data	No non-textual data.	A priori and/or emergent
Complex	One or more units of analysis	One or more levels, according to the unit(s)	Snapshot	One or more types of textual data	No/or one non-textual data	A priori and/or emergent
Compound-Complex	One or more units of analysis	One or more levels, according to the unit(s); constant and time-related attributes	Longitudinal	Several types of textual data	None or several types of non-textual data	A priori and/or emergent

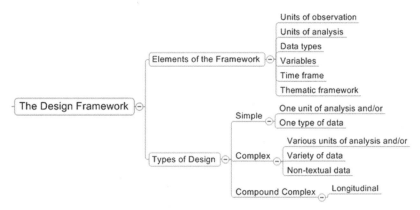

Figure 2.8 Design framework summary

project for any QDAS package, it is essential that whatever program is selected, the analyst understands what tools the software has to support the structure of the project. In the second half of this book, the case examples are from four different QDAS programs. The design framework should be used with all of them but each program has different tools and different terminology to refer to those tools. Table 2.2 illustrates the relevant tools in ATLAS.ti 5, MAXqda 2, NVivo 7 and XSight 2 that relate to the key aspects of our design framework. Appendix 2 offers a more detailed checklist for representing a research design in each of these four packages.

This chapter offers the basics of what you should be doing when setting up a project in a QDAS package and the kinds of question you should be asking. The following chapter discusses wider concerns about qualitative research supported by QDAS. Chapter 4 looks at research design issues when using QDAS in different contexts. The series of case study chapters that follow exemplifies the different types of design articulated in the design framework above. It is our belief that it is best to learn from case examples of different designs. The case studies address more specific issues.

Table 2.2 Research design in software shell framework

	ATLAS.ti	*MAXqda*	*NVivo*	*XSight*
Unit(s) of analysis	Document Families or codes	Text or Text groups or sets	Case nodes	Respondents or subsamples
Attributes	Document Families or codes	Attributes table	Attributes Casebook	Sample characteristics
Data organization	Document Families	Text groups	Document Folders	Use alphanumeric workaround
Thematic frame	Code Manager Code family Manager	Code system	Free nodes Tree nodes	Analysis Frameworks and headings

Note

1   Maxwell cites Mike Agar (1991) who had been asked to review a report on how historians worked. The researchers used *The Ethnograph* to code the interviews into topics and reported across the interviews topic by topic. However, the brief had been to see how individual historians thought about their own work – looking at the links between their thinking, actions and results. This would require a contextualizing strategy. Agar comments that the fault was not with the software package *The Ethnograph* but with its misapplication. Maxwell comments that this has implications for the use of software for data analysis as he states that almost all are designed for coding data and have a bias towards categorizing approaches. However, all the packages have developed significantly since the 1990s when Maxwell and Agar were reporting. Nearly all have contextualizing tools as well as reduction tools. However, it is up to the researcher to choose the tools appropriate to their study and there seems to be an automatic tendency for many researchers to choose coding without thinking through whether it is appropriate for their research questions.

3 Implementation of research design

In Chapter 2, the focus was on the design of the project within the electronic container. But once you have the E-Project developed as a shell, how do you proceed? How do you generate a process and a product that will have meaning and lead to useful results for you, the researcher, the researchee(s), and the many readers that may encounter your work?

Qualitative research in QDAS must still attend to the critical issues that have been developed and explored in the qualitative research methodological literature. A researcher must place him or herself within qualitative research traditions, account for the ways that self and other intersect or fail to intersect, employ credible methods of interpretation, and examine the ways truth(s) are formed, supported and represented, to name just a few of the many topics upon which the methodological literature has touched. These issues are not eclipsed or solved by technology, but they may take new or different forms in an electronic environment. The technology may offer affordances that were not previously available or raise new challenges.

As researchers began to enter the thickets of QDAS use, it was not uncommon for them to refer to the software as explanation for a range of issues – from ethics and coding to interpretation and validity. Evoking the name of a software package, however, cannot be considered an appropriate explanation for researchers' ethical decisions, the coding plan, or an excuse under which to subsume all challenges to validity. Researchers answer these questions, not the software in question. However to do so, they must be able to explain and justify the use of QDAS throughout the research process, just as in an earlier time they would describe the research process as conducted with paper, pen, audio tapes and file folders.

In the following section, we examine several areas that raise special issues for the conduct of the E-Project. This is not an exclusive list of concerns that QDAS raises in the implementation of qualitative research, but can be considered to be a starting point for methodological discussions. Our selected points of focus regarding implementation are:

1 qualitative research traditions;
2 subjectivity and role; access and ethics;
3 interpretation;
4 validity;
5 representation.

Qualitative research traditions

Qualitative research traditions are distinctive, serving to characterize and define examples of qualitative research work at the same time that they are also mutable, pluralistic and highly plastic. Qualitative research traditions are not formulas but evolving social understandings of how to parse the world. These traditions encompass overlapping forms from the post-modern and feminism to critical theory and symbolic interpretation. Some traditions are more exclusive than others. Researchers borrow and marry, exclude and divorce their social theories, and the ways they do so shape the project and its representations in significant ways.

It is critical that each qualitative researcher take personal responsibility for this sociological act of definition, and, in so doing, ensure that there is congruence in the methodological stance throughout process and through the development of product. This is as true in a qualitative research embedded in an electronic environment as it is of qualitative research that does not develop in an electronic environment. In the past, QDAS non-users have hypothesized that their autonomy in this realm could be constricted by the software and that somehow they would be forced to work in an alien tradition. As mentioned earlier, this is not any more true of conducting qualitative research in QDAS than it is in a world lacking QDAS. All technologies have embedded assumptions . . . and all researchers have embedded assumptions. Where they meet is a rich and intriguing 'interpretive zone' (Wasser and Bresler 1996).

Important questions then for the researcher are:

- How do I integrate my methodological tradition(s) within this new tool?
- Are there turning points in the process of conducting research in which my decisions were shaped by the tool?
- If yes, where were these?
- How did I respond?
- Why did I respond in this way?
- What decision would be most in keeping with my methodological perspective?
- How do I make the technology congruent with my perspective?

The choice of which software you use may be dictated by many issues: the tradition in which you work, the site licence your organization purchased, what your colleagues were using, what you first received training in – all are reasonable explanations for choosing to use a particular software. As we have mentioned before, it is up to the researcher, using an iterative technique that connects technology to methodology, to develop 'work arounds' that make best use of the software while continuing to honour the demands of the methodological tradition.

Here is an example of how different researchers working in the same tradition might approach use of various software. One researcher might argue that ATLAS.ti's networked-based presentation lends itself better to his phenomenological perspective. However, another phenomenologist might elect to use NVivo, emphasizing its modelling feature for the same reasons. Finally, a third phenomenologist might prefer MAXqda's grid presentation that allows her to look across codes for a view of density and weakness. All have possibilities for the demonstration of a phenomenologist's perspective.

As with research conducted outside of QDAS, there are several points over the course of a project in which a researcher explores issues related to the traditions within which they are situating their work:

1 prior to undertaking the study in developing the proposal or research protocol;
2 during the study as one thinks about decision-making points and their methodological ramifications;
3 at the conclusion of the study as one seeks to explain and justify actions taken.

QDAS offers many opportunities for doing a better job of understanding the tradition in which one is working and the ways it is connected to a specific project and its products than we could do without the use of these packages. The following are suggestions for the use of QDAS to strengthen one's integration of methodological traditions within the E-Project. These suggestions are made regardless of software brand. Whether one is working in the portraiture method, grounded theory or feminism, the materials still require organization, reflection and interpretation. One's methodological tradition offers suggestions for the ways to do this, and, in this sense, it is a tool to be used in conjunction with QDAS.

Prior to . . .

Assembling the methodological literature

Many researchers opt to start the project in the E-Project shell prior to undertaking the actual research. They begin their reading and studying about topics related to the project within an electronic container. Some of these readings will include methodological items related to the tradition within which they work. For those who are more experienced researchers, with an accumulated library of methodological notes, they may choose to import these notes or in some cases to simply copy a previous E-Project, strip it of the project specific items, and start over again with nothing but the literature notes. For graduate students undertaking a dissertation, the literature review is a beginning point for their study. Beginning the E-Project with the literature review saves time and effort in the long run, allowing students to connect to methodological literature throughout the study. Assembling literature notes related to the qualitative research tradition in which you are working and organizing these notes within your E-Project will provide you with dynamic opportunities to connect this material to the project as you conduct the study. The literature review is where you can begin to interweave the issues of qualitative research traditions into the husk that will be the shell of your E-Project.

Coding the literature

Literature notes are text, and like any other kind of text in an E-Project they can be coded and the codes can be organized under an appropriate heading or meta-code. If your methodological readings are about a particular qualitative research tradition and you read methodology texts with an eye to the fit with your tradition(s), your codes will necessarily build a critical repository of knowledge related to this perspective. Coding your literature notes will provide you quick and easy access to key methodological points for reflection and/or development of subsequent products (papers, dissertations, books, etc.)

Creating a priori codes based upon issues related to the qualitative research tradition(s) within which you work gives you important starting points for understanding the relationship of practice to theory. In developing your a priori codes you should not be surprised to find that it looks like the index of a qualitative research textbook grounded in your tradition, and, indeed, that is what you are writing, your own textbook on the tradition(s) with which you will be working.

During . . .

Coding data to methodological concerns

Many beginning researchers are surprised to learn that there is value in coding their primary or secondary data (interviews, observations and other sources) to methodological concerns. They imagine that the methodological literature got them where they are but it is held in abeyance as they conduct the study, as if it might sully the data itself. Nothing could be further from the truth.

Qualitative researchers are always growing themselves as methodologists through their careful reflection on the process of their research. They enrich their traditions through this action, developing understanding of specific cases' contributions to methodological understanding. Coding is an important tool in this process. Just as you code for the substance of the issue, you should always be coding for issues related to the methodological issues raised by the material.

While this is true of qualitative research in the cut-and-paste mode, it is equally important to code to methodological concerns in QDAS. QDAS has many affordances for search and reflection that, if used appropriately, will enrich your methodological thinking.

Memoing – iterative practice

Connecting the methodological dots takes place in a methodological memo or memos. The hyperlinked possibilities of QDAS allow for actual linking of these items, either at the top level (document to document) or at intermediate levels (to identified parts of documents). There can be a memo connected to the important codes defining your perspective, as well as links to specific passages – quotations and raw data – that support your understanding of the tradition.

Methodological memos are a place to begin to grow your own contributions to the methodological discussion. This is the place where you can ask yourself: What am I seeing here that is relevant to Levy-Strauss' theories on structuralism? How does this relate to Dorothy Smith's concerns about feminism? In a memo you can 'unpack' an incident from practice (the actual study) and reflect upon its lessons for theory and vice versa.

Memos were part of the manual tradition of qualitative research, and, as they enter the electronic world of QDAS, their possibilities (through hyperlinking) are expanded exponentially. In the Microbicide case in Chapter 13, memos were kept by individual team members, providing a critical means of comparing emergent understandings at multiple sites. Moreover, the ability to code the memos, afforded by the software package, allowed project directors to examine the range of issues that faced members in different locations. These differences offer lessons for thinking about methodological traditions – their strengths and weaknesses.

In completion . . .

As you come to the completion of your study, you will want to draw together the understanding you have gleaned about the methodological issues encountered and the ways these provide insight into the tradition(s) within which you are working. If the E-Project was thoughtfully structured from the outset and you have used the software features appropriately during the study, you will be in an excellent position from which to assess these issues. Multiple kinds of search and the use of modelling tools and other features (such as the review of material coded under methodological topics) will now be able to help you develop interpretations about your process and its relationship to the methodological literature, and, in particular, that of the tradition within which you are working. Of particular importance, this review will help you to test your assumptions about methodology and to develop your own methodological discussions, extending the current limits of the literature. For instance, you may be surprised to find some codes went unused and to discover others that, unexpectedly, were heavily used. You may be shocked by the intersections you can discern among methodological codes. *Vis-à-vis* interpretation, this is where the heavy lifting occurs. This is the methodological gold, so to speak.

Conclusions

QDAS adds greatly to our ability to advance the field's methodological discussions through the specificity one can bring to the discussion of methodological issues. Using the coding tools of QDAS, you can quickly assemble incidents and issues from your research for discussion about a methodological issue of concern. If you are coding methodological literature, as well as primary and secondary data, you will be able to see the intersections of the two with ease. Memos then allow you to connect the dots, meaning to develop interpretations related to methodological findings. Ultimately, the multiple layers of reflective practice afforded by the use of QDAS should help you to better understand the methodological tradition you have elected to follow. While there are many parallels in this description of traditions enacted within the E-Project that you could make to traditions as they are enacted without the E-Project, the E-Project offers unique affordances, lending specificity to one's discussion.

Regardless of the tradition within which you are working, if you are to make good use of the methodological literature you have read *and* the data from the study you have conducted, you must have the materials well organized and you must have a systematic way for retrieving critical pieces of those materials. QDAS gives you better systems for doing this. Its possibilities for organizing materials far exceed what can be done without these tools. Sloppy organization will lead to sloppy conclusions. The possibilities of knowing are always strengthened by tools that help us to better organize the materials. The transparency of the E-Project means that, in a future world where QDAS software is the standard, this sloppiness will be painfully apparent to anybody who reviews the project.

Subjectivity and role, access and ethics: a four-fold concern

In talking to students about this cluster of critical methodological issues, I (Davidson) define them as shown in Table 3.1:

Table 3.1 Four-fold perspective on subjectivity

Self	*Other*
Subjectivity (Values, beliefs, assumptions)	**Access** (Acceptance)
Role (Behaviour)	**Ethics** (Permission)

In this table, subjectivity and role are issues under my (the researcher's) control, related to my internal understandings of an issue and the ways my beliefs are present and possibly affecting the interactions at the site. Access and ethics relate to the critical issues arising around the ability to conduct research in the world of others. They (the researchees) must allow you in to conduct the research. Allowing you in is in their control and you must follow their rules or negotiate for others. In a world increasingly dominated by the reach of IRBs and similar ethical governing boards, access and ethics cannot be ignored, but nor can their counterparts – subjectivity and role.

In thinking about QDAS in relationship to this four-part scheme (subjectivity, role, access and ethics) it is critical to consider: 1) how might QDAS use strengthen our attention to these issues; and 2) what new issues does QDAS use raise in relationship to the protection of human subjects?

QDAS as a tool to strengthen responsiveness

As experienced researchers know, it is critical to reflect on these two areas (subjectivity/role; access/ethics) over the course of the study. Many a project has been brought to an unexpected and embarrassing halt by: a) unexamined beliefs that impede understanding; or b) conflicts or unresolved tensions regarding the researcher's presence or activities. If the researcher is the primary research tool, then who the researcher is, what they believe, and how they act are essential areas for reflection. Subjectivity and role (me/us) are equal in importance to access and ethics (them/me) and the issues they raise are necessarily related.

Working in QDAS does not change the relevance of these topics, but it does present you with tools for deepening understanding of these areas. In developing an electronic shell for a project, we would always recommend that you create a methodological sub-code for the two critical areas of: 1) subjectivity and role; and 2) access and ethics. In addition, we recommend creating related memos on the two topics (1-subjectivity and role; 2-access and ethics) to which one can add insights over time.

Memoing on the topics should start well before the implementation of the project. Also, documents related to access and ethics (letters of introduction, memos of understanding, IRB forms) may all be coded to the access and ethics code. You should also code the appropriate sections of your dissertation proposal or research protocol.

Coding to these topics should be ongoing throughout the project. We strongly urge students to reflect regularly on them within the methodological log (see Chapter 2). It is not enough to know the topics exist; it is important to continually exercise that awareness and practise the habit of reflection on these concerns.

It is also important to review periodically the items that have been coded at these locations and to reflect upon the content. When I look within the code for 'subjectivity and role', what do I see? What does the material mean to me? Because it is entirely possible that one's view of oneself and one's actions may change over time (and with good reflection), it is conceivable that there are important incidents that may not have been coded initially, requiring one to review data for material about these topics. In the same sense, when I review the items coded for 'access and ethics', do I hold the same interpretation as I did before the study? Or, has my interpretation changed with experience at the site? These issues are deserving of reflection in the memo on access and ethics. In this way, my experience and the understanding it generates becomes a powerful resource for interpretation.

Everything we are suggesting here was also possible in the manual methods world of qualitative research, but in QDAS the task is made easier and the tool provides increased capacity to bring ideas together through the hyperlinked capacities of the tool. As an example in the contrasts between the two methods (manual methods and QDAS), in conducting my dissertation in the manual methods mode, I (Davidson) kept a methodological log in a medium-sized three-ring binder that I kept next to my computer, adding to it as I worked. When the study was almost complete I paginated and then indexed the (then) four volumes of logs by hand (the index came to about 10 single-spaced pages). Subjectivity, methodological insight, and theoretical insight were the three topics I looked for. It was a labour-intensive process designed to help me achieve 'saturation', and I was definitely saturated by the time I finished. I long held myself to be a kind of superior researcher because of this labour. It is with a certain sadness that as I entered the QDAS era, I realized that if I had been coding throughout the project in a software package, I could have assembled this material in seconds and spent my available time more productively reflecting on the meaning of the passages, rather than spending hours marking with a highlighter and typing the page number into my index. For all those who would argue that the arduous hand process helps you to better reflect on the items – try it once the other way and I think you will quickly agree with me that time better spent is time better spent.

QDAS and the protection of human subjects

Background

Modern standards for human subject protection are built around three principles: '1) Respect for autonomy; 2) Beneficence; and, 3) Justice' (Strike et al. 2002: 45). These principles guide researchers to inform participants fully of possible risks and their rights, particularly the right to refuse to participate. These principles also guide us to do good not harm. Finally, they provide us with considerations in regard to vulnerable populations and the necessity of spreading the benefits and burdens of research equally.

In the last decade, the scope and importance of ethical review boards or IRBs has grown considerably. The reach of these boards extends beyond national boundaries. Researchers must be aware of the standards of their profession, their institution, their funding sources, and ethical review boards of other organizations and agencies with whom they may be working. Where once it was thought that such review was primarily for medical researchers, this is no longer the case, and qualitative researchers in all fields must now pay close attention to these standards and the boards that enforce them.

The unique qualities of QDAS – portability and transparency – raise important challenges to the ethical conduct of qualitative research. These challenges must be addressed if QDAS-conducted research is to gain acceptance within qualitative research circles and beyond.

Enter QDAS

When QDAS first entered the scene, IRBs were not yet the firm presence that they are today. As IRB oversight has grown in the last decade, QDAS was initially overlooked as an ethical issue. This happened, we can presume, because it was considered simply an electronic version of manual methods qualitative research. Therefore, any ethical stipulation for a manual methods project would be extended to the electronic version. Indeed, in those earlier days of QDAS use, many research proposals or protocols explained little about QDAS as a tool in the methodological process.

In the last few years, however, there is increasing evidence that researchers and research oversight boards are giving more thought to the implications of QDAS use for the conduct of qualitative research. Unfortunately, numerous examples have come to our attention of misunderstandings and reactive responses to technology use in qualitative research that point to the importance of opening a discussion among QDAS users and ethical oversight groups so that responsible standards can be established.

As an example of what can go wrong, one QDAS user we encountered was restricted by his IRB from storing his E-Project on the hard drive of his computer, insisting that the electronic project be stored only on his flash drive. Unfortunately, as an ATLAS.ti user, he could not work on the project from his flash drive. The workaround he devised was to copy the project to the hard drive so that he could work on the computer using ATLAS.ti. Then he would save the project and copy it onto the flash drive (using the copybundle procedure in ATLAS.ti). Finally, as the last step he would delete the project from the hard drive. In order to comply with IRB restrictions, he had to go through this procedure every time he worked on his E-Project. This IRB's concerns about the misuse of an electronic database are commendable, but lacking knowledge of the software and the ways qualitative researchers have been addressing these issues, they imposed restrictions that unnecessarily penalized the researcher.

It is not just researchers and review boards that have problems with the ethical dilemmas QDAS raises. Researchees also have important concerns about the use and storage of their information. While they may not be up to date on QDAS issues, they have the right to know that electronic database systems are being used and how confidentiality will be protected.

Just as researchers are never without their subjectivity, they are never free from concerns about ethical issues. In doing research about human social life, we must always be reflective on the effect our work could have on others. In any study, these concerns are with us as we develop the design for the research project, conduct it, and afterwards as we share what we have learned. QDAS raises new wrinkles for the ethical conduct of qualitative research that deserve our careful attention. Because the use of QDAS is so new, we have yet to standardize or codify our responses to these issues. In this section, we present the standards we have developed for our own practices.

Initiating the study: access and informed consent

Developing the research protocol or proposal gives the researcher the chance to imagine the entire study and the ways QDAS will be implemented. As part of that process of imagination, it is critical that researchers include attention to the ways ethical issues might arise from the use of QDAS and how they would plan to resolve them. These issues surface as one thinks about how to gain access to the site and how to proceed with informed consent. Ethical issues that need pre-thinking include identifying the kind of data to be collected, as well as the data collection process itself.

The issue of access and informed consent requires special attention. It is critical that QDAS be mentioned in seeking consent from participants, and researchers will need to create reasonable descriptions of QDAS use that make sense to researchees, as well as ethical governing boards. In particular, in presenting the project to your governing board, you can make use of screen shots from the shell or a demonstration of the program if members are unaware of the functions of the software.

QDAS can be a stumbling block in gaining access to a site if it is not handled sensitively and with forethought. We live in an era of electronic threats – from identity, credit card and bank theft to the databases of credit card companies, surveillance agencies and crackpots. It is not surprising that the notion of electronic records might put off some participants (others, however, can actually be very intrigued by the idea of QDAS). Therefore, it is important that you give your study participants clear, adequate information, but do not flood them with descriptions that will not add to their understanding about what you are actually doing. Assure them of the ways that confidentiality (as you have crafted it) will be maintained as you use QDAS for the study.

Overall in working with the ethical preparations for a study: Do not resist questions, welcome them – the more questions you receive about the establishment of the ethical agreement, the stronger your study will become.

Archiving/destruction of data

The issue of archiving versus destruction of data is one of the murkiest policy areas, and it only becomes murkier with the introduction of QDAS. Until recently, it was assumed that qualitative researchers would store their data as long as they had room to do so. There were no time limits given to most studies. In anthropological studies and oral history studies, these materials might well be catalogued in the vaults of a natural history museum or library. With the rise of qualitative research, meaning research conducted on local populations, as opposed to exotic others as in anthropology, the issue of data storage/destruction became more problematic. Today, ethical review boards consider all studies involving human subjects conducted within their organizational boundaries to be under their purview, and this includes qualitative research. As part of that responsibility they feel it is important to dictate the terms by which the researcher will retain the data. IRB contracts with researchers commonly proscribe how data will be stored and when it will be destroyed (and in some cases you must also describe how it will be destroyed – shredded, burned, ingested, etc.).

Ironically, at the same time that the destruction of qualitative research data has come to be a concern of ethical review boards, there is also a movement afoot to develop archives of qualitative data. An interesting example of this development is the Qualidata project (part of the Economic and Social Data Service) at the University of Essex (www.esds.ac.uk/qualidata). While there is much to be explored in this realm (the archiving of qualitative research data), for the purposes of this discussion we will focus on the topic that is generally much more pressing to the average researcher – the destruction of data.

While ethical governing boards seek to protect participants' rights to knowing how and when their information will be used, they often make this decision based upon their experience with experimental studies and the publication timeline of medical or scientific studies. They are only beginning to recognize that data in social science may be used differently and thus timelines and expectations for destruction of data may need to be designed from a different perspective.

In many cases, ethical governing boards have separate and sometimes conflicting policies relating to the use and destruction of textual data versus audio or visual data. These different policies were often created in an earlier time and may make no sense given the current state of today's technology (digital and computer stored).

With regard to requirements about destruction of data, it is imperative that the researcher should understand what the actual requirement is, rather than speculating on what it could mean or how a potential committee might vote. If there is any ambiguity, you should ask your compliance officer for an explanation. Always rely on the organization's policy documentation, not hearsay from fellow researchers or students. More tears of frustration are shed over ethical hearsay than just about any other challenge in qualitative research. Once you are sure you understand how the terms for destruction apply to your study, you can develop a statement of your needs and the rationale for them. Think carefully about how your use of QDAS will be affected with regard to the destruction policy: Does it mean that the entire E-Project will have to be deleted? Does it mean that the textual documentation can remain but audio and visual records will have to be destroyed? Do all primary materials (raw notes, audio tapes, etc.) have to be destroyed but can field notes and memos (items created by you about the project) be retained? The subtle differences are important. Make sure you understand what is required. It may well be that QDAS use raises policy issues that your governing board is not sufficiently informed about, and, in that case, you will need to help them through the learning process.

Equally important are the clauses in relationship to renewing your rights to the data. Review the policies and procedures of your local review board. If your research project is over and the data has had the identifiers stripped, review whether you need any approval from the board to use the data? Do you need to make a request every year? Every three years? Every five years? Is there an upward limit on the use of the data? If the governing group differentiates between the kind and form of the materials that can be retained with a renewal, this may raise special issues for QDAS stored materials.

Future use of data is closely connected to issues related to the destruction of data. How will you be allowed to use the data? How will the requirements affect your E-Project? Some guardian bodies require that you only use your materials to publish items related to the topic which was identified for the proposal. How will this affect the way you mine your data in the future as you begin to think across projects and their findings? Will you be able to mix and match E-Projects over time? Because QDAS usage is in its infancy, these issues may currently fly under the radar of ethical governing boards, but they may soon surface and it behoves us to think about them now.

Introducing new methodological techniques

It is up to the researcher to do careful background work designing the research protocol or proposal to ensure that it meets the highest ethical standards; this is equally true for the components related to QDAS usage. In cases where the researcher needs to ask for a variance from what the IRB has outlined as expected practice (through policy statements or practice), it is helpful to be able to share examples of the ways that other qualitative researchers, as well as other IRBs or similar governing boards have dealt with similar issues.

Do not be afraid to introduce new techniques or probe new methodological approaches and to use the presentation to the governing group as an opportunity to prepare yourself to face the ethical issues the new methods raise. You do yourself and your organization a favour by experimenting with new approaches, and you will be surprised by how quickly the new becomes standard practice. QDAS is a new tool and while questioning related to its use may be more rigorous in the beginning as ethical governing boards struggle to get a handle on what should be standard practice, this questioning will strengthen the proposals and enlarge methodological and ethical discussions.

It is recommended that you work to develop an open and trusting relationship with your review board representatives. They are there to assist you in meeting the ethical guidelines set out for human subject research for their institution. Good and effective communication is important and often the review committee needs a little more information to better understand your intentions and to hear how their requirements may affect your research project. Often a solution can be reached that both sides can agree on. Most review boards are open to new techniques if they can be assured that human subjects are protected in the process.

Protecting confidentiality during the study

All the ethical guidelines from the manual methods era of qualitative research apply, as well as some new ones. While we can offer some general suggestions, each project has many unique features which will require unique ethical responses.

(a)   Keep confidentiality within the E-Project

If you are working under standard agreements regarding confidentiality; that is, making the participants and location undecipherable to outsiders, then it is critical that you start enforcing this policy from the very beginning. This means your E-Project should contain no materials that could identify the participants or the place. Anything that would breach this agreement (a list of pseudonyms for participants and places; photographs that are identifiable; documents with recognizable information, etc.) should be stored outside of the E-Project. The E-Project should only contain 'anonymized' or masked data. Pseudonyms should be used for participants and places. This means that the files must be labelled using those same pseudonyms, and internally (within interviews, observations and memos), individuals and locations should be referred to with these pseudonyms (even though participants did not use your made-up names). The choice of using pseudonyms as opposed to numerical identifiers is up to the researcher. Personally, we have found that pseudonyms are easier to remember than identifiers such as 'R33'.

If you do the above, you will have a project that can be shared at multiple levels with key individuals – your researcher supervisor, research team members and other professional colleagues with a legitimate right to examine your work. The E-Project will offer little possibility of breaching participants' confidentiality agreements. The portability and transparency of the E-Project lend it to being shared and discussed with others, but without this foundational level of confidentiality it will be difficult to do so in an appropriately ethical manner.

(b) Sharing the E-Project within research circles

There are very good reasons for sharing the E-Project before, during and after the completion of the project. Good researchers need good feedback to do good work. If the materials in your E-Project are properly masked you should be in position to share the E-Project with appropriate 'research others'.

Masking the data, however, is not all that is required. It is important to state the ethical guidelines to viewers and to gain oral or (in some cases) written agreement that they will comply with the ethical guidelines you have agreed to with the participants. For instance, in working with groups of dissertation students, Davidson discusses these ethical issues and seeks agreement among members of the group that they will all act in ethically appropriate ways with regard to their fellow graduate students' materials. Oral agreement works in this case because of her supervisory role and the long-term relationship of the group. di Gregorio, however, in running master classes with relative strangers, requires that participants sign a written agreement with regard to holding the materials they will view with confidentiality. In both cases, outsiders are viewing masked materials, that is, materials that have been stripped for the most part of items that would allow participants and place to be recognized. In many cases, these reviews stick to the top or mid-levels of the projects and may not need to move into the lower levels (primary and secondary data) where issues of recognition might more easily arise.

(c) Showing the E-Project to participants

Whether or not one should show the E-Project to participants is related to the way the relationship between researcher and researchee has been crafted. This is true for manual methods projects as well as E-Projects. With the E-Project, however, there is an added dimension of concern in that all materials for the project are contained within it and all can be visible. If you share the E-Project (for instance if you sent it to a participant), you are sharing everything. In sharing the E-Project, you will need to ask yourself if the recipient needs to see all of it, or part of it, and, if so, which parts. You will also need to assist new users in reading the project, as they may be unfamiliar with this form of software. You may want to craft an E-Project specifically for sharing, keeping your full E-Project for research out of sight.

In this book, for instance, it would have been possible to set up the Ipsos MORI E-Project (Chapter 7) so it could be shared with participants – those citizens who voiced their views on the issues under study. This is a public policy study, as opposed to studies of an individual's practice, and there is little danger of harm (whether intended or unintended) from the sharing of the views. Moreover, no individuals can be identified from the data. The E-Project in this case might be an important vehicle for sharing the results of the study, and ethical agreements would not be at risk. Indeed, sharing the project with selected participants as it is developing might be an important interpretive device for checking assumptions and deepening interpretations. Some study designs, such as action research approaches, may be strongly committed to such openness. However, many studies may not, for a variety of reasons, lend themselves to this technique. In these studies, checking assumptions will take place, but sharing the E-Project may not be recommended.

Reporting on the findings and maintaining confidentiality of materials

There are many ways in which, as interpretations become stabilized, the researcher is called upon to discuss what was learned and how it was learned. The potential audiences for the findings of a study are many and varied, from the research participants themselves to key supporters of the research endeavour (funders, supervisors, etc.) to the wider community of professional colleagues, policy-makers and concerned members of society. Using QDAS raises new ethical issues for qualitative researchers as they seek to disseminate their findings. Following the ethical guidelines above (maintaining confidentiality throughout the development of the E-Project) will do much to ensure that ethical issues will be appropriately addressed. However, research conducted in any mode, whether electronically or not, must be crafted with thorough attention to ethical concerns. As software capacities change, ethical responses will continue to evolve.

Conclusions

Each study presents its own unique forms of ethical issue. These come in the form of topics, populations selected for study, location of study and relationship of researcher to researchee. In this book, for instance, Mandel's study, 'Doing what it takes' in Chapter 11, required that she gain permission from several IRBs, creating a complicated mosaic of permissions – their individual reviews and separate stipulations. The Microbicides case (Chapter 13) presented another kind of complexity in regard to permissions – an international health project operating in multiple countries. In both cases, QDAS raises new challenges for the ethical conduct of the study.

We cannot offer guidelines for each of the ethical hot spots that might arise related to a particular study. Ethics are an ongoing area of emergent concern for a qualitative researcher, making it more important than ever that (in addition to the suggestions above) we follow good principles of iterative practice. This means that we need to document and reflect on our ethical concerns as the project proceeds, seeking expert advice to sticky dilemmas earlier rather than later in the course of the study. With regard to ethics, our iterative practice should be grounded in the three foundational principles that guide an ethical practice to our participants: 1) respect for autonomy; 2) beneficence; and 3) justice.

Interpretation and the E-Project

Interpretation, in qualitative research, refers to the meaningful generalizations that are derived in systematic fashion from analysis of the experiences and materials of the research process. The generalizations emerging from a qualitative research study should be easily traced back to the experience from which they were generated. Indeed, the telling of that experience may be essential to understanding the generalization or finding, to use a term more familiar to experimental research.

Interpretation in qualitative research is built through a carefully layered process that begins long before the actual act of data collection, as one forms the notions undergirding the study and develops the proposal or protocol for undertaking the research. These formative propositions are with the researchers as they gather materials in the form of texts (written, visual and oral). Primarily, these texts are gathered in their naturally occurring locations and recorded (in whatever form of data collection is used) with a sense of preserving the notion of the socially embedded context.

In a qualitative research study, at the same time texts are being collected or accumulated, they are simultaneously being broken down into small chunks of meaning, identified and labelled by the researcher. The size of the chunks, as well as the labels given to them, are determined by the researchers, who make the decision in relationship to their understanding of the question guiding the studies and the literature on this topic. Most researchers refer to this process of breaking down texts into smaller units of meaning as 'coding'.

The breaking-down of texts into chunks of meaning (coding) has a parallel process that follows with the recreation of meaning through the juxtaposition and realignment of labels and texts. This reorganization is a process of clumping and clustering related to emergent meaning. The reorganization proceeds by reviewing the labels given to the chunks of meaningful text and organizing them in different ways. Tables, diagrams and memos may all figure in the process of sorting out possible meanings from the experience and materials recording that experience. (For an in-depth description of qualitative interpretation, see, for instance, Charmaz 2006.)

QDAS offers many tools that help researchers break down texts into meaningful chunks and reconnect them in new meaningful relationships. Different tools, as can be seen in the cases to follow, offer different possibilities for the two critical tasks – breaking down (disaggregating) and rebuilding (contextualizing) the texts related to a study.

In using QDAS, there are two common pitfalls for qualitative researchers approaching the interpretive process in an electronic environment. The first pitfall in the realm of interpretation is the belief that somehow the interpretive features of the software must be aligned in accordance with the qualitative research tradition(s) the researcher will employ. That is, a grounded theorist must use a tool developed for grounded theory, or a phenomenologist must use a tool developed by and/or for phenomenology. As explained in Chapter 1, this is just not a workable assumption. Qualitative researchers need good sturdy software tools that are plastic enough to be moulded to a range of traditions. As we discussed earlier, it is up to the researcher to make the tool fit the method (given that the tool has a good range of capacity and is robust and well tested) through an iterative process that links technology and methodology.

The second major pitfall in the realm of interpretation is that the researcher falls into the trap of using a QDAS tool for code and retrieve functions, forgoing the more challenging uses that are less like the manual methods with which they were familiar. Tom Richards (2004), developer of NUD*IST and NVivo, presented a paper titled, 'Not just a pretty node system: What node hierarchies are really all about', in which he discussed the dangers of limiting

QDAS use at the level of code and retrieve. As he points out, QDAS tools do a very good job of code and retrieve, but they can also do so much more, and in doing more they push qualitative research beyond the boundaries of the old manual methods of the pre-QDAS era. Researchers must be prepared to be able to interrogate their materials and experience using the advanced possibilities QDAS brings to us. These advanced tools include searches that allow us to compare, contrast and juxtapose the chunks of data we have collected and tagged in ways that were not possible without the computer. This means researchers must know how to develop a robust electronic shell that will support reflective searching, *and* they must understand how to think with the logic available to the computer that will allow them to ask informative questions of their data.

For many (certainly those of us who are not from the field of information science), the manner in which one asks questions of the data in QDAS may seem awkward at first. We may forget that sans computer we ask many kinds of question of our data, from the simple to the increasingly complex, as we consider, what happened, why, what does it mean, how are people organized here, what is foreground and background in the scene. The trick, in QDAS, is ensuring that the electronic shell is properly organized and data collection is conducted in such a way that our questioning process can be adequately supported by the software we are using. A good way to ease oneself towards a stance to QDAS that would get one beyond the barrier of code and retrieve is to consider the kinds of thing one wants to ask of your data and how you would ask or phrase the question, then to begin to think about the software tool and its organization to figure out how you would be prepared to ask those same questions using this tool.

In this book, good examples of thinking beyond code and retrieve can be found throughout, but you may want to take a special look at Penna's dissertation study 'Beyond planning a field trip' (Chapter 10) where she set herself the specific task of better understanding the search capacities of NVivo 7. 'Doing what it takes', another dissertation study conducted by Leslie Mandel (Chapter 11), demonstrates how she used ATLAS.ti to get beyond code and retrieve, in a complex health policy analysis. These two provide a useful contrast in the ways two different tools allow researchers to conduct interpretation.

Validity and trustworthiness

It is not the purpose of this book to discuss the intricacies of questions related to the notion of validity and trustworthiness in relationship to the issue of paradigms or traditions. We recognize that these differences in perspectives can be significant. However, we take the stance that the organization and credibility of any claim to validity or trustworthiness rests upon the quality of the data collected, the strength of the organizational system from which evidence is derived from the information gleaned, and the researchers' documented monitoring of the research process and their reflections on that process. Thus, our purpose here is to consider the ways QDAS can be used to strengthen claims for validity and trustworthiness regardless of the paradigmatic stance or perspective to qualitative research traditions taken by the researcher.

As we have stated in many places throughout this book, simply evoking the name of a software package is not a proxy for a claim for validity. QDAS can strengthen validity, but it is not, in and of itself, a guarantee that expectations for validity or trustworthiness have been met. Maxwell (1996) provides a useful rubric for labelling the kinds of validity that emerge from a qualitative research study, employing the terms – descriptive, interpretive and theoretical. Descriptive validity refers to a rendering of the event, scene or location in a manner that would be accepted by insiders or outsiders as a realistic depiction of the time, place and activity. Interpretive validity refers to descriptions of the meaning of the event as it would be understood by insiders to the social setting. Finally, theoretical validity moves to generalizations that seek to make sense of what was experienced in broader terms – finding new ways of understanding that may transcend the limitations of the insider/outsider or emic/etic divide. Although this is a simplified discussion of a complex issue, these three terms – descriptive, interpretive and theoretical – can be helpful in thinking about the ways QDAS could be used as a tool for strengthening validity or trustworthiness.

Building on Maxwell's three-part framework, the issue for QDAS users then becomes, how might QDAS strengthen claims for validity and trustworthiness in these three realms: 1) description; 2) interpretation; and 3) theory? Evaluation of the project's responsiveness in these three realms is understood through review of:

1 the *research design* as depicted in the setup of the E-Project's shell (descriptive foundation);
2 the *interpretive system* developed and its relationship to the data collected (interpretive foundation);
3 the *iterative process* and the use of software functions that go beyond code and retrieve (theoretical foundation).

In order to evaluate the robustness of the project in these three areas, a reviewer must understand how to 'read' the E-Project. This is true whether the reviewer is actually examining the E-Project, hearing a description of the project methodology (as in a presentation) or reading a description of the methodology (as in an article or book). Just as certain methodological descriptions are *de rigueur* for discussion of a manual methods qualitative research project, we should expect a certain level of description with regard to the development of the research design, interpretive system and iterative process of a qualitative research project conducted with QDAS.

In the following section we discuss the expectations for standards in review of the methodology of an E-Project.

Research design

A famous statement attributed to the modern dancer Martha Graham is, 'The body tells all'. In the QDAS world, we might adjust this statement to, 'The shell tells all'. A review of the shell of an E-Project will give an experienced 'reader' of QDAS a quick understanding of the robustness of the project and/or the potential problems with which the researcher may be struggling.

In a review of an E-Project, important questions to consider are:

- Are units of analysis and their attributes properly established?
- How has the data collected been organized?
- Does the organization of these features make best use of the functions of the software in which the E-Project is housed?

Interpretive system

The interpretive system refers to the analytic files or coding system established within the E-Project. Some of this system may be established a priori, but much of it will emerge in relationship to the collection of the data and preliminary analysis of these materials. In reviewing the interpretive system, which is the heart of the project, the critical themes and designation of units of meaning should jump out at the reader making it immediately clear what the important ideas are that have emerged for the researcher.

In a review of the E-Project's interpretive system, these are critical questions to consider:

- Have methodological codes been established, and are they sufficient?
- Were a priori codes established, and if so where are they located?
- Are thematic codes sufficiently rich, and are they organized in a manner appropriate to the software being used?
- In examining the actual data, is the researcher doing an adequate job of coding? Are they working at the appropriate level of fineness of coding? Are they picking up themes appropriately? In other words, is there a good connection between data and interpretive system?

Iterative process

The iterative process refers to the ways the researcher builds the deepest levels of meaning related to the experience of research and the materials representing that experience. Central to the tracking of the iterative process are the use of memos (either in textual or visual form) and the evidence of the employment of search functions of the software.

As mentioned in earlier parts of this book, every E-Project should contain documentation that performs the function of the following memos:

1 coding;
2 methodology;
3 subjectivity/role;
4 access/ethics.

The presence of these items is not sufficient in and of itself; it is also important to examine how the researcher has been making use of these tools:

- Is the researcher making sufficient entries to demonstrate attentiveness to the research process?
- Are interconnections demonstrated between logs and memos and the data itself?

If the research design and interpretive system are appropriately designed, then the researcher should be in a good shape for using the search tools in a creative fashion to probe hypotheses, check hunches and examine patterns. These activities, however, do not emerge on their own. They require a talented researcher who knows how to ask questions of the data using the functions of the software designed for this use. A reviewer of an E-Project should look at the coding journal and methodological journal to better understand the kinds of propositions, questions or hunches that have come to the fore for researchers during the course of the research and the ways they have used the software tools for exploration of these ideas. Information on searches used may also be stored in specific pre-built sections of the software (in NVivo under 'Queries' for example). If the data mining is gleaning results, do the results of these searches lead to new memos (textual or visual, such as with visual representations) and coding?

Conclusions

Reading an E-Project is no light task. As in reading any professional genre, it requires a skilled and experienced person. The task is infinitely complicated if the author of the E-Project elects to use idiosyncratic approaches to the task, ignoring what are emerging as the standards of the genre. Quickly the reader tires, gets lost and becomes irritated at the author, just as one would do in reading a poorly constructed research paper. For this reason, as the qualitative research field delves more deeply into QDAS use, it is critical that standards should be developed and transmitted to those entering the field.

Representation

Discussions of representation within qualitative research have flourished over the last few decades (see, for example, Clifford and Marcus 1986; Denzin and Lincoln 1994.) As qualitative researchers, we have examined ethnography as a genre (Jacobson 1991) and considered the question of the qualitative researcher as author (Geertz 1988). We have increased attention to the rights and voices of the researchee (Fine 1994). These discussions have led to many important experimentations in the presentation of qualitative research and further considerations of representation (see, for example, Barone 2001; Eisner 2002; Ellis 2004; Lawrence-Lightfoot 1997).

There are two important ways to approach the issue of QDAS with regard to representation. First, as a tool to support the E-Project, we are concerned with the ways its functions support the overall development of the project and, in particular, the ways it allows materials to be identified, examined and reclaimed for the purposes of representation in the many forms available to the researcher. Second, what is equally significant about QDAS is that if we take it to be an emerging genre itself, as we do in this book, the E-Project is a representation that must be considered in and of itself, rather than simply as an aid to other forms of representation. In this section we consider the question of QDAS and the notion of representation from these two important perspectives.

QDAS in support of representations

There are several ways that QDAS can serve in support of a researcher's representations, that is, the final products that emerge to tell the story of the project and what was learned.

First, QDAS serves representation in the way it supports identifying and extracting key pieces of information from the study's materials. Quotations from interviews or pithy segments from observations or documents are easily located to be used in papers or other presentations. The Ipsos MORI study using XSight (Chapter 7) is a good example of this capacity, in which quotations are at the heart of the work and the subsequent presentation of the study. The Audit Commission study (Chapter 6) is another good example of the ways QDAS served in this capacity.

Another way QDAS serves representation is through the generation of materials linked to the unique capacities of the software. These capacities include the creation of matrices, numerical findings and tables based upon cases/families and attributes. These capacities allow for the revisualization of the materials and the ways they are related to each other.

A third QDAS support for representation is through the incorporation of QDAS representations into other forms of representation. Screenshots are one of the most common ways of doing this. With a screen shot, viewers have access to a still photo of the inside of the E-Project related to a specific feature under discussion by the author.

Finally, depending on the QDAS package, researchers may be able to use active models (such as the NVivo modeller) to present new visual representations of the project. Because these models are 'live', the presenter may dip into the actual project through icons that allow them to bore under the surface of the E-Project. Figure 12.9 in the 'Follow-along study' (Chapter 12) shows an ATLAS.ti network view that could be used in this way.

QDAS as representation

As QDAS becomes increasingly integrated into one's practice and the practice of the field, you will find yourself working with the E-Project as a representation in and of itself. Indeed, it may come to eclipse or at least loom larger than other forms (articles, traditional presentations or books) during the course of the study and even upon completion. In other words, you no longer go to the E-Project to find the materials to present in these traditional forms; rather you simply present the E-Project as the significant form. This is the place where the E-Project becomes a genre to the researcher. In doctoral programs, for instance, where the adviser is comfortable with QDAS and there is a community of QDAS users established, discussion of the project is made visible through QDAS. It is not unusual for groups to gather to examine an E-Project and to comment upon the strength of its design; at the same time they examine the actual data, the coding system and its application to segments of data. Portability and transparency, two key features of QDAS, make this possible. For experienced QDAS users, the software design and the substance are inextricably interwoven.

When the E-Project is used as a genre with communicative functions, a researcher examining the work of another researcher will expect to find standardized forms within the E-Project, reflecting the norms of the field. The research design system we propose in this book (units of analysis, characteristics of the units, type of project, data collected, iterative process markers, communication documents for other researchers) is an attempt at defining the meta-standards in the QDAS E-Project. We have sought to develop standards that can be used across packages, rather than assigning standards for a specific package. In this way, researchers examining an E-Project in an unfamiliar package will, once the significant design features of a program are explained, be able to draw upon these shared understandings of what constitutes a good E-Project.

The more comfortable researchers become with the use of QDAS, the more important a peek into the E-Project becomes if they actually are to make sense of what they are being told about a project by another researcher. In master class sessions, di Gregorio leads analysis of E-Projects presented by project leaders to small groups of qualitative researchers seeking to improve their skills in QDAS and qualitative research. She weaves together attention to software design with identification of the impact design has on the research process, demonstrating the ways the two are connected. At Davidson's university, doctoral students typically come together in a similar fashion to review their dissertation projects and help each other to improve the substance of the findings through improving the structure of their E-Projects.

Conclusion

The topics examined here with regard to the implementation of a QDAS research design are not meant to be exhaustive. Indeed, we feel there are vast areas of territory to explore with regard to issues related to this topic of which we have only scratched the surface. This is an area where the methodological literature has much room for growth.

For this reason it is more important than ever that researchers mine the QDAS potential for supporting an iterative practice linking technology to methodology and making full use of the capacities of the software tool for providing in-depth methodological analysis and reflection upon practice.

4 | Research design in context: the E-Project and communities of research practice

Introduction: why context is important

The previous chapters introduced the E-Project as a genre, the design framework as a guide when working with any QDAS package, and new issues that researchers need to consider when developing research in any QDAS package. We consider these factors as fundamental to all research using QDAS. However, research does not take place in a social vacuum and depending on the various contexts where research takes place, other context-specific factors need to be considered. This chapter explores critical context-specific factors that impact on conducting research using QDAS, in particular the impacts on research design, and considers a number of different kinds of context.

Figure 4.1 illustrates the different kinds of context researchers are embedded in, from the macro- to the micro-level. This conceptualization is an adaptation of Layder's (1993) research map. Layder's original map was designed to help in planning and developing field research which has theory generation as its aim. It helps to focus research questions on one or two contexts with the others in the background. di Gregorio has adapted this framework as a map to help researchers situate themselves and consider contextual issues relevant to their use of QDAS.

Starting at the macro-level, there are different cultural norms relating to standards and legal requirements that vary across national borders and sectors. For example, in the USA getting approval from IRBs (discussed in Chapter 3) is *de rigueur* for all social science researchers. In particular, those doing research within the public health sector are under strict controls regarding transferring data from one location to another. In the USA, IRBs are within the legal framework. They are governed by Title 45 CFR (Code of Federal Regulations) Part 46 and are regulated by the Office for Human Research Protection within the Department of Health and Human Services. In the UK, IRBs are not enshrined within the legal framework. However, the impact of European Union Directives led the Department of Health in 2001 to produce a standards framework for the ethical review process of all research conducted within the National Health Service (NHS). Regulations were put in place in 2004 over clinical trials involving medicines. There has also been recent legislation to protect those with limited mental capacity. In April 2007, the National Research Ethics service was established within the NHS to formalize and standardize guidance for ethical reviews across the NHS.

The Economic and Social Research Council or ESRC (2005) (which is the

Figure 4.1 Types of context

largest funder of social science research in the UK) produced a Research Ethics Framework which provides minimum guidelines for ethical considerations that need to be addressed by any social science research that is funded by the ESRC. This framework came into effect on 1 January 2006. While ethics is important in both countries, the different legal structure of the two countries and differences between sectors within each country impacts differently on researchers. US social scientists are currently under more legal restrictions than social scientists in the UK. As mentioned in Chapter 3, the destruction of data is very much a concern for US social scientists, whereas there is a strong movement for archiving qualitative data in the UK, which is supported by the ESRC. The implications of data transparency in QDAS have not been fully worked out in either country.

The setting where the research is located is another context that can have a differential impact on research design. The organization, whether a university, government agency or market research company, has its own procedures and standards relating to research and research design. One key aspect is the availability of support and training for the use of QDAS. Another aspect is whether procedures and standards have taken account of the implications of the use of QDAS by researchers in the organization. These issues are considered later in this chapter in relation to universities' procedures and standards for doctoral students and instruction in QDAS. If more than one organization is involved in the research – such as collaboration among a number of universities – then variations in support and standards across the universities need to be taken into account. The Microbicide project discussed in Chapter 13 is an example of a multi-site project across organizations in different countries.

Moving on to more micro-level processes, situated activity refers to the inter-actions between the various parties involved in the research. For doctoral students, this would not only include their relationship with their supervisor, but also members of their dissertation committee, and other faculty members and students who may have input on their research as well as the participants of the research itself. For larger projects involving teams, communication processes among team members would be added to this mix. The freelance commercial analyst would need to address the process of communicating the research with their client. All these issues are discussed in detail later in this chapter.

Finally, each researcher needs to consider their own strengths and weaknesses when designing an E-Project. In addition, their position and relative power within their research environment can impact on their ability to be successful when using QDAS.

This chapter focuses mainly on issues with regard to setting and situated activity. It begins with looking at teamwork and the issues that need to be considered when designing an E-Project for teams – whatever the larger context is; for example academic, commercial or public sector. Then it considers two issues specific to academic contexts – dissertations and instruction in QDAS. It then addresses QDAS in commercial contexts. Finally, the chapter ends with ideas about the future of QDAS in other contexts.

Teamwork when using QDAS

Introduction

The biggest challenge for any research organization when contemplating the introduction of the use of a QDAS package is how to reorganize the way they work in teams. Typically QDAS is considered when there is a large project with a lot of qualitative data to manage. One of the researchers who may not even be the principal investigator decides that the project needs to be analysed in a QDAS package. There is no experience of using a package in the organization; one, or less typically, a few of the researchers on the team get some basic training in the software (it is not unusual for a researcher to first try to learn it from a manual) and they are then on their own. Little thought is given to how the introduction of a software package will impact on their current ways of working as a team. Many just opt for one researcher on the team to use the software but this in itself does not avoid the implications of working as a team. If the other researchers on the team (particularly the senior members) do not understand what a QDAS package can do, they will be pulling the researcher using the software back into traditional ways of analysing qualitative data. Often the use of the software is abandoned or just used to manage and organize the material. Careful thought must be given into how to integrate the use of the software in the team if the research organization wants to reap the benefits of using a software package. In order to do that, they first need to examine their current working practice for team research and then decide what needs to be changed to integrate the software package into their research process. This also requires knowledge of what QDAS packages can do by those managing the research. Research organizations – whether academic institutions, public sector research departments or commercial organizations – work in a variety of ways. We first look at current models of research teamwork in such organizations before suggesting ways they need to be modified.

Current models of teamwork

One of us (di Gregorio) has extensive experience consulting with commercial, public sector and academic research organizations in both the USA and the UK. Davidson has also worked for several years for a US not-for-profit research organization. Together we have seen a variety of ways research organizations organize their qualitative research teams. The discussion below is not exhaustive but indicates some of the more common traditional ways of organizing teamwork for qualitative research.

di Gregorio was brought in to introduce a QDAS package half-way through a traditional cross-state evaluation study by a leading US commercial research organization (di Gregorio 2001). There were 17 case studies spread within five states across the USA. There were four research teams with 2–3 analysts each who collected the data and wrote up the 17 site reports. The principal investigator had designed the site report structure that formed the template into which each analyst had to summarize the data they collected. The analysts had to synthesize the analysis of three focus groups for each site, numerous interviews with the key stakeholders involved with the implementation of this new policy, and local and state documents regarding the new legislation. Only one analyst had included full summaries of the focus groups she conducted as appendices to the site reports. This was her preferred practice, but it was not required by the principal investigator. It is typical practice, however, for commercial organizations to work with summaries of qualitative data. For large projects, the cost is high for full transcriptions, both in money and time. The use of summaries, as opposed to full transcripts, depends heavily on the quality of the analysts involved and the skill of the principal investigator in devising an appropriate framework for the site reports and ensuring consistency across the analysts. QDAS was brought in during the middle of the project at the insistence of the client. Once in the package, it was easy to see (thanks to the transparency provided by QDAS) that there was unevenness in the quality of the site reports with some giving very good detail and others very scant in some areas. This unevenness in quality would not have been so evident using traditional methods. It would be the job of the principal investigator to pull together conclusions from the 17 site reports into one overall report. In a situation such as the one described above, the principal investigator may become aware of the deficiencies while organizing the analysis, but it would not be evident in the final report to the client.

To be fair to this organization, they were fairly new to qualitative research. Their expertise and reputation had been built on their surveys and more quantitative techniques. Qualitative work had been done previously on a much smaller scale. Since the mid-1990s there has been an increase in the demand for large-scale qualitative work to be done in evaluation studies, and research organizations have had to struggle to cope with the new demands this development places on them.

In the UK, di Gregorio had the opportunity to discuss the question of adopting a QDAS package with the British Market Research Bureau (BMRB) who have been involved in the analysis of qualitative data for quite a while. They use what they call 'Matrix Mapping' which is based on the Framework method of analysis which was developed by Britain's National Centre for Social Research (Ritchie and Lewis 2003). This method was developed originally as a paper method to approach methodically the analysis of qualitative data and is quite popular with some commercial researchers, particularly in the UK. It involves using a matrix table with the first column listing the identifier for each case and the first row listing the questions or topic areas. The researcher summarizes the information for each case and question in the appropriate box. This original method was done by hand on large sheets of paper but later has been used with an Excel spreadsheet. However, after the data has been inputted in Excel, it still involves printing out large amounts of paper and eyeballing trends in the data.[1] Using the Framework Approach in Excel, BMRB had developed a structure for dealing with large-scale qualitative analysis. It involved outsourcing the extraction of the summaries from tapes of interviews using independent consultants. The Excel sheets were then sent back to the BMRB analysts who eyeballed the data for trends and produced the final report. However, they were not satisfied with this method as Excel is not a flexible medium for qualitative analysis.

Once the structure of the Matrix Framework is set it is difficult to alter. In addition, there is a limit to the amount of words that an Excel cell can hold which could compromise the quality of a summary. In addition, it was awkward to spread out the printouts of the Excel spreadsheets which would involve placing several sheets of paper side by side on a long table. The sheets of paper often did not align which is important in order to track across the responses for a particular case. It was an awkward method and BMRB were looking for a better solution. However, they wanted the new solution to fit the existing structure they had for organizing teamwork. This would mean that the independent consultants would have to be trained in the use of the software, and had to be willing to use a QDAS package which often involve a higher level of computer skills than using Excel. BMRB would have had to negotiate a limited licence for these external people and would have had to put in place procedures to ensure the software was used just for their project. Ideally, BMRB wanted to find a QDAS solution to fit their current teamwork structure. However, they realized that their working methods would have to be altered if they adopted a QDAS package. As they needed to learn a QDAS package themselves, they could not see initially that their existing working practice was geared around a particularly unwieldy method and some of these practices would not be necessary when using a QDAS package. Making the transition to using a software package would involve new learning at all levels – from project managers to junior analysts – and would require time.

The previous discussion described two common ways commercial researchers analyse qualitative data. They both involve extracting summaries of the information from tapes, notes, or, less typically, transcripts. The summaries can be either organized immediately into a pre-defined site report or they can first go through a more methodical approach of summarizing each case in a matrix of case by topic area. The material will then be scrutinized for patterns and pulled together into a report. Both methods tend to rely on junior members of the team or data collectors to do the extraction of summaries. These summaries are the raw material that the more experienced researchers use to produce their reports. Once the pre-defined site report or matrix framework has been designed by the more senior researchers, the 'summarizers' are usually left alone to extract data.

Teamwork models when working with QDAS

As can be seen by the previous discussion, introducing a software package in a large-scale qualitative study with a team of researchers requires a reappraisal of working practices. The two examples in the previous section came from commercial research but the same issues are relevant to academic large-scale research. There are a number of different models for restructuring teamwork using a QDAS package. An organization needs to consider resources in terms of time constraints, financial constraints, geographical location of staff and staff expertise (in terms of both qualitative analysis and QDAS knowledge).

The QDAS supremo

Regardless of resources and existing teamwork structure, the key for successful management of a team using QDAS is the appointment of a QDAS coordinator or supremo to each project (di Gregorio 2001). This person should have a thorough knowledge of the software package. They are in charge of ensuring the design of the research is reflected in how the project is set up in the software. They create the 'shell' of the project in the software. They design how the raw data is organized in the software, how ideas should be catalogued, and they design the templates for any material that will be imported into the database. They allocate work to team members and send a common shell of the project to each team member who will be working with the software package. They are responsible for quality checking team members' work on a regular basis. Figure 4.2 illustrates the workflow for the QDAS Supremo.

This person does not need to be the most senior member of the research team, but they should have a key role in the management of the research process. This is not a role to be given to a novice. The supremo needs to have skills in: (a) the analysis of qualitative data; (b) using the QDAS package; and (c) in managing a team. If this role is not taken by the most senior member of the team, then that person needs to have a working knowledge of the QDAS

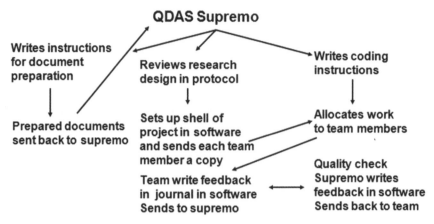

Figure 4.2 Example of QDAS supremo flowchart

package. Otherwise, they will be in danger of making requests that will pull the QDAS supremo back into a traditional way of working. Senior team members need to understand what a software package can do and make requests for information accordingly. Ideally, they should be able to 'read' the project in the software and pull out the information they want themselves.

How the work is divided among the rest of the team depends on the approach to the analysis, the experience level of team members and the complexity of the design of the project.

Division of labour – data collectors summarizing information

As mentioned earlier, some researchers do not work with transcripts but directly with tapes or from notes. They do not code the raw data but extract the key points and summarize them. In a large-scale qualitative study, it is not unusual for those who collect the data to summarize the information. There are good reasons for this strategy. The data collectors have a live memory of the interview or focus group discussion and can add more detail regarding the tenor of the discussion. Working from tapes is far superior to working from notes as tapes give the data collector a chance to refresh their memory; the tapes are also required for quality control. However, some researchers, particularly within a commercial context, just work from notes (Ereaut 2002). Usually, but not always, the data collectors will be given a template into which they will record their notes. These notes will be scrutinized by a more senior analyst who will put a report together.

There are two ways this approach can be adapted using a QDAS package.

Approach 1: The software supremo will devise a template for the data collectors to record their summaries. When the summaries are returned to the supremo they will import them into a QDAS package and use its tools to analyse them. The advantages of this approach is that the data collectors do not need to be trained in the QDAS package – only the supremo or senior analysts involved need to know the software. The disadvantage is that there is more work for the supremo or analysts in organizing and analysing the data.

Approach 2: The data collectors will record their summaries directly in a software package. This is similar to the BMRB model discussed above, except the software would not be Excel but a dedicated QDAS package. The Ipsos MORI project discussed in Chapter 7 adopts this approach. They used QSR's XSight, which was designed specifically for market researchers who use summaries of data. In this approach, the supremo designs the 'shell' of the project with frameworks where data collectors can directly record their summaries. In addition, a journal is created for each data collector to record issues that arise during the data collection. The training of the data collectors can be integrated with their briefing meeting on the project. The supremo gives copies of the 'shell' of the project to each data collector. The Ipsos MORI team stipulated that the data collectors (in this case, the moderators of focus groups) write up their summaries listening to the tapes within 48 hours of the focus group. They also emailed their project back to the supremo at regular intervals. The supremo would read through the data collectors' journals, note and deal with issues. The supremo would also quality-control the summaries and feed-back areas for improvement. If necessary, the 'shell' of the project can be altered by the supremo to capture emerging issues. At the end of the data collection period, the supremo can merge all the work of the data collectors into one overall project in the QDAS package. Then the supremo and/or senior analysts can review the journals for key issues that the data collectors see emerging and then check them out using the querying tools in the software.

The advantage of this approach is that the summaries are being directly recorded in the software package and changes can be made for emergent issues globally by the supremo. The disadvantage is that the supremo needs to monitor closely the data collectors and feedback on a very regular basis. The supremo needs to be skilled in coordinating and managing teams as well as being a good analyst.

Division of labour – based on the profiles of coders

Where the research team decides to code from transcripts (as opposed to working with summaries of the data), then all members of the team need to learn the QDAS. A supremo will set up the 'shell' of the project. The supremo will also decide how to divide up the coding work among the members of the team. The way the supremo should divide up the work varies according to the experience of the analysts in the team.

Table 4.1 shows a matrix of the type of skill combinations a team of coders can possess. This matrix table should be three-dimensional. The third axis would be whether they have experience of using QDAS. In an ideal world they should all be experienced qualitative analysts, specialists in the topic area under study and have experience of using QDAS. However, that is rarely achieved even within an academic context. In a commercial context, the coders would often be the data collectors. Data collectors – particularly in individual interviews – are often chosen for their specialist knowledge, not

Table 4.1 Matrix of analysts' experience profiles

Qualitative analysis	Subject area specialist	Subject area generalist
Experienced	Experienced analyst Subject specialist	Experienced analyst Subject generalist
Novice	Novice analyst Subject specialist	Novice analyst Subject generalist

their analytical skills. Sometimes, because of the difficulties in getting a team together at short notice, the supremo may have to manage analysts who are both novice analysts and subject generalists.

In order to use QDAS effectively in the team, all team members need to be trained in the software. The QDAS supremo should have experience of using the software and if not should be working in conjunction with a consultant to ensure that the project is set up to reflect the research design.

There are other considerations which are hidden in the above matrix table. It is possible for an analyst to be a novice in qualitative analysis but experienced in quantitative analysis. This profile can be either a positive or a negative – it depends on the individual analyst. The negative aspect is if the analyst is inflexible in their thinking and insists on taking a quantitative approach to coding. It may not be a wilful strategy; it could simply be that the analyst cannot see or understand any other way of approaching the analysis. The positive aspect is if the analyst has an open enquiring mind and is interested in developing new skills. Their experience of quantitative analysis will stand them in good stead in terms of the discipline of looking out for patterns in the data (albeit in a different way). The supremo needs to assess these variables in the team they have to manage and divide the work to make the most of their skills.

Experienced analyst and subject specialist: When the supremo has this dream team of highly experienced analysts, it may be best to divide the work so that each analyst is only coding for their specialist areas. They can be free to develop their thinking by creating new codes and writing analytical memos. They will be drawing on their wealth of knowledge in their subject area and experience as qualitative analysts and will be focused on fully developing their part of the analysis.

Novice analyst and subject specialist: This is not an unusual combination found in teams, particularly in cross-disciplinary research where the need to find subject specialists is a priority. The supremo needs to take advantage of this strength and divide the work, as in the previous example, so that the subject specialist is only coding for their subject area. While dividing up the work by coding was a recommendation in the previous example, it is a necessity for analysts with this profile. The analyst here is a novice in qualitative research – they will need a lot of direction and guidance from the supremo and careful quality checking. They will gain confidence by focusing on coding and reflecting on what they know and the supremo will get the best out of them.

Experienced analyst and subject generalist: An experienced qualitative analyst should be able to tackle any subject area. However, they will need to develop a feel for the area and spend more time, perhaps, than a subject specialist in immersing themselves in the data. For this reason, it may be best to divide the work by documents, so that they will be coding in all areas. This strategy will help them to get to grips with the wider picture and use their analytical skills to develop analysis memos which cross-relate topic areas.

Novice analyst and subject generalist: This profile is best avoided but it sometimes happens due to difficulties in getting a team together. In a more positive light, it can be seen as an apprenticeship role. The best use of someone with this profile is to limit their coding to broad topic areas – where the coding decision is pretty much straightforward. The division of the project will be by documents. They should keep a thorough coding journal and be asked to record insights they get as they code broadly. This will stop the coding process from becoming mechanical and the recording of insights should help to develop their analytical skills.

Research teams can have analysts with a mixture of the above types of profile. The Audit Commission study (Chapter 6) is one such example. In that case, there was a combination of novice generalists and experienced specialists. The division of work was done so that the novice generalists focused on the broad coding and their work was then passed on to the experienced specialists for finer coding and analysis.

This system worked very well and the team was able to turn around the report in three weeks. However, di Gregorio was involved in the training of this team and as part of the training developed this work flowchart with them. For any teamwork, it is important to attend to an understanding of the strengths and weaknesses of the team, an understanding of the data collection process, and the features of the work environment. Thinking through and creating teamwork flowcharts are important to get right from the beginning of the project.

As a result of this trial use of NVivo, Laura Richards-Gray, the supremo in this project, prepared a briefing paper on conducting a consultation for the Audit Commission (Laura Richards 2005). Included in this paper was a protocol for managing the data from consultations which were to be analysed using NVivo. She established new guidelines for teamwork when using a software package within the Commission.

Division of labour – multiple sites

Since the mid-1990s, our sense is that there has been an increase in the number of very large-scale qualitative research projects. There are no statistics that we are aware of supporting this statement, but it is a reflection of our experience and the experience of other consultants and trainers that we know being asked to advise or consult on extremely large projects (Lyn Richards 2006). Most of these projects are evaluation studies. Evaluation studies are done by both academic and commercial organizations. Regardless of who they are done by, they all face the same kinds of issue regarding how the QDAS impacts their working practice for team research.

These large projects consist of several teams located in different sites. The Microbicides project (Chapter 13) is an example of this kind of large-scale qualitative study. It is being managed overall by the principal investigator and his social science coordinator in London while the teams are based in South Africa (three teams in three separate locations): Uganda, Zambia and Tanzania. The principal investigator is the overall supremo of the project. He is an experienced anthropologist and an experienced user of the QDAS package. He designed the QDAS shell of the project and allocated the coding tasks to the six teams. Each site has its own mini-supremo who has knowledge of the software and allocates the work to other team members. They quality-check the work and then send back the coded project to London where the principal investigator performs another quality check and merges the various site projects to perform analysis. As you can imagine, managing such a large project is challenging. To add to its complexity the qualitative team in each site also liaises and feedbacks information with the medical team on the site who also collect data on the people who are part of the trial.

The principal investigator and the social science coordinator keep close contact with the various sites by visiting them on a regular basis. Each team had analysts with different kinds of coding profile (as discussed above). Part of the brief of the project was capacity building. The principal investigator organized a series of week-long retreats for the whole team focusing on different aspects of qualitative research. di Gregorio was brought in on two of these sessions to enhance the teams' use of the QDAS package they were using (NVivo 2). These sessions were important opportunities for team members to discuss ways of working with the software and helped to instil a sense of being part of a qualitative social science team among such geographically dispersed sites.

The point of this example is that multiple site research projects add another level of complexity. They are harder to manage, especially when they are geographically dispersed. It is important to allocate budget money to bring the teams together for an analysis 'retreat' so they can create links with other teams and gain an identity as part of a bigger whole. QDAS can help in this process but teams need to be brought physically together occasionally to work with the software. In between 'retreats' the overall supremo can directly communicate with teams via software such as Webex or GoToMeeting where via the Internet you can have conference calls with the additional advantage of seeing the computer screens of participating members. The overall supremo will be able to look at a site supremo's project and explore what has been done with the site supremo. This is a more direct form of feedback than monthly emailing projects. So there are a number of ways that such multi-site teams can be managed and new technologies are making it possible to do so without travelling. However, this needs to be mixed with face-to-face sessions to develop positive team dynamics.

Academic contexts

QDAS was created primarily as a tool for academic research, and many of the accounts of QDAS focus on these uses. However, there are two special circumstances for the use of QDAS in academia that do not fall under this banner and that bear special consideration. These are the use of QDAS in: 1) dissertations; and 2) instructional purposes.

Dissertations and QDAS

Dissertations represent a unique academic genre. In conducting a dissertation, a novice (the doctoral student) is apprenticed to an expert (the faculty adviser). The goal for this dyad is the production of a single complete research project, conducted primarily by the student but with the scaffolding of the faculty member, and, as students and faculty know, the quality and quantity of that scaffolding differs widely from dyad to dyad and program to program.

The dyad is also embedded in other critical groupings: 1) the dissertation committee; 2) the program; 3) graduate studies at the institution; and 4) the discipline(s). Each of these groupings have standards or evaluations that are related to the conduct of the dissertation and, hence, the use of the tools that are used in production of the dissertation.

In today's academic world, while qualitative research is gaining increasing recognition and popularity in diverse academic fields, the use of QDAS in qualitative research dissertations lags behind. This leads to special tensions at those sites where QDAS use is pushing forward. As mentioned above, it is not the purpose of this chapter to discuss how QDAS can be scaled up within higher education: see Chapter 14 for information on this topic. What we wish to focus on here are the ways student, faculty adviser and dissertation committee can make the best use of QDAS in the dissertation process, providing information on how one might address the mixed-use problems (QDAS users and non-users working together) that are the present state of QDAS use in higher education.

In the ideal world, the adviser of qualitative research dissertations would be skilled in QDAS use, as would the members of the dissertation committee. This, however, is not always the case. There are many instances where graduate students may forge ahead alone in the use of QDAS. Regardless of whether yours is the ideal case or not, it is essential if you choose to make QDAS foundational to your work that you get the formal training you need in the tool and seek out the support you will need as you implement your study. The ground floor of good QDAS training is to understand research design in QDAS, the focus of this book.

Let us assume, however, you are one of the lucky ones with an adviser who is skilled in qualitative research and QDAS use. In this situation, you should be able to use QDAS in a full manner that will enhance the depth and quality of your study and introduce you to new ways of understanding the communicative potential of QDAS. Here are suggestions for QDAS use you and your adviser might consider:

1 *Start development of the E-Project as early in the process as possible*

As soon as the project is a 'gleam in your eye' is about the right time to set up an E-Project in which to house your thinking. Think of the E-Project as a virtual organizational and analysis centre, in which everything related to the project will be stored and in which you will conduct the bulk of your work when you are not in the field. Therefore, as soon as you start to muse about the topic, begin to store these thoughts in the E-Project, using memos and/or models. Your musings may be related to readings, and these notes can be imported and serve as the beginnings of your literature review section. Depending on the topic, you may have artefacts that are important to your thinking (newsletters, policy documents, handouts, meeting minutes, etc.). These should also be entered into the E-Project in some form. In our experience, when students put off the development of the E-Project, hoping for just the right moment to enter the materials, it is often a sign they lack confidence in their technical skills or an understanding of the E-Project as a research design feature. If you have a research idea and find yourself avoiding the task of setting up an E-Project, seek help from your adviser, a QDAS consultant or colleagues with experience in the QDAS product you will use.

2   Include full explicit discussion of the E-Project in the dissertation proposal

If you started the use of QDAS from the very beginning moments of your project, then it is already integral to the research process and needs to be described in the dissertation proposal as part of the history of the development of the proposal. In addition, because you will use QDAS throughout the conduct of the study, just as you would envision and describe the research process in a non-QDAS mode, it is essential that in shifting to the use of QDAS you uphold the same standard of full disclosure.

Talking about the future – the 'what I will do' – is often hard for doctoral students, because for many this is the first time they will have experienced the full research process from start to finish. They are not sure of what lies ahead. This is true whether they are working in QDAS or a non-QDAS mode. As advisers, we have often marked in the margins of the methodology section, 'Tell me more'. 'Be more explicit'. 'Add more detail about what you will actually do'. Nothing has changed really, but now the adviser is assuming that 'Tell me more' includes not only how you will conduct the interview, with whom, and how you will organize and analyse it, but what role QDAS is playing in the process, particularly in the organization and analysis of the data.

In writing about QDAS in the dissertation proposal, a typical failing of the doctoral student is to describe the features of the technology without linking these features to the research they will be conducting. The result is that the QDAS sections of the proposal read like an advertisement for a particular QDAS product, but provide little information about the research to be conducted with this product. This is a normal beginner's quandary, as in many cases the student lacks the necessary experience to imagine the connections between the technology and the methodology. Again, this is a place where the adviser needs to probe and nudge to deepen students' reflections. As a rule, the more natural and less jargony the QDAS descriptions sound, the more you will realize that you are 'thinking within' the package rather than 'thinking about' it.

Screenshots can be very helpful to include in the dissertation proposal itself, especially in a situation where some of the committee members are not familiar with QDAS.

3   *Ensure that your IRB submission addresses issues of the E-Project*

Because the E-Project will be integral to all aspects of the conduct of the dissertation, it will necessarily be related to issues concerning the use of human
subjects, the arena of the IRB. Moreover, the E-Project is not only of interest as
a place where confidentiality could be breached; it is a place where one is
expected to reflect upon the key issues of concern in relationship to conducting research in natural social contexts: subjectivity, role, access and ethics. We
discuss these concerns in depth in Chapter 3. As a reminder here, we suggest
you think hard about the ways the E-Project is both a challenge and an
opportunity to the conduct of research that is good and safe for researcher and
researchee. What are the possible dangers you could expose your participants
to? How will you set up protections in advance? Have you thought through
the possible ethical situations you could encounter and how you would
respond? What features have you put in place for reflection on your subjectivity, reactions and the ethical repercussions? Specifically, how are these issues
reflected in the research design of the E-Project? Ethics are not something that
take place outside of the container of the E-Project. If ethics are intertwined
aspects of the project, they are part of the E-Project.

There are several cases in this book where researchers had to deal with complex issues regarding access and ethics. In particular, Chapter 11 – Mandel
and Chapter 13 – Pool and Montgomery are interesting examples in this
regard.

3   *Integrate the actual E-Project in the dissertation committee proposal deliberations*

In the future, perhaps, qualitative research proposals will be submitted as
E-Projects, that is, the E-Project as designed up to that point with an embedded
proposal will be shared with committee members. The doctoral student will
receive comments back from committee members related to the structure of
the E-Project and the proposed research design, which they will incorporate
before completing the final submission. Then, the E-Project will serve as the
central point of discussion at the dissertation proposal hearing. Rather than
the classical oral presentation with overhead transparencies or PowerPoint,
the candidate will discuss the project from within the E-Project, using models
and other items embedded in the E-Project to describe what the research is and
how it will proceed, thus providing committee members with evidence of the
quality of their research design.

Very few places in the academic world, if any, are at this point yet. Because
most of us exist in the era of mixed practices, QDAS and non-QDAS users, this
will not be the scenario most doctoral students encounter. In most cases, the
student will be lucky if the adviser has knowledge of the QDAS package. In
these circumstances, most students will deliver a standard presentation on the
dissertation proposal, but should have the E-Project ready and waiting in
the wings if committee members have questions about it.

4   *Make the E-Project the common medium of exchange between adviser and advisee*

Throughout the conduct of the research project, from the 'gleam in the eye'
moment through to the end of the dissertation hearing, the E-Project should
serve as the common medium of expression and exchange between adviser

and advisee. If they are truly capable of reading and writing in this genre, then they should be conducting their work within it at most times. This means that the E-Project is sent regularly from the student to the adviser as the work evolves, and the adviser has access to the student's full range of materials and thought. This is a new and perhaps scary proposition for adviser and advisee, as both are visible in new ways to each other.

For this process to work, it is critical that students develop projects with reference to commonly accepted standards for research design in E-Projects. Furthermore, it is essential that adviser and advisee 'rope off' a certain area of the E-Project for their joint communication. A memo of some sort that provides a road map to each new version of the proposal will be important for helping the reader understand the evolving directions of the author.

5 *Advisers: review and reflect on the E-Project with the same intensity that you spend on the final draft of the dissertation*

The use of the E-Project as the common medium of exchange places important new responsibilities on the shoulders of the dissertation adviser. In an earlier era, doctoral students in their later stages were pretty much left to their own to conduct research, analyse data and develop findings. While they might have conversation about the project with the adviser, they would see little of the actual materials or the analysis items. This was due in large part to the technology of research – paper, and lots of it – that dominated the process. It was simply too cumbersome to march back and forth to meetings with the wealth of materials one gathers in a full-blown project, even a small one.

The E-Project, with its qualities of transparency and portability, however, provides a way to connect doctoral student and adviser during the critical phases of the conduct of the dissertation research. Wherever the student is, they can email the project as an attachment to the adviser, and the adviser can review the unfolding of the research design as it is represented in the E-Project. As an adviser you can see the quality of the data that is being collected, review the coding that is accumulating, examine the strengths and weaknesses of the coding scheme and read the coding journal for description of what the student thinks they are doing.

Doing this kind of review requires the adviser to be fluent in the use of the genre of the E-Project. To be a good critical reader, you must understand the author's dilemmas – the substance and the technology, and be able to understand how to structure the research design in this medium.

In using the E-Project with doctoral students, we have come to enjoy this opportunity to work hand in hand with students through all phases of the research. However, we are well aware of the shift this makes on an adviser's time and responsibilities. This kind of intensity may require that an adviser should have fewer doctoral commitments. Or it may be that the program needs to consider the ways qualitative research training is conducted in the pre-dissertation part of the program, and where the bar is set; that is training for students may need to be more thorough and there may need to be higher expectations for the level of skill they should achieve before undertaking a qualitative research dissertation.

6   *Make opportunities for public review and critique of E-Projects among advisees*

Although the dissertation is often represented as the lonely work of an isolated researcher, in truth, this research benefits much from being drawn into community. It is through community with other rising scholars that doctoral students will be able to practise their new skills as users of the E-Project genre, and in this way learn, grow and expand their reach in this new arena. Everyone benefits when there can be public review and critique of E-Projects.

As an example, at the University of Massachusetts Lowell's Graduate School of Education, E-Project review was made into a tradition, through the Super Wednesday dissertation advisory groups. A dissertation group composed solely of students working in qualitative research and using QDAS met five times over a semester to provide members with community and critique. E-Projects were shared and discussed throughout the semester. In this way the representation of the research design was always considered part of the technology of QDAS. Indeed, it would have been hard for this group to imagine a qualitative research project, without mentally imaging the features of the QDAS program.

As mentioned in Chapter 3, before this kind of public review can be undertaken, there must be careful attention made to the rules for participation so that the participants in the research projects will not be harmed through careless disclosure.

7   *Include full explicit discussion of the E-Project in the dissertation*

Again, in a future world, the dissertation may be produced and live within the womb of the E-Project, rather than the way it currently exists, as a document separate and apart from it. Given that the current state may continue for some time, it is important to address this reality.

If the research design has been developed within the E-Project, then it is critical that there is full disclosure about its role in the research adventure. This means that the description of the research at every stage should provide information on the organization of the project within the E-Project and the ways this organizational tool shaped the conduct of the research. If the student has been diligent in keeping the coding journal and methodological log, as well as memoing as ideas emerge, they should have ample material for creating a picture of the research process that expertly welds the technical and the substantive together.

Most students find it much easier to create an integrated discussion of the E-Project as the mode of research in the final dissertation stage than they do in the proposal. Having done the research with the QDAS tool, they are not in the same tentative mode that they were when proposing the research. There are still instances, however, where special attention needs to be paid to full disclosure of the role of the E-Project and the discussion of validity is one of these areas. Students need support to go beyond invoking the name of the QDAS product or the processes it affords as a warrant for validity. They need a nudge to take the next step in creating a link for the reader between theoretical discussions of validity (and any of the other questions of qualitative research methodology for that matter) and the use of the QDAS tool that are specific to their research project.

8 *Integrate the actual E-Project in the dissertation committee deliberations*

Again, in a future world, the relationship between dissertation and E-Project may well be reversed, and the E-Project/dissertation will be the subject of a dissertation committee's deliberations. In today's world, however, the dissertation, that unique genre, still reigns as queen/king of the academic world, and probably will reign supreme for some time to come. Although there have been some small changes – dissertations are now read and edited in electronic copy, and on many campuses colour illustrations are no longer considered suspect – the finale, however, the public presentation of the dissertation where committee members and others debate the merits of the candidates work, is still based upon the hard copy.

If the integration of the E-Project and the research process is adequate, there will be much of interest to committee members that is embedded in the E-Project. In the dissertation itself, they will have had access to descriptions of the E-Project's role in the shaping of the research, and they may well have questions about the structure of the E-Project. Thus, it is important to have a copy of the project up and running, ready to go, so that the E-Project can be called upon to add its information to the mix.

Here, though, the dissertation adviser, like the student, runs risks with the committee. Just as the dissertation is seen to be a reflection of the adviser, not just the student, so, too, the E-Project can also be seen as a reflection of the adviser. A poorly structured E-Project, just like a poorly structured, dissertation, could reflect poorly on an adviser. For this reason, it is important that the adviser should be thoroughly knowledgeable of the advisee's E-Project, in the same way that they are aware of the ins and outs of the hard copy dissertation.

Among committee members and in the discussion at the final hearing, it is important to make sense of the dissertation in light of the E-Project.

- Does the E-Project contain all the necessary materials of the project? Did the student fail to enter certain kinds of data? Why?
- Does the coding warrant the assertions made in the dissertation? What can be learned from the coding journal about the development of the analytic system?
- Was the E-Project structured to make appropriate use of the search tools? And did the student do so? To what end?
- Overall, how does the E-Project support the assertions of validity?

9 *Recognize exemplary QDAS use in the dissertation*

Many academic programmes, colleges or universities award students for exemplary dissertation work. As qualitative researchers know, these awards are far more likely to go to quantitative dissertations than qualitative, unless special provision has been made for the recognition of qualitative work. In those cases, where qualitative research dissertations are elected to receive university recognition, it will be important to consider QDAS use as part of the criteria of exemplary work, and not only QDAS use, but the quality of that QDAS use. In an age of digital tools, this is only reasonable and responsible.

Conclusion

In this book, we include three examples of dissertation research: Siccama (Chapter 9), Penna (Chapter 10) and Mandel (Chapter 11). All three represent examples of dissertation studies conducted in the USA. We recognize that there are differences between the US dissertation process and that followed in the UK, Europe and other locations. In particular, in the UK the thesis is examined both by an internal and an external examiner, an individual from another academic institution who is a specialist in the field, which is the subject of the thesis and who has no prior knowledge of the doctoral student's work. This person is asked to make an independent judgement of the dissertation – its substantive and technical competence and quality. As the external examiner is not brought into the doctoral process until the very end, we feel that the internal process recommended for the US system is also relevant for the UK system. We would recommend that *A Guide for the Examination of E-Projects* should be prepared for the benefit of external examiners who may not be familiar with QDAS or the notion of E-Projects. A short glossary of QDAS specific terms should be included in this guide as well as the internal criteria for judging an E-Project. We also recommend that in the case where the external examiner is not familiar with QDAS that they should be matched by an internal examiner who is familiar with QDAS.

Instruction in QDAS

One reason that QDAS integration has lagged in qualitative research is that qualitative research instructors have been slow to make these new technologies part of their course curriculum and instructional goals for learning. Faculty who teach qualitative research may not have received training in these tools and so feel uncomfortable showing them to others. Recognizing the need for exposure, in many cases qualitative research faculty will schedule one class session for an introduction to one or more QDAS tools during the course. This brief introduction may be provided by another faculty member or a graduate student. It may take place in the computer lab and the instructor of the class may not even attend. Exposure, however, falls far short of integration, and integration is what is critical if we are to make full use of QDAS in the field of qualitative research.

A qualitative research course in which QDAS is fully integrated will exhibit the following characteristics:

1 *The instructor will be a competent reader and writer in the E-Project genre*

It is possible to learn on the job as you teach, and that may be the case the first time around, but in the long term it is essential that qualitative research instructors possess the skills and competencies of skilled E-Project users. This means that they understand the best ways to structure E-Projects, are aware of the items that can and should be standardized across projects, and have the ability to integrate knowledge of qualitative research methodology with the structure of the QDAS tool.

It is *not* necessary for a qualitative research instructor to know every QDAS package that is available. It is critical, however, that they have strong knowledge of the QDAS package they will use with their classes. They must also accept the reality that this field of software development is highly dynamic, and they will have to make frequent adjustments as software packages change over time.

A skilled reader and writer of the E-Project genre is flexible, recognizing the multiple features that can be used to achieve a research goal. They possess experience that helps them to understand what happens when they choose one path over another and, thus, can guide students towards productive, rather than unproductive, paths.

2 *The instructor teaches from within and across the E-Project – the E-Project is integral to every part of the course*

As an instructional tool, a useful way to consider the E-Project is as an electronic notebook or portfolio that you grow across a semester. You can pass it between instructor and student, adding to it with each assignment, creating a full record of all the work that is conducted over the term, the responses and the reflections. In this sense, the E-Project is truly a kind of sophisticated E-Portfolio, possessing advanced tools for reflection (coding and linkages) that are not available in the standard E-Portfolio program.

Because the E-Project should be constructed from the earliest inception of a project idea, it makes sense that an instructor would model using the E-Project from the very beginning of coursework. This helps students to practise good E-Project use. Building a project slowly over a semester (whether it is a research project or simply the course as project) provides students with opportunities to start small, reflect frequently, and get feedback about good structuring technique early on before the project has become too cumbersome.

Just as Microsoft Word has become the reality for any kind of writing project, so, too, the use of QDAS will touch upon all parts of a qualitative research undertaking. For instructors of the future, it will be necessary then to 'think in' rather than 'think about' these tools. As teaching becomes more and more digitalized (online and blended forms of online and offline instruction becoming commonplace), it will become increasingly advantageous to have an electronic package like this that can be easily transported between teacher and student or student to student.

3 *The instructor provides students with adequate supports for learning the basic technical aspects of the QDAS package used in the class*

In the early days of the packages, the interface was often off-putting for the average user, but this has changed considerably. As QDAS tools have evolved over time, there has been increasing attention among developers to create user-friendly interfaces. Bearing this in mind, it must be stated that QDAS is complex software. Even those who are intuitive and fluid with the use of software may lack the deep knowledge of qualitative research methodological issues that will allow them to use the tool in a way that is commensurate with the best qualitative research practice. A skilled user is essential for guiding new users to understand QDAS in light of qualitative research methodological discussions.

There are a range of ways a qualitative research teacher can structure technical instruction in the tool. Here are suggestions for providing that assistance:

- integrating instruction in technical features throughout the semester;
- requiring a text with up-to-date technical information on the required QDAS package as a course requirement;
- providing a QDAS lab that is to be taken along with the course;
- offering a special QDAS-intensive workshop for course participants;
- requiring QDAS training prior to undertaking the class (from the software company or a skilled consultant);
- offering QDAS support institution-wide that is available to graduate students;
- requiring students to review the tutorials provided by the software developer.

Students worry about their technical capacity, and these anxieties, if not attended to, can derail a good class. Moreover, down the road you will see better use of the software if students develop a good foundation in the technical features early on.

4 *The instructor makes creative use of QDAS features to teach qualitative research topics*

As with any tool, the more you use it the better you get, and you will find innumerable opportunities to integrate these valuable tools into qualitative research coursework once your mind is tuned in this direction. Some interesting uses that we have found to have value with students include:

- *Use of automatic coding*: If students use Microsoft Word headings for content sections in papers, they will be able to import a paper into NVivo and code automatically; that is, code the headings and their subsequent content sections. Many graduate students struggle with understanding the function of headings in social science writing, and we have found this to be a powerful way of helping them to understand this concept.
- *Coding as reflection*: When students code their own writing or the writing of others it brings them into a new level of understanding with the text and their ideas.
- *The E-Project as collaborative dialogue*: Having students share an E-Project composed of just one interview, in which the reader codes and comments on the interview and then discusses it with the author of the field notes, has had powerful impact in our experience.
- *Logs or journals*: By having students keep logs of research activities (coding journals, methodological logs, etc.), they learn the techniques of good housekeeping in qualitative research. They come to recognize the importance of making entries on a regular basis . . . and the dangers of failing to do so.
- *Literature review*: Many students have told us that the use of QDAS for literature review was a profound turning point for them. Through entering and coding reading notes they began to understand the role of literature in the development of the project in ways they had been blind to before.
- *Accountability*: Simply having everything together in one place has a profound impact on most students. They can see the full range of what they

have produced, and are accountable for what is there (and what is not there)!

With thought, each technical feature can yield different kinds of instructional opportunity, whether it be coding, merging, reporting or creating cases or sets. These are tools to be used on text and visual images, which are the heart and soul of qualitative research. Thinking creatively with QDAS tools has value for both instructor and student.

5 *Students' achievement in content learning is assessed in the context of their demonstration of QDAS facility*

If QDAS is truly integral to the qualitative research course, then assessing the quality of students' QDAS achievement will be a necessary and meaningful activity. By assessing what is good structure and not such good structure and pointing out the difference early on and consistently through the development of their work, students will learn best how to use QDAS. They will learn to distinguish what is important and why; they will learn how to make good choices, and avoid inefficiencies or choices that will impede their progress down the road.

It is important to note that learning QDAS, just like learning any other skill, is a developmental process. What students are aware of and attend to at the beginning is different than what they will be aware of and attend to at the conclusion of the semester. Assessments should be structured to recognize this difference and acknowledge developmental change in students' understanding of QDAS.

6 *Students leave the class understanding the value and importance of developing strong literacy skills in the E-Project genre*

Just as instructors must contend with the constantly changing landscape of QDAS, so, too, must students. As graduate students leave a course in qualitative research, they need to understand that the QDAS skills they possess will need to be added on as they proceed to the next stages of their work. They should have knowledge of the ways they can continue to grow their skills in the institution (user groups, special workshops, etc.) and outside of the institution (conferences, web sites, developers' activities and professional organizations). This will be critical for their continued professional development in the field.

7 *The instructor supports other faculty to better understand students' use of QDAS*

If QDAS, the primary digital tool created exclusively for the conduct of qualitative research, is not accepted by many qualitative researchers, then there is no reason to expect that faculty who are not dedicated qualitative researchers would understand or use these tools. For this reason, it is important that qualitative research instructors work within their programs and institutions to support other faculty to understand the possibilities of QDAS use.

It is not unusual in this era of mixed use to hear faculty who are non-QDAS users make statements like these:

> Does this mean that everything that was done before without QDAS cannot be trusted?

I've never done it this way, and I do an excellent job as a researcher. I don't think I should have to change.

If they want to use it, that's fine with me, but I will only accept copies of materials (paper or electronic) that are available in Microsoft Word.

QDAS can be threatening. It represents a major change in practice and, thus, in our identities as professionals and researchers. We owe it to our students, however, to lead the way towards best practice. In a digital age such as ours, it is inconceivable that these tools will not become essential. We need to help our students make the transition in a way that will support them to grow as future leaders of our field.

Going outside of the box

Because QDAS was developed by qualitative researchers for the use of qualitative researchers, our eyes are often clouded to the fundamental purposes of the tool and the ways these purposes might be more generally applicable in academic or other environments. When looked at dispassionately, QDAS is essentially a text analysis tool, whether that text is alphabetic markings, sound or images. Analysing texts is something students must do across multiple disciplines. English majors analyse poetry, short stories and novels. High school students must learn how to read textbooks in science, social studies and other subjects. Students in many kinds of class must conduct literature reviews and write informative papers. Art students must keep track of images of various kinds and analyse the style, materials and expressive techniques of particular artists. Students in the communication fields must study texts they and others have created (in all manner of forms) to understand how to better express themselves. All of these and many, many more school tasks call out for the application of QDAS. QDAS does not have to stay within the box constructed for it by qualitative researchers. It could 'bleed' across those boundaries to serve much broader purposes within school environments.

Currently, QDAS use is confined almost exclusively to doctoral students. If QDAS is a tool that can serve needs of undergraduates, secondary and even middle schools' students, there is no reason that it should not be used in these other environments. Indeed, it could prove valuable to a broad range of tasks that K-12 students encounter.

As QDAS becomes more broadly accepted, we can assume that it will also begin to spread to a wider range of audience who will apply these tools as they see that it could be useful. This happened with many of the office productivity tools that were introduced to schools (Microsoft Word, Excel and PowerPoint are examples), and we can assume it could happen here, given the match between tool purposes and school tasks. We urge researchers and teachers to explore the use of QDAS outside of the box. This is an arena where we anticipate seeing much creativity. We also urge software developers to consider these new audiences for their products. Indeed, we hope for the day when sophisticated text analysis tools are an assumed feature of standard word-processing programs.

Commercial contexts

Background

QDAS was originally developed by academic qualitative researchers for their own use and for other academic qualitative researchers. While the history of their development goes back to the early 1980s, they have been slow to develop into commercial products. Part of that can be explained by an anti-commercial culture inherent in academia as well as the developers themselves not having the commercial and business skills (or sometimes even the inclination to develop them) to promote their products. The first attempt to promote QDAS products widely was in 1995 when the newly formed company – QSR International (developers of NUD*IST and subsequently NVivo and XSight) – approached Sage Publications (which had an established reputation in publishing books on qualitative research) to market NUD*IST. Sage Publications had an extensive mail order list in both the UK and US academic markets and were soon marketing a range of QDAS. However, they were reluctant to move outside of their known market area, although there was discussion about moving into more commercial markets beginning with market researchers. In the end, Sage Publications moved out completely from marketing QDAS and marketing the software went back to the individual software companies – most of them just micro-businesses. The period that Sage Publications was marketing these products contributed greatly to their dissemination and adoption in academia. However, they made little, if any, impact, on commercial markets.

As a result, there is little awareness of these software packages in the commercial arena. QSR International has been trying to reach the market research market with the launch of XSight in 2004, which was designed with the needs of market researchers in mind. They have had some success but it is still early days in this market. Ruth Rettie of Kingston University surveyed 400 market researchers from the UK Market Research Handbook about their use of QDAS. Of the 153 who replied only 13 (9 per cent) used QDAS. More had heard of QDAS, and the software with the highest brand recognition was NUD*IST (Rettie et al. 2007). QSR dropped the NUD*IST name in 1999 and finally stopped developing it with the launch of NVivo 7 in 2006. The persistence of NUD*IST as the most mentioned software package among market researchers indicates how out of date this sector is with developments in QDAS.

di Gregorio together with Gill Ereaut have presented the case for the use of QDAS at several Association for Qualitative Research (AQR) conferences – the UK qualitative market research association (Ereaut and di Gregorio 2002, 2003). di Gregorio also presented at the annual Business Intelligence Group's (BIG) Business-to-Business Researchers Getting Together (B2B) conference in the UK (di Gregorio 2005). The general reaction by market researchers is one of caution: concern that the software may somehow interfere with the analysis; concern of the amount of time needed to prepare data and to code; and whether the time needed to learn the software is worth the effort.

In North America, the situation is not much different. The Virtual Chapter of the Qualitative Research Consultants Association (QRCA) ran an online discussion on qualitative research analysis tools in May 2007 (Walkowski and Nordgren 2007). Thirty-three QRCA members took part over three days. di Gregorio analysed the transcript of their discussion, which included both the existing ways these researchers conduct analysis and what they would expect from a QDAS package and finally their reactions to demonstrations of some of the packages. Figure 4.3 maps out the current research practice of the QRCA members who took part in the discussion.

This online discussion demonstrated that the software tools most QRCA members used was Microsoft Word with a few using Excel and PowerPoint. Several still use exclusively manual methods such as flipcharts and post-it notes. Extracting or reducing the data included writing a page per subject or using the interview guide as a template. However, they were far from happy with their existing methods. Many described analysis as a big job, requiring a lot of space. They found it hard to handle lots of data and to keep track of where quotes came from.

Figure 4.4 maps out the QRCA participants' wish list for how software could help them. What is interesting is that QDAS already meets most of their wish list.

All the features included under 'organizing data' and 'analysing data' have been available for some time from most of the popular packages. Reporting features are rapidly improving but it has always been easy to export to Microsoft Word or PowerPoint. A few of these researchers never use transcripts and were not aware that some of these tools could be used without full transcripts or any transcripts at all. (Partial transcripts, summaries and/or notes can be used with all packages and QSR's XSight allows the inputting of quotes and summaries directly into a thematic framework without any transcripts or summaries at all.) An important fear was the amount of time it would take to learn a new package. It would have to be intuitive to learn.

On the final day of this online discussion, the participants saw a variety of packages demonstrated. They were pleasantly surprised at how user-friendly some of them looked. Those packages which imitated a Microsoft interface were most favoured. The ability to analyse video was seen as a positive. Many were interested in trying out a few of the packages. Their earlier scepticism seemed to be based on what they had heard about earlier versions of the package and not being clear about how the packages could support analysis.

With each passing year more market researchers are considering that the benefits outweigh the disadvantages. The packages, themselves, are becoming more user-friendly over time. The success that Ipsos MORI have had with XSight (Chapter 7) is spreading. The Ipsos MORI team have been presenting their experience at a number of conferences (Vince and Sweetman 2006). As more companies start to use the software, the more it will become a 'must have' technology.

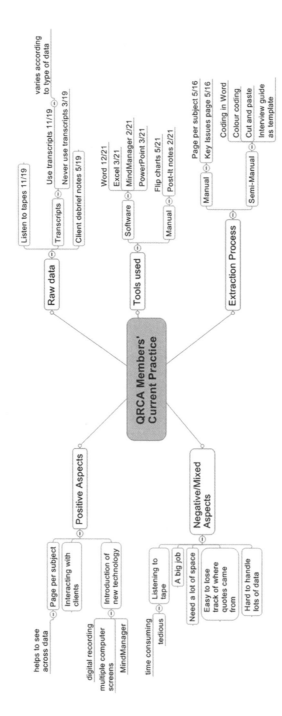

Figure 4.3 Current research practice of some QRCA members

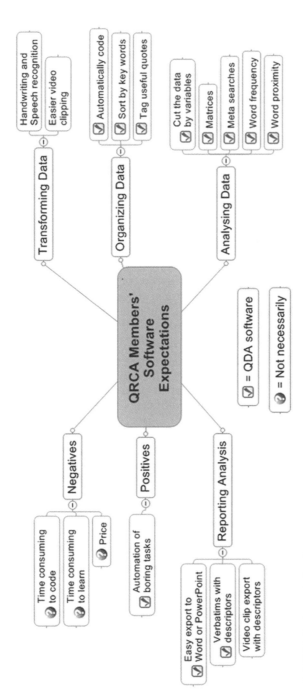

Figure 4.4 Wish list for analysis software

Initial impetus for using QDAS

In the UK there has been an increase in the government commissioning market research companies to conduct evaluation and policy research including research involving qualitative data (Sin 2006). Government departments require accountability, and market research companies involved in this kind of research are required to make more transparent the evidence for their conclusions. This pressure has led a few market research companies to try using a QDAS. The Ipsos MORI project reported in Chapter 7 is an example of a market research company's need to satisfy the demands of a government department. The size of the project (78 focus groups) was another consideration that led them to try out QSR XSight. The success of that project led to the software being used in other projects at Ipsos MORI. Slowly, a core group of users has developed and expertise is being shared across the company about changing working practices in order to maximize the use of the software. It could be that QDAS could be incorporated in the working practice of market research companies through their increased involvement with policy research.

In order for software to become part of the working practice of a company, there is a need for a strong champion or champions within the company who push for the adoption of software. di Gregorio has been involved in a number of projects where the initial champions for the use of software either left the company or were promoted too early in the adoption process, so no one was able to take over the promotion of the software once they left.

The adoption of QDAS in the commercial arena is at an earlier stage than in the academic sector where although still not part of the mainstream has institutions with core groups of users. The commercial sector has still to develop those organizations with core QDAS users. However, as they are starting to consider the software at a later point in time, they are looking at far more user-friendly software and the adoption process is likely to be much shorter than in the academic sector. However, as within the academic sector, adoption will have to come hand in hand with reorganizing working practices. This will vary according to the type of organization.

The E-Project in a commercial context

The implications of the E-Project in commercial research are wide-ranging. Yet, as QDAS packages are not well understood in this sector, the value of having everything in one place pertaining to a particular brand, or to a particular client, or to a particular market sector, are lost to potential users. Part of the problem is that these products have been marketed emphasizing the tools in each package. As many of these packages have developed their own vocabulary for naming different features, the use of these tools are lost to those trying to get a sense of whether a package would help them or not. If QDAS were promoted showing their benefits and end use, we feel that more commercial companies would be eager to take advantage of their benefits.

Key benefits of the E-Project

The E-Project is best conceptualized for the commercial market as a management tool – one that manages both data and ideas. It is an electronic container of all your material as well as your ideas and analysis. Instead of having tapes, notes and reports stored in different locations, they are all immediately accessible in one place. This enables the commercial researcher to:

- immediately access detailed information about a particular client or brand;
- build on and add to existing knowledge;
- respond quickly to clients' requests for additional information;
- produce an additional deliverable for the client – an archive about their business issues.

Market researchers and consultants strive to develop a continuing relationship with their clients. They can build up a wealth of knowledge of their clients over the years. For individual consultants, the ability to be able to access this information is valuable; using a QDAS package is far better than relying on memory or information scattered across several files. For an organization, it is crucial; staff are promoted, move on to other departments or leave an organization – and with them goes the wealth of knowledge they have gleaned over the years. Whereas if that knowledge is held in a QDAS package, not only is that information available for the organization but the way that information has been interpreted and used is also available. The tacit knowledge of key employees which seems so elusive and difficult for organizations to retain is made much more accessible.

Regular clients often ask for similar types of research to be done over the years. Often this can lead to time wasted 'reinventing the wheel' – going over ground that had already been established in previous projects for the client. Working with QDAS, previous work is easily accessible and can be reviewed. More time can be spent on building up from existing knowledge. Again, for organizations, it is easier for a new team to pick up and build on work that a former disbanded team had developed. It gives the client an added incentive to stay with a particular consultant or market research company. The client knows that consultant or company knows their business. It is not unusual for clients to ask for additional information once a report or presentation has been done. The query features of QDAS packages make it quick and easy to look at information in a new way. The consultant can provide the additional information very quickly, even if the request from the client is several months down the line.

Finally, the E-Project itself – as an archive – is a new deliverable to a client which should not be underestimated. It is a more substantial deliverable than a report as it offers the client the opportunity to look *inside* the data. As QDAS packages are becoming more user-friendly, this is not so far-fetched. A *Guidance for Clients* document can be written and contained within the E-Project to help them navigate through the archive. It is a deliverable that can be added to the digital library of company knowledge.

Challenges posed by E-Projects

While QDAS provides new benefits to commercial researchers, it also offers some new challenges. A key challenge is the flip side of the benefits provided by ease of access to information and ideas. It also makes it easy to access confidential material. As raw data is visible, the identities of key informants are exposed. If informants are company employees, the consequences of negative attitudes could lead to dismissal. This would have a negative impact on future research as potential key informants would be reluctant to express their true views.

There is also the danger of industrial espionage. As the E-Project is very portable, it could be easily emailed to a rival company. As the E-Project contains all the raw data, ideas and analysis around a particular topic, this is far more damaging than a leaked document.

In addition, there are the growing rules and regulations about the storage of personal information. This is particularly true in Europe. The Data Protection Act (Office of Public Sector Information) 1998 is the relevant legislation for the UK. The USA has no overarching privacy law. It relies on a mix of legislation, regulation and self-regulation. The European Union (EU) requires the creation of governmental data protection agencies and the registration of databases with those agencies. What data is stored, who has access to it, and where it is stored are all issues that need to be carefully addressed. The digitalization of all forms of data has prompted European governments to legislate to protect the rights of individuals. The European Commission's Directive (95/46/EC) on Data Protection (1995) prohibits the transfer of personal data to non-European countries that do not satisfy their privacy criteria. In order to continue trade with the EU, the US Department of Commerce created a voluntary scheme – Safe Harbor – where companies self-certify themselves annually that they comply to the Safe Harbor principles of notice, choice, transfer to third parties, access, security, data integrity and enforcement. Commercial researchers need to keep abreast of these developments and put in place procedures to conform to these requirements.

Design issues

Does size matter?

A common question I (di Gregorio) have had from market researchers is: What number of documents do you need to have in a piece of research to make it worth while to use a QDAS package. Market researchers can see the need for software when dealing with large amounts of data but find it hard to see the benefits when working with a small dataset. Time is usually limited and they are concerned that by the time they start to get to grips with a software package, they could have had the report written and delivered to their client if they had stuck with their tried and tested traditional methods. Ironically, it is much easier to learn software with a small dataset than with a large dataset. You can see much more easily what the software is doing, and you are more likely to start playing with more of the tools the software has to offer. The question should not be about the size of the project but about the level of complexity of the project design. A small project of six focus group discussions where participants are asked to respond to television ads of a number of brands and then fill out individual open-ended responses to those brands before a group discussion could be quite complex to analyse, whereas 100 open-ended responses to five basic questions could be a straightforward sorting job.

Levels of complexity

In market research, in contrast to academic research, there are two types of complexity to consider; the range of complexity in the research design (which is common to both academic and commercial research) and the range of complexity in the topic to analyse. By definition, academic research, including doctoral theses, consider complex topics. Market researchers tend to look at a wider range of complexity, from very basic topic areas (from an academic viewpoint) to very complex areas. It could be argued that companies where the emphasis is mostly on quantitative techniques with the occasional foray into qualitative work may not see the need to invest in learning a QDAS package. A few open-ended questions, for example, could be looked at using traditional methods. There is also an issue that if the qualitative work is irregular, the package would have to be relearned each time it is used. In any area, learning is reinforced through repetition or repeated use. If only a small amount of simple qualitative work comes up once a year, then maybe using a package is not efficient. However, if a piece of work is complex (not necessarily large in size), then it may well be worth the effort.

Managing the data

As mentioned previously, QDAS is a data management tool. Commercial researchers should think through the relevant data required for a project. They should consider both primary and secondary data.

Primary data for market researchers commonly would include interview records, respondent-produced materials, field notes and observations and the client's perspective (Ereaut 2002). Increasingly, they could also include video diaries, vox pop (Firefish), blogs, bulletin boards, online forum discussions and other forms of multimedia and online data. Audio-recording of focus groups and depth interviews are standard as is video-recording for fieldwork conducted in viewing facilities (Ereaut 2002). The decision facing the researcher is whether to transcribe audio and video data or work from notes. This decision could be dependent on budget, time and the complexity of the topic under study. Most QDAS is flexible – transcripts are not required for its use. Summaries and notes can be analysed in the software.

Much commercial research relies on setting respondents tasks often incorporating projective techniques. These respondent-produced materials can also be analysed, although often they are interpreted with the respondent and the data would be the resultant notes or tape of that discussion with the researcher. This data can also be organized in QDAS. Most packages have facilities for working with graphics and photos and increasingly video. Notes can be linked to the graphics they refer to.

The client's perspective is also data to be organized. This would include the project brief, any briefing sessions with the client, background material, email/telephone communication, and so on. Background material, company reports and the like are secondary data that can enhance the analysis.

Some commercial research could be geared more towards secondary analysis. The analysis of newspaper ads, television commercials and company brochures are examples of this kind of data. With commercial researchers expanding their repertoire of analysis techniques into areas such as semiotics, this kind of data will become more important (Ereaut and Segnit 2006).

The type of data that will be collected is known at the start of the project and just as described in Chapter 2, a 'shell' of the project can be constructed before any data has been collected. The different types of data can be organized into folders, or sets, or families, dependent on which QDAS package is adopted. These can be created beforehand, ready for the data, whether transcripts, notes, tapes, and so on. Background information and protocols can be imported into the E-Project at the start. Working with the E-Project right at the proposal stage will help commercial researchers become familiar with the notion that QDAS can be used as a thinking tool as well as an organizing tool. It will also help them in keeping the project organized right from the start.

In addition, at the beginning of a brief or proposal, it is possible to think of the characteristics that you will be collecting about the subjects of research – whether they are people or documentary material. This information such as gender, age, job, and so on for people or type of document, date, source for secondary material can be set up beforehand in the package, ready to be allocated as data is collected.

Managing ideas

QDAS is also an ideas management tool. It can be used as a virtual whiteboard to start brainstorming ideas. Most of the packages have a modelling tool, where you can flesh out your initial ideas about a particular brief. It can also be used to map out relationships in your data as well as to map out the structure of a report. More worked out ideas can be incorporated into a catalogue. These themes can be coded. The code and retrieve function of QDAS is both the most understood and misunderstood aspect of how the software works. It is understood partly because coding is an activity that quantitative analysts do. It is also understood because the software makes the coding of documents very transparent. All the packages allow you to see the coding in the 'margins' of the on-screen transcript. The packages also make coding very easy to do – just a question of highlighting the relevant text and dragging it to a code. However, this ease of coding can lead to over-coding and in doing so the purpose of coding in the first place can be lost (Gilbert 1999; Declercq 2002). For novice users coding becomes an end in itself and the crucial process of reflecting on the data gets lost (di Gregorio 2003). Instead, coding should be best conceptualized as 'indexing' ideas in a catalogue. (It is interesting to note that QSR NUD*IST originally described its catalogue system as an 'index system;' however, coding is the terminology that has stuck.) It is a way of cataloguing your ideas about themes or categories in the data in order to retrieve them later on. Your catalogue of codes is an efficient way of managing your ideas about the data. However, it needs to be used in conjunction with tools that support reflection and holistic thinking, such as memos and maps.

Many qualitative market researchers, however, do not bother coding. Ereaut

(2002) describes how it is not only a time investment issue but that it 'feels wrong' to some commercial qualitative researchers. There is a feeling that it is counter to a 'holistic' approach which is valued by some market researchers; that a sift-and-sort approach fragments data and certainly cannot get at the interactive processes in the analysis of focus group discussions – a common technique among market researchers. Other commercial researchers do code or at least summarize their data according to categories. Whether to code or not and how much to code depends very much on the approach to analysis. Contrary to popular belief QDAS can be used without coding at all. Ideas can be represented by maps and by memos. QSR XSight is a package designed especially for market researchers which offers a solution for categorizing summaries of ideas without the need for detailed coding. The point is that regardless of whether an analyst codes or not, QDAS provides tools for organizing and managing ideas about the data. If some of these ideas are known at the start of the research, they can be represented in the E-Project as initial codes or memos. As more ideas emerge they can be added to the 'shell' of the project. An audit trail of the analysis process can be created by keeping a journal in the E-Project where analysts can record their work on the project and date-time stamp the entries. This is key when working in teams (discussed earlier) but also for the sole researcher as a way to reflect on their thinking process and as an aid when pulling together findings for a report.

Commercial contexts other than market research

Challenges in understanding what qualitative analysis can do for you

In a commercial context, the term 'qualitative data' has little meaning. One of the problems in the commercial world is that people do not recognize the material that they try to manage as 'qualitative data'. Customer records, letters, emails, company brochures, web-site content, and so on are all forms of qualitative data. QDAS can be used both to organize this material and mark it up so retrieval is facilitated.

While the value of organizing this kind of material for easy retrieval may be self-evident, what to do with all this material may not be so evident. Commercial organizations need help in not only recognizing what is qualitative data but also in what they can do with it. It is very early days in the application of QDAS to this sector but there are a few visionaries who have seen the possibilities. Below are some ideas.

Customer relations departments

CMS Cameron McKenna are an international law firm who value being client-focused. The client relations team had been gathering client feedback on their relationship for four years. They wanted to get an in-depth view so they had been outsourcing the interviews to specialist qualitative market researchers. These researchers conducted the in-depth interviews and produced very detailed summaries which included direct quotations into a template. The template varied according to the market research company. While Cameron McKenna were happy with the quality of these feedback reports, they were faced with a massive amount of data and found it difficult to retrieve the information they needed. They first turned to their IT department for a solution but the development time was too lengthy. Then they discovered QDAS.

Cameron McKenna wanted to use the material they gathered from clients in a number of ways (Coia 2006). Business development managers would ask for information to help them pitch for new clients. Previous feedback provides valuable information on approaches used in past projects and how clients assessed these approaches. This evidence is used to get new business. The information was also used within the company to analyse the strengths and weaknesses of approaches used by different partners or different sectors of the business. This information would be fed back in order to improve perform-ance. The information is also used in their quarterly reports to the company. The customer relations team already had a vision of how they wanted to use the qualitative data. They just needed to find the right tool to help them realize that vision. QDAS has now enabled them to manage their client feedback data so they can retrieve information quickly in order to win new business as well as help to continue to raise the standard of their workforce (di Gregorio 2006b).

Complaints and helplines

Another aspect of customer relations is managing complaints. In addition, companies, particularly technological companies, have helplines to assist customers who are having problems with their products. IBM's Tokyo Research Laboratory have been developing their own text mining software called TAKMI (Text Analysis and Knowledge Mining) in order to support a variety of issues key to the company. The software packages they have developed are state of the art and to date are for internal use only. They are not commercially avail-able. However, IBM have visionaries who understand both what qualitative data is and can see how this information can help the business.

They have seen the value of analysing the records of customers from their call centres around the world. Analysis of these records would help them in a number of areas. It would help improve:

- sales productivity – by analysing good contact patterns with customers; this could be fed into an education programme to enhance operators' skills;
- marketing – by extracting potential customers for a particular marketing campaign from contact logs;
- customer intelligence – by extracting reputation from customers about products and services;
- contact centre business process – by extracting customers' most frequent questions to be used to create FAQ log and to aid in producing monthly reports.

In order to aid the collection of information from their call centres, IBM have developed a voice recognition software that needs no training and recog-nizes multiple voices over a phone line. di Gregorio saw this software demon-strated at a workshop sponsored by the National Centre for e-Social Science in Manchester, UK and can vouch for its accuracy. This software is not available commercially but as IBM have proved it is technically possible, it is something to watch out for in the future.

IBM have found TAKMI particularly effective in PC help centres where it has been able to identify product failures in its early stages. It identified a paint peeling problem in one of its computer models very early on in its release. IBM estimate that they saved millions of dollars by identifying this problem early on in the production process through the analysis of customer complaints coming through their PC Help Centre in Raleigh, NC (Nasukawa 2006).

Online talk boards, blogs

Web sites offer another rich source of qualitative data for customers. Many companies have feedback forms for customers. Some even have their own customer forums or discussion groups. This data is already digitalized so it would be easy to import into a QDAS package. Although an academic study, the 'Buying birth' case (Chapter 8), analyses how hospitals and natural birth providers market their services through an analysis of their web pages. Companies could do the same in order to position themselves differently from competitors.

Summary

While the use of QDAS is relatively new in market research and commercial research agencies and it is hardly known in commercial companies, it is gaining a foothold. A big push is the increase in the number of large-scale evaluation projects that are using qualitative data. More of this research is being done in the commercial sector and they need software tools just to manage the sheer amount of data. However, as argued in this chapter, they need to be aware that they will also need to change their working practices when they adopt a piece of software. In commercial companies, there are a few visionaries who are starting to see the benefit of analysing their unstructured data. Once these benefits become more widely known, others could well jump on the QDAS bandwagon.

Conclusion

As indicated earlier in this chapter, research does not take place in a social vacuum. Researchers and users of QDAS need to situate themselves within a variety of contexts. Starting with themselves, they need to look at their experience and predispositions, their strengths and weaknesses and their power to influence, given their position. These are important factors in order to gauge their likely success when designing a piece of research within QDAS and the implications QDAS has for the other contexts in which they are embedded. Moving on to 'situated activity', QDAS users need to reassess their current working practices and modes of communication with others involved in the research. QDAS itself can be used as a mode of communication. The research design should be represented in the software and so QDAS can be a vehicle to examine the design (as mentioned earlier in relation to the dissertation committee) and to change it. Protocols for teamworking need to be revisited. It is no good introducing QDAS into an existing system for teamworking which was designed to work with an earlier technology. New forms of working practices need to be designed using the new affordances QDAS brings. However, designing new practices has to take account of the wider context of the setting where the research takes place. Organizations have their own rules and regulations and criteria for standards. Designing new practices may be easier in some settings than in others. There needs to be an understanding and acceptance across whatever the setting the research is embedded that new protocols are required when using QDAS. Finally, different overarching contexts such as the sector the research is located; for example academic, public sector, commercial and the national context pose differing constraints on the design of research using QDAS.

In Appendix 1 you will find a series of questions to help researchers think through the contexts in which they are embedded and the kinds of issue they may confront when designing research using QDAS.

Note

1 The National Centre for Social Research released a Framework QDAS package to support the Framework Approach in September 2008.

PART II
Exemplars

5 Introduction to the cases

Introduction

The first part of this book discussed the special issues that need to be considered when using QDAS. We have argued that the E-Project is a container that holds all the relevant materials relating to a specific piece of research. In order to use the tools that support analysis, the research design needs to be represented in this container. We have proposed a framework of questions about the research design that need to be considered when setting up an E-Project. In addition, the transparent and portable nature of the E-Project raises new ethical and privacy issues that researchers need to address. Finally, the context in which researchers are adopting QDAS – whether within a university or commercial context, whether as part of a team or dyad – requires new thinking about ways of communicating the research to that wider context.

We believe the best way to illustrate our arguments is through examples of real research projects. Our principles of research design are relevant to any QDAS package. Table 5.1 identifies the chapter, project title and researchers for each of the eight E-Projects we examine. For brevity's sake, in this chapter we refer to each E-Project primarily by the name of the researcher. Thus, Chapter 6 may be referred to as the 'Audit Commission' and Chapter 9 as 'Siccama'.

We have examples from four QDAS packages – ATLAS.ti, MAXqda, NVivo and XSight. However, in deciding which case is relevant to your situation, the type of software used should not be your guiding principle. All these projects could

Table 5.1 Table of case chapters, project titles and researcher(s)

Chapter	Title	Researcher(s)
Chapter 6	The Framework for Comprehensive Performance Assessment (CPA) of District Councils from 2006: an analysis of a consultation	Audit Commission
Chapter 7	Views of New Deal for Communities (NDC): focus group study	Ipsos MORI
Chapter 8	Buying birth: consumption and the ideal of natural birth	Rutherford and Gallo-Cruz
Chapter 9	Faculty support staff in online programs	Siccama
Chapter 10	Beyond planning a field trip	Penna
Chapter 11	Doing what it takes	Mandel
Chapter 12	Follow-along study	Hamner
Chapter 13	Microbicides Development Programme (MDP) case study	Pool and Montgomery

have used any of these software packages or other QDAS packages not included in this section on cases. You should be guided by looking at cases that best reflect the research design you are adopting.

Note: We have chosen cases (with the exception of Rutherford and Gallo-Cruz) that Davidson (Penna, Siccama) or di Gregorio (Audit Commission, Hamner, Ipsos MORI, Mandel, Pool and Montgomery) have either been involved with in a supervisory or in a consulting capacity.

Guide to cases

Researcher contexts

Starting from the macro-level, you could look at the cases according to the cultural contexts in which they are located (see Figure 5.1). At the national level, there are five projects from the USA (Hamner, Mandel, Penna, Rutherford and Gallo-Cruz, and Siccama); two UK projects (Audit Commission and Ipsos MORI), and one multinational project (Pool and Montgomery). The multinational project is funded by the UK Department for International Development and is administered by the Medical Research Council Clinical Trials

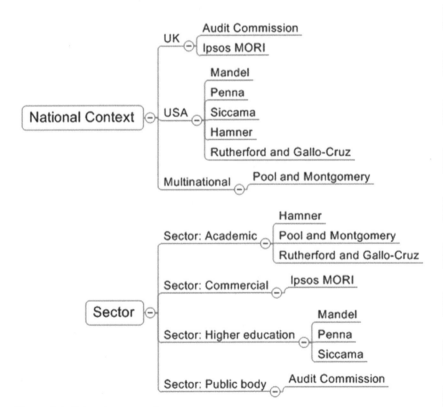

Figure 5.1 Cultural context of cases

Unit and Imperial College London. There are six research sites in four African countries – South Africa, Uganda, Zambia and Tanzania. Among the cases in this section, four sectors are represented: three higher education dissertations (Mandel, Penna and Siccama); three academic pieces of research (Hamner, Pool and Montgomery and Rutherford and Gallo-Cruz); one public sector research project (Audit Commission); and one project from a commercial market research company (Ipsos MORI).

In terms of research settings, the majority are located within individual organizations (Audit Commission, Ipsos MORI, Hamner, Mandel, Penna and Siccama). One is a multi-organization network (Pool and Montgomery) and another is a collaboration between two academics located in different organizations (Rutherford and Gallo-Cruz).

In terms of situated activity, Mandel, Penna and Siccama were all doctoral students and communicated not only with their adviser but with their dissertation committee and other students. In addition, Penna and Siccama had additional support as they were in an environment where the software they were using (NVivo 7) was supported by staff who were knowledgeable about the software and had set up specific regular seminars (see Chapter 4) where students presented and discussed their research using the software. The Audit Commission, Hamner, Pool and Montgomery and Ipsos MORI were all large team research projects. They had to set up their own structures for dividing up the teamwork using the software and for communicating with the software. The projects from the Audit Commission and Ipsos MORI were the first projects that these researchers had tackled using QDAS as a team. Rutherford and Gallo-Cruz are an example of a dyad who had to develop their own system for collaborating using QDAS. They were first time users of their particular software.

Research contexts

The cases represent a number of different approaches to qualitative analysis. Three of them take an ethnographic approach. Penna and Siccama take an exploratory ethnographic approach while Rutherford and Gallo-Cruz take an ethnographic content analysis approach. There are three evaluation studies. Ipsos MORI did an evaluation of a national programme at one point in time; Hamner and Pool and Montgomery are longitudinal evaluations. Mandel took a case study approach while the Audit Commission study is an example of an analysis of a public consultation.

In terms of the development of their thematic frameworks, Siccama and Rutherford and Gallo-Cruz had a very emergent approach; Penna and Mandel referred to existing literature and had a semi-emergent approach; Hamner and Pool and Montgomery are examples of the principal investigator developing the thematic framework with inputs from the larger research team, while the Audit Commission and Ipsos MORI had developed the thematic framework in advance for their teams (see Figure 5.2).

The unit of analysis is one of the key factors that need to be considered when setting up a project in any QDAS. Only one project had one unit of analysis

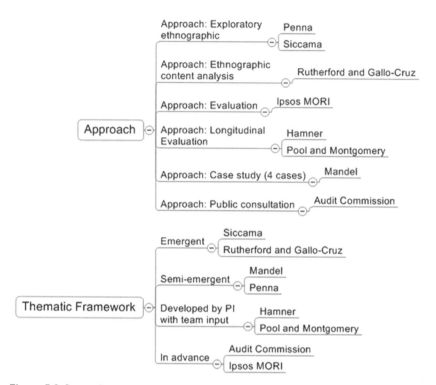

Figure 5.2 Research approaches and thematic framework

(Audit Commission). Their unit of analysis was the public consultation response. All the others had multiple units of analysis, although three of them (Hamner, Penna and Rutherford and Gallo-Cruz) had mainly one unit of analysis. Figure 5.3 locates each case in terms of the number and type of units of analysis in their study.

A large number of types of variable were used across the cases (see Figure 5.4). The most common type of variable was characteristics of individuals, such as gender, job position, and so on. Penna and Pool and Montgomery also looked at variables related to the behaviour of the individuals in their research, such as use of lesson plans (Penna) and use of gel (Pool and Montgomery). Responses to closed-ended questions (Audit Commission) are also variables relating to individuals. Partnership values, provider characteristics and programme values refer to the characteristics of organizations or programmes. Finally, Rutherford and Gallo-Cruz through their ethnographic content analysis were able to characterize the web sites they studied according to dominant and supplementary themes and classified them accordingly.

Half of the eight cases used only one type of data in their study while the other half used multiple types of data (see Figure 5.5). In-depth interviews were the most common type of data collection method, used by five out of the eight research projects. Focus groups were used by two of the projects (Ipsos MORI and Pool and Montgomery). Logs/diaries kept by respondents were used by

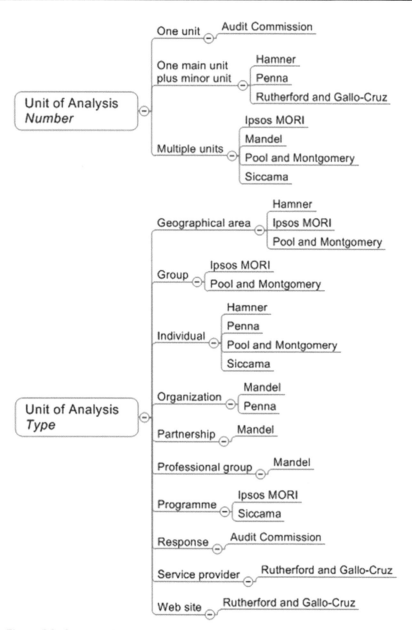

Figure 5.3 Cases and their units of analysis by number and type

three of the research studies (Penna, Pool and Montgomery and Siccama). Other data collection methods included artefacts, observations, field notes and questionnaires. A few cases included multimedia data collection methods. Penna and Siccama used photos taken by respondents while Rutherford and Gallo-Cruz analysed web sites. The Audit Commission's data were replies to a public consultation. The replies took various forms; some were emails, others

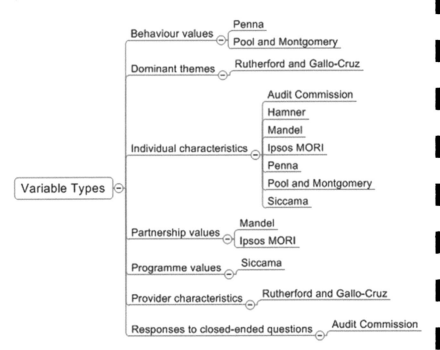

Figure 5.4 Types of variables used in cases

letters, and others followed the line of questioning provided in the consultation document.

Special features

Each case also illustrates several special features and lessons to be learned from the case. Figure 5.6 illustrates the special features in the cases.

Coding

Penna and Siccama illustrate the use of automatic coding for structured data in NVivo 7. Both Penna and Siccama prepared their interviews and Siccama prepared her activity logs in Microsoft Word with appropriate style features so they could automatically code them for these broad topic areas in NVivo. In addition, Siccama and Pool and Montgomery used the 'coding on' technique where it is possible to initially code broadly, then through reading through a broad code it is possible to code more finely within the broad code itself.

Institutional review boards

In Chapter 2, we have already discussed how Leslie Mandel had to have her study approved by several IRBs which led to some modification of her research design.

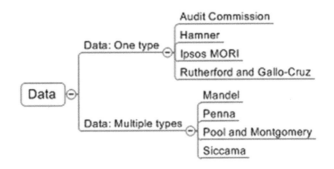

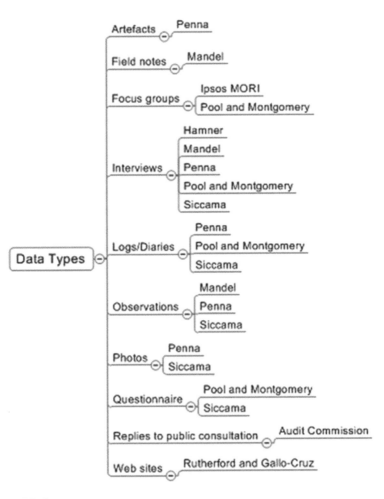

Figure 5.5 Data types

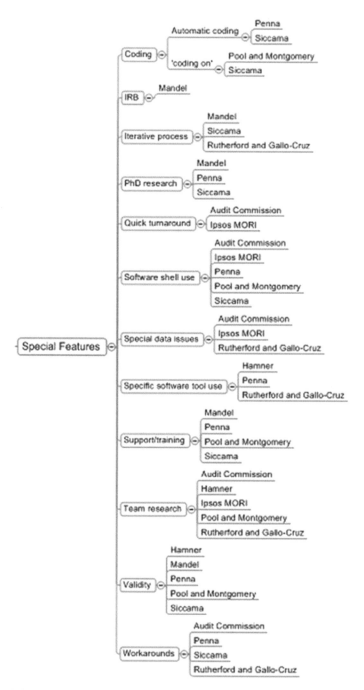

Figure 5.6 Special features

Iterative process

Discussions about the iterative process when analysing qualitative data in QDAS can be found in Mandel, Siccama and Rutherford and Gallo-Cruz.

PhD research

Mandel, Penna and Siccama are the three cases of doctoral students using QDAS for their dissertations.

Quick turnaround

The Audit Commission study and the Ipsos MORI study are both examples of projects which required a quick turnaround in the analysis in order to meet deadlines.

Software shell use

We discussed in the earlier chapters the importance of starting with the research design and reflecting that design in the initial stage of the research. The Audit Commission, Ipsos MORI, Penna, Pool and Montgomery and Siccama are the projects which began with the creation of the E-Project software shell.

Special data issues

Three projects exemplify special issues relating to how they managed data in QDAS. The Audit Commission study was an analysis of a public consultation. The responses to a public consultation come in a variety of forms – decisions had to be made on how to handle this fact. Ipsos MORI had time constraints on the turnaround of their analysis and did not have the time for transcribing their focus groups. Instead, they designed a system whereby the focus group moderators directly input data into QDAS while listening to the focus group tapes. Rutherford and Gallo-Cruz were analysing web sites, which currently cannot be directly imported into QDAS. They had to devise a workaround to represent their data.

Specific software tool use

The Hamner case illustrates the use of the super code tool and the network tool in ATLAS.ti. Penna illustrates the use of some of NVivo 7 searches as well as how the software shell was used in the defence of her dissertation. The Rutherford and Gallo-Cruz case illustrates the use of the code matrix browser to identify dominant codes.

Support and/or training

Mandel, Penna and Siccama discuss issues of support/training in QDAS for doctoral students. The Pool and Montgomery case discuss capacity building for a large team using QDAS.

Team research

The Pool and Montgomery case is an example of large-scale multi-teamwork. There are six teams based in six different geographical areas that are coordinated by one principal investigator. The Audit Commission, Hamner and Ipsos MORI cases are examples of a single team using QDAS. Rutherford and Gallo-Cruz are an example of a dyad (team of two).

Validity

The Hamner and Pool and Montgomery cases discuss their procedures for quality control and validity when working with QDAS in a team. Mandel, Penna and Siccama address this issue within PhD research.

Workarounds

The Audit Commission study looks at how new versions of a programme dispense with the needs of a previous workaround. In this case, it is the use of sets as a workaround in NVivo 2 and the new feature of document folders which dispenses with this use of sets as a workaround. Penna and Siccama discuss the use of a workaround to represent their photos in NVivo 2 and 7. This workaround will no longer be needed with the introduction of NVivo 8 which allows for the importation and direct coding of photos. Rutherford and Gallo-Cruz discuss their workaround for representing web sites in MAXqda 2007.

The design framework

In Chapter 2, we introduced the design framework as a guide when representing the research design in QDAS. We categorized types of design into simple, complex and compound complex (see Figure 5.7). We present the eight case examples in this book in the order from the simplest design to the most complex design.

A simple design is where there is one unit of analysis or one type of data. The Audit Commission study (NVivo 7), Ipsos MORI study (XSight) and Rutherford and Gallo-Cruz (MAXqda) fall into that category (see Figure 5.8). Complex designs are where there could be more than one unit of analysis or a variety of

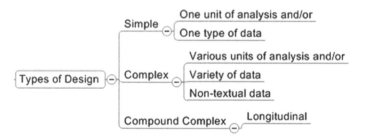

Figure 5.7 Types of design

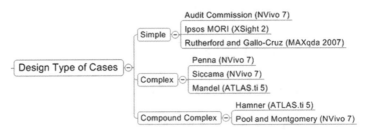

Figure 5.8 Design type of cases

data which could include non-textual data which is directly imported in the software. Penna (NVivo 7), Siccama (NVivo 7) and Mandel (ATLAS.ti 5) are examples of complex designs. Compound complex designs are projects which have a longitudinal element. Managing longitudinal data in QDAS requires use of more tools. Hamner (ATLAS.ti 5) and Pool and Montgomery (NVivo 7) are examples of compound complex designs.

A figure with a summary about the key features of the case is shown at the beginning of each case chapter.

Conclusion

We hope these hands-on case examples provide readers with concrete details to help them efficiently organize their specific projects. It is also our desire that by reviewing the cases with the lens of the research design framework provided here, readers will move forward in their understanding of the issues related to integrating the rich body of qualitative research methodological literature with the practice of using QDAS. We hope our efforts will contribute to the development of standards for practice in this new world of qualitative research where QDAS and other digital tools play such an important role.

6 The Framework for Comprehensive Performance Assessment (CPA) of District Councils from 2006: an analysis of a consultation[1]

The software that was used in the original project was NVivo 2.

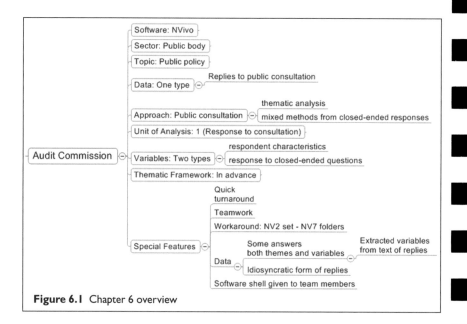

Figure 6.1 Chapter 6 overview

For the purposes of this discussion, we have converted the Audit Commission's study into the latest version of NVivo at the time of publication – NVivo 7. In making the conversion to NVivo 7, we have also undertaken some reorganiza-tion of the project in order to demonstrate the important features of the NVivo 7 version that were not available in earlier versions. Currently, researchers at the Audit Commission use NVivo 7.

Background of project

This project is an analysis of a consultation by the Audit Commission on five proposed options for a new Comprehensive Performance Assessment (CPA) framework for assessing District Councils. There are 238 District Councils in England which provide a range of services including street cleaning, housing, sports and leisure, and parks and open spaces. District Councils have a statutory duty to ensure the continuous improvement of their services with regard to economy, efficiency and effectiveness. The Audit Commission has a statutory duty to assess how well authorities are fulfilling this requirement for continuous improvement.

In 2005 the Audit Commission decided to redesign the way it assesses the performance of local councils. The Commission prepared a consultation paper outlining five options for a new CPA framework for District Councils. This project is an analysis of the responses to the consultation paper which formed the basis for the new CPA framework.

Design of project

The Audit Commission prepared a Consultation Paper which was published on 6 September 2005. In the paper they discuss the background to the consultation, the guiding principles for the new framework, the key elements of CPA (use of resources assessment, service assessments, corporate assessments, direction of travel statements, developing options for CPA of District Councils), the options for CPA in District Councils (two broad options – Group A and Group B; Group A has three sub-options; Group B has two sub-options), quality assurance and review, and opportunities for getting involved. It ends with a list of the consultation questions. There are five broad topic areas with specific questions under each. The five broad topic areas are:

- guiding principles for overall district council CPA framework (two specific questions);
- key elements of CPA (six specific questions);
- recategorization (four specific questions);
- quality assurance (one specific question);
- other comments (one specific question).

The consultation period was from 6 September 2005 to 30 November 2005. The Consultation Paper was published on the Audit Commission's web site from which it could be downloaded. Anyone could respond to the consultation paper. In the end written responses were received from the following:

- 168 district councils;
- 7 regional agencies;
- 6 local government associations;
- 4 national agencies;
- 2 government departments;
- 2 county councils;

- 2 professional organizations;
- 2 individuals;
- 1 charity.

As it was a public consultation, the form of the written responses varied. Some responses followed the structure of the list of consultation questions at the end of the consultation paper. However, others responded to some of the questions only or responded in more general terms. The form of the written responses varied as well. Some responses were emails; others were in the form of non-digital letters.

In addition to the written responses, the Commission held six regional events which discussed the consultation paper. The responses made at these six events were written up in a consistent way following the structure of the list of consultation questions at the end of the paper.

Constraints on project

As already mentioned, the form of the consultation response was beyond the control of the team. The team had prepared a structured framework of questions for people to answer but the nature of a public consultation process is that District Councils decide how they reply – whether to the whole set of questions, just the questions they feel strongly about or a general response without regard to the structured questions posed. In addition, the form of response was also out of control of the team. Some people downloaded the structured questions and answered them as one would answer a questionnaire. But many others replied by email or by written letter.

The Audit Commission runs many public consultations and they know from experience that most people respond just before the deadline. They anticipated that the bulk of responses would arrive a few days before the deadline and up to a week after the deadline. In the event, they received at least half of the total number on the deadline day and about a fifth more in the few days after the deadline.

The deadline for the report on the consultation was three weeks after the end of the consultation period. Because the bulk of the responses would come at the very end of the consultation period, the team had approximately two weeks to input and code the responses in NVivo.

The team

The analysis of the consultation was done mainly by the research team within the Local Government Improvement and Performance Directorate with Laura Richards-Gray as the NVivo supremo who set up and managed the project. In addition, Emmeline Cooper did much of the fine coding of the responses with some help from Mark Wardman from the studies team. An additional source was brought into the team from outside – a PhD student. She was able to help with the easier broad coding of responses. A very bright GAP student was also trained in NVivo as a backup – in the end

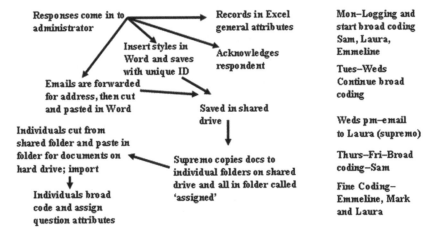

Figure 6.2 Teamwork flowchart for CPA study

his services were not needed. The team had to be tightly coordinated in order to make their deadline for the report. Figure 6.2 illustrates the flow of the teamwork.

The consultation responses were sent to the administrator for the project who: (a) acknowledged the respondent; (b) inserted styles in Microsoft Word for letters; and (c) forwarded emails so that the sender's name and address would be recorded; then copied and pasted them into a Microsoft Word document and then applied styles as needed; (d) saved responses with a unique ID for both (b) and (c) in a shared drive; and e) extracted the variables for each response into an Excel file, which later would be imported into NVivo.

Laura (the NVivo supremo) copied the documents into individual team member's folders on the shared drive and then cut all of them from the administrator's folder into a folder called 'assigned'.

Individual team members cut the responses from the shared drive and pasted in a document folder on the hard drive and then imported them into their NVivo project. (Given the computer network setup at the Audit Commission, documents could not be imported directly from the network drive.)

Given the time constraints, the schedule for coding was very structured. Mondays and Tuesdays and Wednesday morning were allocated for broad coding by all team members. On Wednesday afternoon the projects were emailed to Laura so that she could merge their work into one project. She would note any comments and issues from the other team members and respond to them. On Thursday morning she emailed the newly merged project to each team member. The more experienced members of the team would fine-code on Thursday and Friday while the less experienced members would continue with broad coding new responses.

Representing the design in the software shell

Organizing and preparing source material

As can be seen in Table 6.1, the source material for this project is of two types – responses to the consultation and notes on the regional events discussing the proposals. In addition, the researchers had access in their E-Project to the consultation questions, instructions on the setup of the project, and how they were to proceed. Each researcher also kept a journal to record their progress and any questions or insights they had. Figure 6.3 illustrates how this material can be organized in folders in NVivo 7. The original project had been done in an earlier version of NVivo which did not have the folders as an option to organize the material. However, the icons representing the different types of data were colour coded. Once colour coded, it was possible in NVivo 2 to filter them into sets as illustrated in Figure 6.4.

No matter which software package you use or which version of a package, you need to understand the tools it has to organize your material. As can be seen above, the tools can vary not only between packages but also between versions of the same package. However, whatever tools the package has, it is possible to organize the raw data in a way which makes it easily accessible.

Table 6.1 Design framework of CPA project

Unit(s) of analysis	Attributes	Time frame	Data: textual (primary or secondary forms of data)	Data: non-textual (primary or secondary forms of data)
Response to consultation	*Respondent values* • Region • CPA Category • Political control • Respondent type *Response values* Questions 1.1, 1.2, 2, 3.1, 3.2, 3.3, 3.4, 4.1, 5	Snapshot	Emails, letters Notes on regional events	No non-textual data

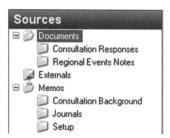

Figure 6.3 Source folders in NVivo 7

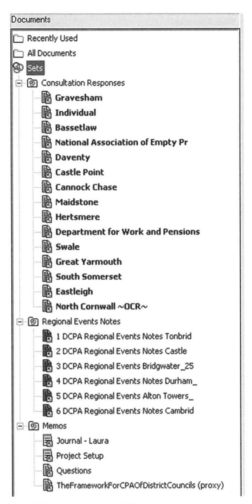

Figure 6.4 Colour coded document sets in NVivo 2

As mentioned earlier, the form of the consultation responses was outside of the control of the Audit Commission. Figures 6.5 and 6.6 illustrate some of the variety of the structure of the responses. For this reason, it was not worth the time to format the responses in Microsoft Word for automatic coding. They were simply imported into NVivo as they were received.

When assessing the value of preparing transcripts for automatic coding in the software, the main rule is to assess where the responses lie in the range of totally structured to totally unstructured responses. If the responses lie closer to the totally structured end of the continuum, then it is worth spending time in Microsoft Word applying the features in order for the software to recognize structured questions. (In the case of NVivo, this would be to use the styles feature to apply heading levels.) In the Audit Commission case, the consultation questions were structured. If they had commissioned a

Dear Sir/Madam

District Council CPA Consultation

My authority is very grateful for the opportunity to respond to the consultation document provided in September 2005. The matter was discussed by all 60 Councillors at a full Council meeting earlier this month.

In terms of the guiding principles set out in your consultation document, this council is in full agreement. However it does not feel it appropriate to have peers involved in the assessment activity. It is believed this may introduce a greater subjectivity into the process. The experience of peers can and will vary greatly. This is not seen as advantageous.

My council is very much of the opinion that re-categorisation of all councils over a period of between 18 and 36 months is the right approach. Option 3 is preferred but only if the 2003/04 CA result is replaced with a revised CA which is carried out as part of the inspection. This to include resident satisfaction, equality/diversity work, performance focus, local and national priority work and civic renewal. Therefore the framework should consist of the following elements (with priority in brackets)

Corporate Assessment as set out above	(Priority 1)
Use of Resources **and** Direction of Travel	(both Priority 2)
Service Assessment	(Priority 4)

Figure 6.5 Extract of letter-style response

CONSULTATION QUESTIONS

1. Guiding principles for overall district council CPA framework.

1.1 We have outlined some guiding principles in section 3; are there any others you think we should be following?

Response: **Agree with the guiding principles outlined in the consultation paper.**

1.2 Do you think that peers should play a part in our assessment activity and if so what do you think is the best way of using them?

Response: **Peers are useful in the CPA process specifically in relation to conducting a 'reality check' on the Councils Corporate Assessment or Direction of Travel Assessment prior to the formal CPA inspection. This gives Councils the opportunity to update their self-assessment based on feedback from Peers prior to submission to the Audit Commission.**

2 Key elements of CPA
2.1 How do you think that the key elements of CPA should be used in relation to district council CPA? Please indicate the relative weighting or priority each element should have:

2.2 Use of resources assessments?

This should be a high priority. How you manage your resources is a corporate issue that affects the whole council. High priority, high weighting.

Figure 6.6 Extract of structured question-style response

---

straightforward questionnaire which they administered, then they could have created a Microsoft Word template in which they would have recorded the responses ready for automatic coding in the software. However, the consultation process is a response to a proposal paper. While there were structured questions that the Commission wanted addressed, the consultation process

allows for flexibility of response. As there was no consistency in the way councils responded, it was not worth the time to prepare them in Microsoft Word in
a consistent format. It was more efficient to import them into NVivo the way
they were received, and spend the time coding them directly in NVivo.

Organizing cases and units of analysis

This case has a simple design. The unit of analysis is the consultation response as is the unit of observation. In NVivo 7, each response would be
represented by a case node as illustrated in Figure 6.7. They are organized as a
simple list.

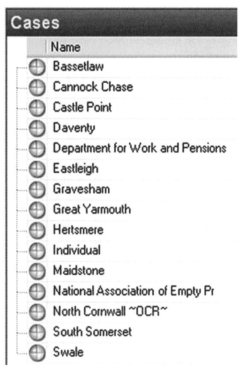

Figure 6.7 Case nodes

Attribute variables – two types

The attribute variables in this case are of two types – *characteristics of the
respondent* and *the values of responses to various questions in the consultation*.
Respondent characteristics which could aid in the analysis are the region of
the country, the current CPA score for the District Council, the political
makeup of the District Council and respondent type (note: anyone could
respond to the consultation, not just District Councils, so it was important

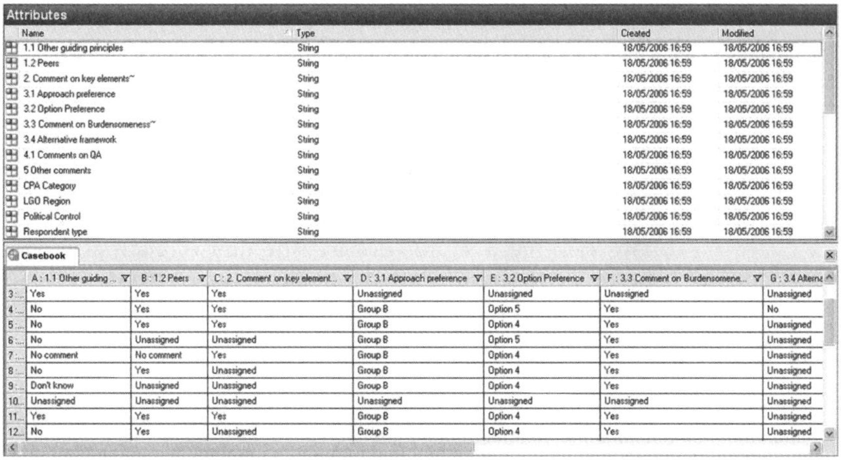

Attributes

Name	Type	Created	Modified
1.1 Other guiding principles	String	18/05/2006 16:59	18/05/2006 16:59
1.2 Peers	String	18/05/2006 16:59	18/05/2006 16:59
2. Comment on key elements~	String	18/05/2006 16:59	18/05/2006 16:59
3.1 Approach preference	String	18/05/2006 16:59	18/05/2006 16:59
3.2 Option Preference	String	18/05/2006 16:59	18/05/2006 16:59
3.3 Comment on Burdensomeness~	String	18/05/2006 16:59	18/05/2006 16:59
3.4 Alternative framework	String	18/05/2006 16:59	18/05/2006 16:59
4.1 Comments on QA	String	18/05/2006 16:59	18/05/2006 16:59
5 Other comments	String	18/05/2006 16:59	18/05/2006 16:59
CPA Category	String	18/05/2006 16:59	18/05/2006 16:59
LGO Region	String	18/05/2006 16:59	18/05/2006 16:59
Political Control	String	18/05/2006 16:59	18/05/2006 16:59
Respondent type	String	18/05/2006 16:59	18/05/2006 16:59

Casebook

	A : 1.1 Other guiding ...	B : 1.2 Peers	C : 2. Comment on key element...	D : 3.1 Approach preference	E : 3.2 Option Preference	F : 3.3 Comment on Burdensomene...	G : 3.4 Alterna
3 :...	Yes	Yes	Yes	Unassigned	Unassigned	Unassigned	Unassigned
4 :...	No	Yes	Yes	Group B	Option 5	Yes	No
5 :...	No	Yes	Yes	Group B	Option 4	Yes	Unassigned
6 :...	No	Unassigned	Unassigned	Group B	Option 5	Yes	Unassigned
7 :...	No comment	No comment	Yes	Group B	Option 4	Yes	Unassigned
8 :...	No	Yes	Unassigned	Group B	Option 4	Yes	Unassigned
9 :...	Don't know	Unassigned	Unassigned	Group B	Option 4	Yes	Unassigned
10...	Unassigned	Unassigned	Unassigned	Unassigned	Unassigned	Unassigned	Unassigned
11...	Yes	Yes	Yes	Group B	Option 4	Yes	Unassigned
12...	No	Yes	Unassigned	Group B	Option 4	Yes	Unassigned

Figure 6.8 Attribute variables and casebook in NVivo 7

to keep track of the type of respondent). The second type of attribute – values of responses to specific questions – is one which may not be immediately recognized as an attribute by qualitative analysts. However, the fact that a respondent is favourable or not to a certain proposal or prefers one option over another is a variable which is different from coding text about what the respondent *said* was favourable about a proposal or what they *said* about what they disliked about a particular option. Keeping track of these variables allows not only for simple counts of how many favoured or not certain options but also for contrasting respondents who held particular views with themes that emerged from qualitative analysis of the responses. Figure 6.8 shows the setup of the attribute variables for this case in NVivo 7.

The casebook at the bottom of the screenshot shows which values have been assigned to the different respondents.

Organizing thematic framework

The last section of the consultation paper on CPA for District Councils consisted of the five main questions and sub-questions that they wanted responses. These questions were:

1 Comments on the guiding principles of the framework

  (a) Whether there were others that should be considered
  (b) Whether peers should be part of the assessment activity

2 How should the key elements of the CPA be prioritized

  (a) Use of resource assessments
  (b) Use of service assessments
  (c) Corporate assessments
  (d) Direction of travel statements or scored judgements
  (e) How should they be brought together to allow recategorization

3 Recategorization – which of the two broad approaches proposed is preferred

    (a) Which of the five options is preferred and why
    (b) How burdensome is each option
    (c) Is there an alternative framework

4 Comments on the approach to quality assurance
5 Other comments

The report on the consultation was to be structured around these questions, so the structure of the thematic framework in NVivo 7 and for the analysis had already been predetermined by the consultation paper. As the analysis had a very specific purpose, the thematic framework could be and was created in advance. Figure 6.9 illustrates the nodes in NVivo 7. The nodes that relate to specific questions in the framework are numbered 1–5.

What is coded at these nodes is what respondents *said* in relation to these topics as opposed to just indicating whether or not they were in favour of a particular option or whether they saw an option as burdensome or not. Those latter types of response are variables and are captured in the attributes section of the software package, as discussed earlier. In addition, there are nodes for burdensome level and priority level, as specified in the questions. These nodes were used with the query tool which enables the analyst to combine, for example, the coding for option 4 with the coding for high burdensome level and see what respondents *said* about that compared with combining low burdensome level and option 4 to see what respondents *said* about why they did not see it so burdensome. Figure 6.10 illustrates the matrix query that results from combining the codes mentioned above. You can see the *words behind the numbers* in each cell of the matrix table in order to understand better the differences.

There were some other issues that the Audit Commission were interested in understanding that were not covered by the specific consultation questions. These were to do with culture, housing and environment. These were issues that the team thought might be mentioned by those responding to the consultation and they needed to collect those responses systematically. Additional nodes were created for them.

Key aspects of the analysis process

The nature of the consultation process is that the bulk of the responses arrive at or just after the deadline. The expectation of a consultation is that the findings should be reported soon after the end of the consultation period. The Audit Commission team had a very short time frame to input the responses to the consultation in NVivo, to analyse the data and write a report. The design of this research was simple with just one unit of analysis which was the same as the unit of observation. The questions were structured and focused. The responses were idiosyncratic in their form and content but the nature of the consultation is that respondents choose which aspects of the consultation they want to address. The key for smooth analysis was the setup of the project

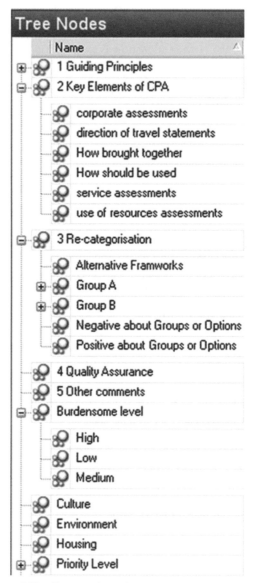

Figure 6.9 Themes in NVivo 7 tree node catalogue

in NVivo to reflect this simple design. As the Audit Commission was trialling the use of the NVivo software at this point, they used di Gregorio to consult on project setup and training of the research team. The setup in the software was done well in advance of the arrival of the bulk of the responses to the consultation. The training of the research team was done well in advance, as well. With the structure of the project set up and the team trained, the team were in a good position to check the initial setup and team processes with the few responses that came in during the early phase of the consultation period. This

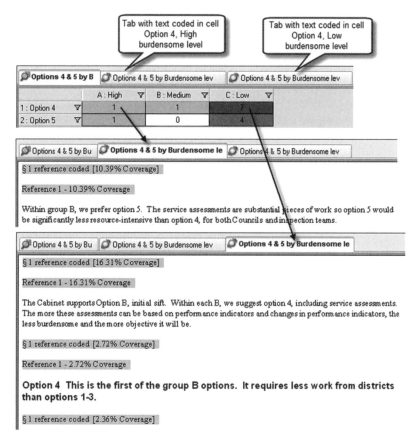

Figure 6.10 Matrix query – comparing options 4 and 5 and burdensome level

allowed for fine-tuning the setup and teamwork procedures in readiness for the bulk of responses they knew would come in at the end of the consultation period. The division of labour of coding with the fine coding allocated to the more experienced analysts, enabled a picture of the results of the consultation to emerge early in the form of memos. Simple matrix queries as illustrated in Figure 6.10 enabled quick comparisons to be made of the reasons behind the preferences for different approaches and options discussed in the consultation paper.

A key aspect in the analysis of this project is to understand that answers to some of the questions were *both* variables (represented in attributes) *and* thematic codes (represented in nodes). Figure 6.11 illustrates how the attribute whether or not peers should play a part in the assessment can be used in a matrix to see whether that impacts on the preference for particular options. This contrasts with the purpose of the matrix table in Figure 6.10 where the focus is to understand the reasons for perceptions of the burdensome levels of the different options.

Peers and Option p		A : Option 1 ▽	B : Option 2 ▽	C : Option 3 ▽	D : Option 4 ▽	E : Option 5 ▽
1 : 1.2 Peers = Yes	▽	1	1	1	6	3
2 : 1.2 Peers = No	▽	0	0	1	0	0
3 : 1.2 Peers = No comment	▽	0	0	0	1	0
4 : 1.2 Peers = Mixed reaction	▽	0	0	0	0	0
5 : 1.2 Peers = Don't know	▽	0	0	0	0	0

Figure 6.11 Matrix query – attribute peers important and option preference

Lessons for this case

This case illustrates how a QDAS package can be used to good effect outside of the context of academic research. Public consultations are a key component of UK policy-making.

> Involving the public in the work of government has become an integral part of the policy-making process. It is not simply about more open-government, although that too is important, it is about making policies more effective by listening to and taking on-board the views of the public and interested groups.
>
> (Cabinet Office 2007)

The challenge of these consultations is to do justice to the analysis of the large amount of responses they generate in a timely fashion. Their design tends to be simple but they generate a large volume of responses at the end of the consultation period. However, as has been shown, by setting up the structure for the analysis in the QDAS package beforehand and fine-tuning the approach with early responses, the team will be well prepared for the bulk of the responses when they arrive.

Another feature of consultations is that they are public. The QDAS project is a public record that can be easily interrogated at a later date. A subsequent consultation carried out by the Audit Commission produced some surprising results. The research team had been asked to review the analysis. The transparency of the analysis in NVivo (or any QDAS package for that matter) made it easier for the research team to check the integrity of the original analysis.

Laura Richards-Gray who was the NVivo 'supremo' for this consultation, advocated the use of QDAS at a lunchtime seminar at the Audit Commission (2006). She valued the fact that the software managed large amounts of data in an efficient way while maintaining the flexibility to allow for emerging ideas. Most importantly, it kept an audit trail of the analysis process. Richards-Gray had written a briefing paper for the Commission on conducting consultations which included using NVivo for the analysis (Laura Richards 2005). She established new guidelines for teamwork. The Audit Commission has subsequently used NVivo 7 in a number of consultations and other projects.

For more information on this project see Audit Commission (2005, 2006).

Note

1 This exemplar is based on a public consultation by the UK Audit Commission.

7 | Views of New Deal for Communities[1]

The software that was used in the original project was QSR XSight.

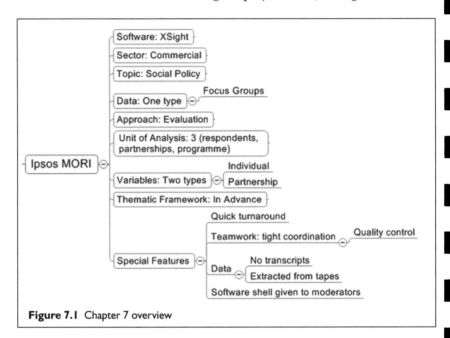

Figure 7.1 Chapter 7 overview

Background of project

The New Deal for Communities (NDC) is the UK government's flagship regeneration project targeted at 39 deprived areas in the UK. Around £50 million a year has been allocated over 10 years to fund projects to improve the areas. The five key issues to be tackled are crime, health, education, employment and housing/physical environment. The scheme is run by local partnerships in the 39 areas. The composition of the partnership varies from area to area but comprises local people, community groups, public agencies, local authorities and businesses.

Ipsos MORI was commissioned to conduct an evaluation of the programme. In addition to the qualitative research reported in this case, a household survey was conducted in the 39 areas with 500 face-to-face interviews in each area – a total of 19,500 people were surveyed. The aim of the qualitative side of the study was to supplement the survey by providing an in-depth and contextualized understanding of the factors which informed participants' views of their local areas, the NDC partnerships and recent change. The specific research questions the qualitative side of the study addressed were:

- What factors inform participants' views of their local area and NDC Partnership?
- What are their attitudes towards change in their local area, and which, if any, changes do they ascribe to the NDC?
- How informed are they about the NDC Partnership?
- How do they judge the impact and success of their NDC thus far? Which factors inform their views?

Design of project

In order to examine the views of residents in the target areas, two focus groups were conducted in each of the 39 programme areas. One group consisted of a cross-section of the general population in the area having a range of mixed profiles based on age, gender, ethnicity and working status. The other group consisted of a targeted population group relevant to the particulars of the programme in the area. These consisted of one of four targeted groups: beneficiaries of particular projects; volunteers delivering NDC projects; children between the age of 11–16; or a particular sub-section of the community, such as those over 55 or those seeking work. (Those who took part in the Household Survey side of the study were screened out of the focus groups.)

There were three units of analysis: individual respondent types/groups; each partnership (39); and the programme as a whole. A separate report had to be prepared for each of the 39 areas in addition to the overall report evaluating the programme as a whole in the five key theme areas.

The variables collected were: (a) demographic information about the individuals; (b) the type of focus group – general or targeted – and within targeted, type of targeted group; and (c) the region where the partnership was located.

Focus groups were the only data type collected in the qualitative side of the study. There were 78 focus groups conducted (two in each of the 39 areas). The moderators used a structured Topic Guide. The focus groups were taped but not transcribed due to time constraints. The moderators of the focus groups had 48 hours to review the tapes and to extract information from them into a predesigned analysis framework set up in QSR XSight.

A summary of the research design is in Table 7.1.

The team

The Ipsos MORI team responsible for this project were Jaime Rose, Associate Director, Sara Butler, Associate Director (Qualitative Hot House) and Jessica Vince, Senior Research Executive. All three moderated some of the groups – Jessica moderated the most (20). In addition, there were seven others who acted as moderators, including Bobby Duffy, the Research Director, who moderated two of the groups.

Table 7.1 Design framework of NDC project

Unit(s) of analysis	Attributes	Time frame	Data: textual (primary or secondary forms of data)	Data: non-textual (primary or secondary forms of data)
Individual respondent type/ group type NDC area (39) National programme	*Individual* Age, gender, ethnicity, working status *Focus group* General, beneficiaries, children, volunteers, sub-section of community *Region* NE, NW, Yorks. and Humber, E. Midlands, W. Midlands, SE, SW, London	Snapshot	No textual	Focus group audio tapes – structured topic guide (78)

di Gregorio trained Jaime, Sara and Jessica in the QSR XSight software and together they set up the shell of the project in XSight. Time constraints meant that there would be no time to transcribe the interviews. The focus group topic guides were quite structured, so the framework for organizing the data could be developed by the team in advance. QSR XSight had been chosen by the team as its simple structure meant that moderators could easily input summaries and quotes from listening to the tapes of the focus groups directly into the predefined analysis framework.

The core team of three piloted the design in XSight with a few focus groups before finalizing the structure of the analysis frameworks. The training of the moderators in the software was included in their overall briefing for the project. di Gregorio provided the very targeted training in XSight using the pilot work already done. The training was focused on inputting the data, recording reflections in a journal kept in XSight and in the process of backing up and saving and reporting back to the Ipsos MORI core team. Sara was the XSight supremo in this project and she was the one to whom the moderators reported back. She was responsible for quality control and made any changes and adjustments that were needed in the framework in XSight.

Representing the design in the software shell

Variables

In QSR XSight, variables are called 'sample characteristics'. The variables can be set up in the shell beforehand. They enable the research team to cut the analysis according to the different units of analysis specified in Table 7.1. They needed to be able to analyse separately the focus groups from a cross-section of the general population from those in targeted groups (see Figure 7.2).

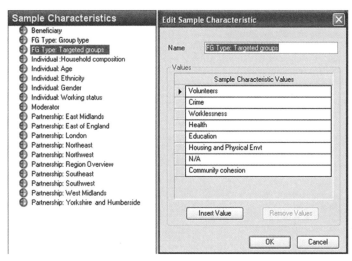

Figure 7.2 Attribute variables showing the values for FG type: targeted groups

They also wanted to be able to distinguish differences in the general population according to age, gender, ethnicity and work status. In addition, they had to write separate reports on each of the 39 partnerships, so those partnerships needed to be quickly identified. A variable for moderators was included, so that the work of individual moderators could be quality control checked.

Thematic framework

As the moderators had to follow a structured topic guide, it was possible to set up the framework for the themes beforehand. In addition, there was no time for transcription, so the moderators needed a structured framework to input their observations and quotations. QSR XSight was a good software choice for the team as it enabled the moderators to directly type in their summaries and verbatim quotes in the relevant slot for their topic area. The place for constructing the thematic framework in XSight is called an 'analysis framework'. Figure 7.3 illustrates the analysis framework that explores the five main areas the moderators had to explore in the focus groups.

In the XSight shell, the core team specified the framework for where the moderators had to input their information. They would select the relevant focus group in the first column, then select the topic heading in the second column and directly write their summaries or verbatim comments in the third column. Note that the core team had set up in the shell instructions for the moderators. In Figure 7.3 you can see that there is an instruction as to where to add comments about crime that does not fit into the framework.

Figure 7.4 shows the framework the core team set up for the part of the focus group which discussed people's views of their local area. The different sections

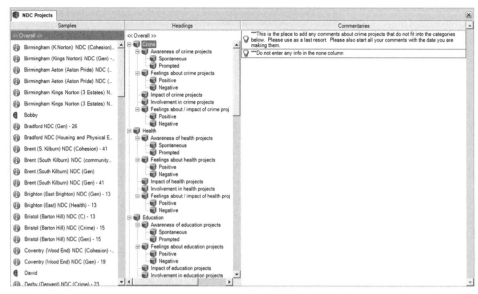

Figure 7.3 Analysis framework for discussion on the five NDC project types

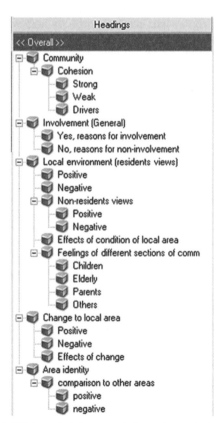

Figure 7.4 Headings in XSight analysis framework for topics on the local area

of the focus group topic guide were represented by analysis frameworks in QSR XSight. They could all be opened at the same time, and the moderator could click on the tab of the relevant section and input information as they listened to the tape (see Figure 7.5).

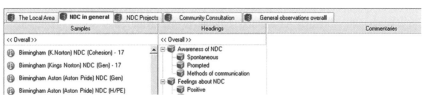

Figure 7.5 Analysis frameworks

Journal

Finally, a journal was set up for each moderator (see Figure 7.6). This was the place that moderators communicated with Sara, the XSight supremo. Any problems with using the pre-existing analysis framework were recorded here. Sara gave feedback there on the quality of the moderators' work and clarified any issues to do with interpretation.

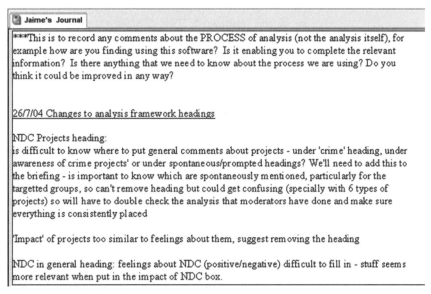

Figure 7.6 Jaime's journal

Key aspects of the analysis process

The moderators' role was limited to running the focus groups and recording their summaries and verbatim quotes in the analysis frameworks in QSR

XSight. They were encouraged to record any insights in their journals. However, the analysis of the data was done by the core team of Sara, Jessica and Jaime.

Sara, as mentioned above, was the XSight supremo for the team. She kept very tight tabs on the moderators. She was responsible for quality control and needed to ensure that the moderators were working in a consistent manner. The moderators had 48 hours after each focus group to listen to the tape and record mainly their summaries within the analysis frameworks in XSight. They would then e-mail their XSight project to Sara. Sara had stipulated that verbatims (quotations) were to be used judiciously to illustrate key issues. There had been a discussion in the core team about whether to emphasize verbatims – in order to keep close to the original data, or summaries – which would enable a quicker analysis. Given the volume of data that 78 focus groups could generate and time constraints, it was decided that summaries would facilitate the core team's final analysis task. It was also felt that by writing summaries, moderators would be forced to reflect on the data, rather than just mechanically record verbatim quotes.

Figure 7.7 illustrates the way the Ipsos MORI team worked. After each focus group was recorded in XSight it was sent to Sara, the supremo. She reviewed the work and fed back to the moderator any comments she had about how they summarized the focus group, allocated the summaries to the framework and addressed any questions the moderator had. If necessary, she altered the framework if she felt that recommendations a moderator had merited a change in the framework. This change would be fed back to all the other moderators. Only Sara could make changes to the XSight shell. Each project was merged into the master project which Sara had. From the master project, the core team could analyse each of the 39 programme sites and across all the sites.

The core team were able to use queries to cut the data in the various ways they needed for the analysis. They had to produce a report for each of the 39 NDC areas. This was easily done by restricting queries to just a particular area.

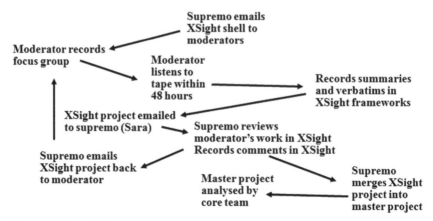

Figure 7.7 Ipsos MORI teamwork flowchart

Hackney feelings on NDC Impact ✕

Heading Name (2)	Sample Name	Commentary Text
Feelings about / impact of NDC\Positive	Hackney (Shoreditch) NDC (Cohesion) - 43	Programme is a step in the right direction, although results won't be realised for a long time - definitely a long-term programme.
Feelings about / impact of NDC\Positive	Hackney (Shoreditch) NDC (Cohesion) - 43	Several people feel that the investment in programmes for young people, education and health make long-term benefits for the area.
Feelings about / impact of NDC\Positive	Hackney (Shoreditch) NDC (Cohesion) - 43	Programmes will benefit the next generation. Start improvements now, but the real change will be in years to come.
Feelings about / impact of NDC\Positive	Hackney (Shoreditch) NDC (Cohesion) - 43	We can see they've started improvements now, but it's really geared for our kids and their kids. That's who it's really geared for.

Heading Name (2)	Sample Name	Commentary Text
Feelings about / impact of NDC\Negative	Hackney (Shoreditch) NDC (Cohesion) - 43	Most had heard of Shoreditch NDC, but hadn't really seen what it has done for the area. People not sure how the money is being spent and haven't seen much in the way of tangible change.
Feelings about / impact of NDC\Negative	Hackney (Shoreditch) NDC (Cohesion) - 43	I'd like to know, what's this New Deal? Who is it for?
Feelings about / impact of NDC\Negative	Hackney (Shoreditch) NDC (Cohesion) - 43	Changes are bitty - nothing hugely substantial or significant.
Feelings about / impact of NDC\Negative	Hackney (Shoreditch) NDC (Cohesion) - 43	People not quite sure how much money is left or what it has been spent on.
Feelings about / impact of NDC\Negative	Hackney (Shoreditch) NDC (Cohesion) - 43	Changes are more the result of the influx of private developers who are attracted to a trendy area, rather than NDC. Not seen as having a huge impact, although most see the initiatives as steps in the right direction.
Feelings about / impact of NDC\Negative	Hackney (Shoreditch) NDC (Cohesion) - 43	Some view the success of NDC on its progress in terms of structural, physical improvements to the area.
Feelings about / impact of NDC\Negative	Hackney (Shoreditch) NDC (Cohesion) - 43	Some concern that the programmes will not be long-lasting enough - need for follow-through or long-lasting impact is impossible.
Feelings about / impact of NDC\Negative	Hackney (Shoreditch) NDC (Cohesion) - 43	People do not feel that they understand the decision making process.
Feelings about / impact of NDC\Negative	Hackney (Shoreditch) NDC (Cohesion) - 43	Need for more information provision - better communication about how decisions are made, why and how can people get involved.

Figure 7.8 Hackney's views on positive and negative aspects of NDC

Heading Name (2)	Sample Name	Commentary Text
Feelings about / impact of NDC\Positive	Bradford NDC (Gen) - 26	One person had positive feeling about Trident. They cleaned up teh area, fences for houses were put up.
Feelings about / impact of NDC\Positive	Bradford NDC (Gen) - 26	One girl felt that Trident had made a difference and given the area a good facelift
Feelings about / impact of NDC\Positive	Bradford NDC (Gen) - 26	People have changed around our area, more open and friendly, you can talk to people. The place is cleaner and people feel better about it. People have changed beca
Feelings about / impact of NDC\Positive	Bradford NDC (Gen) - 26	There was some scepticism at first when first hearing about Trident as to what impact it could have.
Feelings about / impact of NDC\Positive	Bradford NDC (Gen) - 26	Some residents said there had been some positive changes, and while it is easy to focus on the negatives about the area, should recognise these positives too.
Feelings about / impact of NDC\Positive	Bradford NDC (Housing and Physical Enviornment)	NDC has made a difference but some felt it was only superficial - focusing on external appearances.
Feelings about / impact of NDC\Positive	Bristol (Barton Hill) NDC (C) - 13	Felt by most to be a good idea, provided it is spent on improving the area in tangible ways. This specifically relates to provision of community focal point, particularly for young people, and moving on the housing issue.
Feelings about / impact of NDC\Positive	Bristol (Barton Hill) NDC (C) - 13	They have done lots of small things that I don't think they get credit for.
Feelings about / impact of NDC\Positive	Bristol (Barton Hill) NDC (C) - 13	Feeling amongst 3 of the them that the NDC is more effective in small things rather than large capital projects. For instance, 1 had been helped into educational courses by provision of transport and paying for fees. Another has had safety bars installed in his house so feels safer. Indeed, all had benefited from the Locks & Bolts project which they felt helped them to feel safer, although of course, the fear of crime remains.
Feelings about / impact of NDC\Positive	Coventry (Wood End) NDC (Cohesion) - 19	Difficult for NDC to improve community cohesion as the decline in neighbourliness has been for so long, that it will be difficult to break people out of the mind frame that prevents them from engaging with the rest of the community for fear of hostility. All agree that if people saw activities going on, some might get interested in getting involved.
Feelings about / impact of NDC\Positive	Coventry (Wood End) NDC (Gen) - 19	The community centre is really the only thing that people were unequivocally positive about [and the new school].
Feelings about / impact of NDC\Positive	Coventry (Wood End) NDC (Gen) - 19	People are most positive about substantial changes to the physical enviroment and this is how they will measure the impact/success of NDC.
Feelings about / impact of NDC\Positive	Coventry (Wood End) NDC (Gen) - 19	Things like that [the new school] are actually regenerating the area because its a new, modern building for the kids.
Feelings about / impact of NDC\Positive	Hackney (Shoreditch) NDC (Cohesion) - 43	Programme is a step in the right direction, although results won't be realised for a long time - definitely a long-term programme.
Feelings about / impact of NDC\Positive	Hackney (Shoreditch) NDC (Cohesion) - 43	Several people feel that the investment in programmes for young people, education and health make long-term benefits for the area.
Feelings about / impact of NDC\Positive	Hackney (Shoreditch) NDC (Cohesion) - 43	Programmes will benefit the next generation. Start improvements now, but the real change will be in years to come.

Figure 7.9 Positive impacts of NDC across the whole dataset

Heading Name (2)	Sample Name		Commentary Text
Feelings about / impact of NDCVPositive	Coventry (Wood End) NDC (Cohesion) - 19		Difficult for NDC to improve community cohesion as the decline in neighbourliness has been for so long, that it will be difficult to break people out of the mind frame that prevents them from engaging with the rest of the community for fear of hostility. All agree that if people saw activities going on, some might get interested in getting involved.
Feelings about / impact of NDCVPositive	Knowsley (N. Huyton) NDC (H/PE) - 30		Initiatives like the street lights and walls have made a difference to the appearance of the area and to health (i.e., protect against rats), but need to be rolled out to other areas.
Feelings about / impact of NDCVPositive	Knowsley (N. Huyton) NDC (H/PE) - 30		Initiatives can have a long-lasting impact if the residents don't destroy the work that has been done. Again refers to the feeling of 'intruders' who have come into the area without a sense of community pride or spirit.
Feelings about / impact of NDCVPositive	Walsall (Blakenall) NDC (Health) - 21		The woman who received the Christmas hamper was extremely touched by the gesture and felt as though people cared about her. She feels more willing to use NDC and sees them as providing important services to the area to make it a better place to live.
Feelings about / impact of NDCVPositive	Walsall (Blakenall) NDC (Health) - 21		Seen as a good thing for the area, as they have not had a formal effort such as this to try to regenerate the area in many years.
Feelings about / impact of NDCVPositive	Walsall (Blakenall) NDC (Health) - 21		There's more pride in the area. It shows that they are doing something for us.
Feelings about / impact of NDCVPositive	Walsall (Blakenall) NDC (Health) - 21		Recognition that regeneration is a long-term process which has only just begun, but all are hopeful that the effect will be positive and long-lasting as pride will be reinstilled in the community.
Feelings about / impact of NDCVPositive	Walsall (Blakenall) NDC (Health) - 21		By the time they finish this area, people will be proud to live here.
Feelings about / impact of NDCVPositive	Walsall (Blakenall) NDC (Health) - 21		Efforts to take away the dirtiness and improve the overall neglect of the area is key to making people take pride in the area - that is how long term change will happen; once people take ownership for both the area and the changes within it.
Feelings about / impact of NDCVPositive	Walsall (Blakenall) NDC (Health) - 21		Happy with the work that NDC has done - only sticking point is the housing issue, but not really seen as NDC responsibility - more of a council WHD thing.
Feelings about / impact of NDCVPositive	Walsall (Blakenall) NDC (Health) - 21		We're happy with the work they've done because there has been progress. Except with housing as they are knocking all the properties down instead of repairing them.
Feelings about / impact of NDCVPositive	Walsall (Blakenall) NDC (Health) - 21		It's progressing and they're doing alright, but there are still some things in the area that need doing. But you can see people's sense of pride coming back. It was very depressing before. This is the starting point and that's nice.

Figure 7.10 Positive impacts of NDC across all areas restricted to over 55s

Figure 7.8 is a query restricted to just Hackney's views on positive and negative impacts of NDC. In addition, they were able to compare areas across particular topics. Figure 7.9 is a query looking at positive impacts of NDC across the whole dataset. It is possible to distinguish between verbatims 📝, summary statements (called articulations) 💬 and the moderator's ideas or explanations 💡.

Figure 7.10 is the same query as Figure 7.9 but restricted to the views of the over 55s.

Lessons from this case

This case is a good example of how to set up and manage a team project with a large number of fairly structured focus groups. The thematic framework can be set up beforehand. Transcripts are not necessary as information can be recorded directly into the thematic framework. QSR XSight has been designed specifically so it can be used in this way. (Although it can also be used with transcripts.) The key to the success of this project was the tight coordination of the project supremo, who ensured quality and consistency by having the team members' work sent directly to her. She also provided immediate feedback if any issues were raised. The use of the journals in the software enabled good communication between team members.

Once all the data was collected the core team were able to explore themes and patterns in the data. The sample characteristics were key in identifying differences between programmes or populations with different characteristics.

For more information on this project, see MORI Social Research Institute (2005) and Vince and Sweetman (2006).

Note

1   This exemplar is based on a National Evaluation focus group study conducted by Ipsos MORI for the Neighbourhood Renewal Unit, Office of the Deputy Prime Minister (UK) – (2005).

8 | Buying birth: consumption and the ideal of natural birth[1]

The software that was used in the original project was MAXqda 2007.

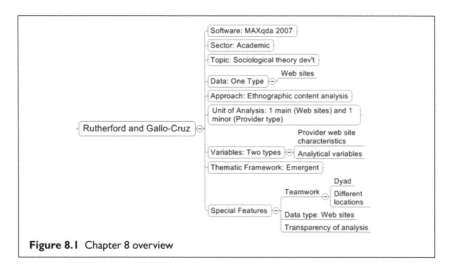

Figure 8.1 Chapter 8 overview

Background of project

This study looks at how the process of birth in the USA has undergone drastic changes mirroring the changes in the role of women and the normative expectations of sexual behaviour over the past two hundred years. It looks at the natural birth movement as a consumer movement that has influenced the providers of childbirth services. The questions this study examines include:

- Is the idealized birth experience treated as a commercial commodity?
- How much do care providers – both hospitals and natural birth providers – market their services to appeal to the consumers' image of an idealized birth experience?
- What are the similarities and differences between hospitals and natural birth providers in how they communicate through the language in their ads an idealized birth experience?

This is a joint project between two sociologists.

Design of project

This study is an ethnographic thematic content analysis of web sites of 58 hospitals and 40 alternative providers of childbirth services. The sample has been regionally stratified. Other variables included were urban/suburban, average income level and level of competition faced by hospitals within a 20-mile radius. The web site is the unit of observation. There are two units of analysis – the web site itself and the type of provider (hospitals or alternative provider) (see Table 8.1).

Table 8.1 Design framework of buying birth project

Unit(s) of analysis/ units of observation	Attributes	Time frame	Data: textual (primary or secondary forms of data)	Data: non-textual (primary or secondary forms of data)
Web sites (UA and UO) Provider type (UA)	Provider type Hospital Alternative • Birth centres • Midwives Region Urban/suburban Average income Competition level	Snapshot	Web sites	Links to web sites with photos

Representing the design in the software shell

Preparing and organizing source materials

The source materials for this project are web sites. Currently, MAXqda could only support the importation of textual files saved in rich text format (.rtf). It was not possible to import the web sites directly. However, Rutherford and Gallo-Cruz were able to create a *text* within MAXqda and copy and paste the words from the web site into this *text*. They also included the hyperlink to the web site in the MAXqda *text*, so it was possible to access the web site directly from within MAXqda. They also described any photos, graphics or videos in the MAXqda representation of the web site. One *text* represented all the relevant pages in a web site.

Figure 8.2 shows the original web page of one of the web sites in the study. Figure 8.3 illustrates that web page's representation in MAXqda.

The representation of the web site cannot simulate the impact of viewing the actual web site. However, all the words from the web site have been included and formatting features, such as bold, italics, and so on, can be used to mimic the formatting used in the web site. Rutherford and Gallo-Cruz use square brackets to indicate the name of each page in the web site, for example [family birth centre]. However, the inclusion of the hyperlinked web site address ensures direct access to the web site to remind the analyst while coding of the web site's impact. This representation is a good example of a 'workaround' (see Chapter 1) to manage data that cannot (currently) be used directly by the software package.

Middletown
Regional Hospital
the right care in the right here

about us | our services | visitors' guide

find a doctor | jobs | for physicians | programs & classes | contact us | home
news & events | health library | volunteering | make a donation

search our site

family birth center

PRINT THIS PAGE

Whether this is your first baby or your fifth, the birth of your child is one of the happiest, most memorable moments of your life. At Middletown Regional Hospital (MRH), we want to make this experience as perfect as possible.

The Best Medical Care
All parents want the best for their babies. That's why we offer comprehensive medical services and highly skilled physicians dedicated to giving you and your baby the best quality care available. Our skilled nurses are equally committed to providing outstanding patient care. They're experienced in providing both normal and high-risk care, and many are certified by the Association of Women's Health/Obstetric and Neonatal Nurses.

Your Home Away From Home
At Middletown Regional Hospital, we'll help you feel right at home. When you arrive at the hospital, you'll go directly to the Family Birth Center. After a brief registration, you'll be escorted to one of our five private birthing suites specially designed to meet your labor and delivery needs.

Our birthing suites provide a comfortable, home-like environment for your special delivery. You'll have your own bathroom and shower, a TV and VCR and a state-of-the-art birthing bed. Each suite has an attractive décor with wall coverings, paintings and hardwood floors even a cozy seating area for your family and friends. But most importantly, all suites are equipped with the latest medical technology to support you and your baby all neatly tucked away out of sight until it's needed.

Throughout your labor, you'll receive the best possible care and the personal attention you deserve. You may choose natural childbirth or a wide range of anesthesia options, including epidural. And should you require a Cesarean section, our medical professionals are prepared to make this a safe and special birthing experience, as well.

Come See for Yourself
Years of experience have earned us a reputation for providing quality care with a friendly, personal touch. If you would like more information about the Family Birth Center, call (513) 420-5069.

For dates and times of our childbirth education classes, please call CareFinders at (866) 608-FIND (3463) or Click Here.

Back to Services

online nursery!
click here

related links

- Introduction
- Prenatal Care
- Childbirth Education
- Special Care Deliveries
- Security
- Special Services

Links

- Online Nursery
- Childbirth.Org
- Labor Resources
- The Administration for Children and Families Dept. of Health and Human Services
- The American Medical Women's Association
- La Leche League Health Topics
- International Lactation Consultant Association
- Academy of Breastfeeding Medicine
- American Academy of Pediatrics

Figure 8.2 Web page of Middletown Regional Hospital Family Birth Center

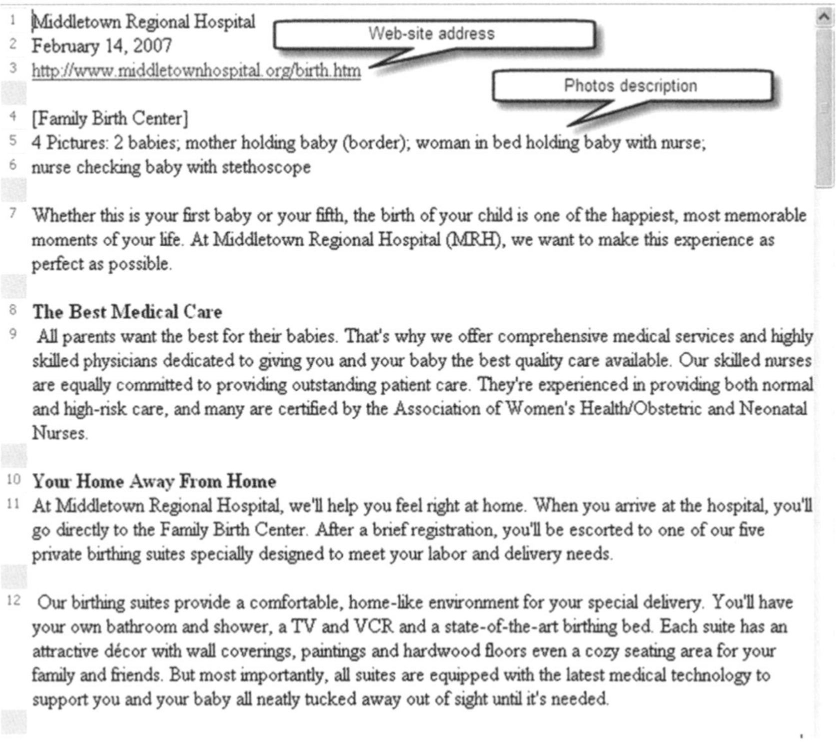

1 Middletown Regional Hospital
2 February 14, 2007   Web-site address
3 http://www.middletownhospital.org/birth.htm

                                                                          Photos description

4 [Family Birth Center]
5 4 Pictures: 2 babies; mother holding baby (border); woman in bed holding baby with nurse;
6 nurse checking baby with stethoscope

7 Whether this is your first baby or your fifth, the birth of your child is one of the happiest, most memorable
   moments of your life. At Middletown Regional Hospital (MRH), we want to make this experience as
   perfect as possible.

8 **The Best Medical Care**
9 All parents want the best for their babies. That's why we offer comprehensive medical services and highly
   skilled physicians dedicated to giving you and your baby the best quality care available. Our skilled nurses
   are equally committed to providing outstanding patient care. They're experienced in providing both normal
   and high-risk care, and many are certified by the Association of Women's Health/Obstetric and Neonatal
   Nurses.

10 **Your Home Away From Home**
11 At Middletown Regional Hospital, we'll help you feel right at home. When you arrive at the hospital, you'll
   go directly to the Family Birth Center. After a brief registration, you'll be escorted to one of our five
   private birthing suites specially designed to meet your labor and delivery needs.

12 Our birthing suites provide a comfortable, home-like environment for your special delivery. You'll have
   your own bathroom and shower, a TV and VCR and a state-of-the-art birthing bed. Each suite has an
   attractive décor with wall coverings, paintings and hardwood floors even a cozy seating area for your
   family and friends. But most importantly, all suites are equipped with the latest medical technology to
   support you and your baby all neatly tucked away out of sight until it's needed.

Figure 8.3 Representation of web page in Figure 8.2 in MAXqda

The text group area is where source material can be organized in MAXqda. In this study, the web sites were organized by both types of provider and researcher who analysed them, so the 'filing system' was alternative-Selina, alternative-Kelly; hospital-Selina, hospital-Kelly. Originally, Rutherford and Gallo-Cruz each had their own version of the MAXqda project and worked on different *texts*. Figure 8.4 represents what the document organization of their merged project looked like. *Text groups* provide a quick way of just restricting the analysis to the *texts* in that group, by selecting the text group and right clicking in order to *activate* them for analysis. Figure 8.4 shows how Rutherford and Gallo-Cruz organized their source material.

The document system window in Figure 8.4 gives the analyst some immediate information. The column of numbers on the right-hand side indicates the number of *coded segments* (passages) there are for each *text*. The yellow icon □ indicates that there is a memo linked to the adjacent *text*. In addition, *texts* can be colour coded in order to differentiate them in some way. The colour coded *texts* can be filtered for analysis purposes. In Figure 8.4, the *texts* in the *text group* 'alternative-Selina' have been colour coded. The colour is indicated as a square in the lower right-hand corner ▤ of the *text* icon.

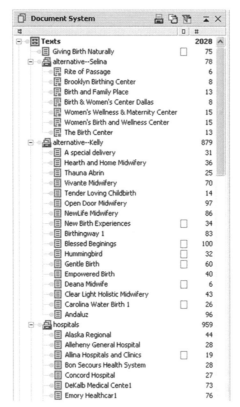

Figure 8.4 Organization of source material into text groups

Representing units of analysis and attribute variables

The unit of observation and one of the units of analysis are the web site. The other unit of analysis is the type of provider – hospital or alternative provision. In this study, the *text* itself represents the web site as a unit of analysis. The *text groups* represent the unit of analysis of the provider group.

Attribute variables are attached to *texts* in MAXqda. Variables in this study include region, urban/suburban, income level and level of competition. Type of provider was also included as a variable in order to compare web sites when they were the unit of analysis. In MAXqda, attributes are represented in a spreadsheet style. Figure 8.5 shows some of the texts in this study and the attribute values assigned to them.

Once the variables have been set up and values assigned, it is possible to restrict the analysis to any combination of them. Figure 8.6 shows how by combining the attribute values 'urban' and 'midwife', MAXqda activated for analysis all the urban midwives' web sites. Activation is shown by the red arrows pointing to the relevant texts (also in red) in the document system.

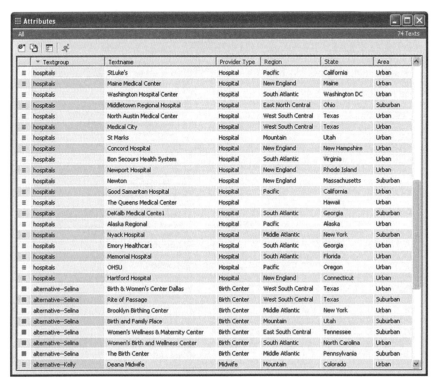

Figure 8.5 Display of research design attributes

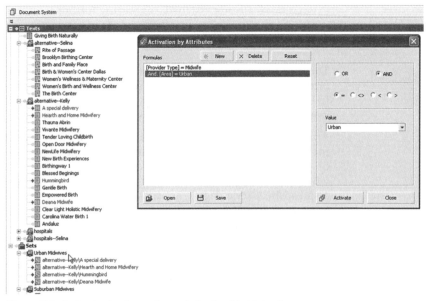

Figure 8.6 Activation by the attributes 'urban' and 'midwives'

⊞ Code System

	Code-ID	Position	Parent Code	Code	Creation Date	Author	All Coded Segments
■	2	5	physical labor\safety	natural	17/02/2007 22:39	Kelly	78
■	3	2	physical labor	safety	17/02/2007 22:40	Kelly	22
■	4	14	physical labor	environment	17/02/2007 22:40	Kelly	16
■	6	3	physical labor\safety	expertise/training/prestige	17/02/2007 22:41	Kelly	123
■	7	9	physical labor\safety	technology	17/02/2007 22:41	Kelly	90
■	10	52	social labor	individual empowerment	17/02/2007 22:42	Kelly	11
■	11	62	social labor\relational connection	partners & family involv...	17/02/2007 22:43	Kelly	205
■	12	60	social labor	relational connection	17/02/2007 22:44	Kelly	9
■	13	21	physical labor	pain & anxiety	17/02/2007 22:46	Kelly	2
■	17	6	physical labor\safety	risks/complications	17/02/2007 23:07	Kelly	99
■	18	1		physical labor	17/02/2007 23:09	Kelly	0
■	19	51		social labor	17/02/2007 23:09	Kelly	0
■	20	68	social labor	symbolic meaning	19/02/2007 11:58	Kelly	0
■	21	11	physical labor\safety	baby care/parenting	19/02/2007 11:59	Kelly	78
■	23	8	physical labor\safety\risks/complications	Cesarean	19/02/2007 12:24	Kelly	13
■	24	7	physical labor\safety\risks/complications	neonatal unit	19/02/2007 12:25	Kelly	20
■	25	10	physical labor\safety	Newborn screening	19/02/2007 12:28	Kelly	17
■	26	65	social labor\relational connection	visitors, friends	19/02/2007 12:40	Kelly	19
■	27	64	social labor\relational connection	provider's vocation of care	19/02/2007 14:17	Kelly	59
■	29	4	physical labor\safety	experience	24/02/2007 12:10	mrutherf	48
■	30	15	physical labor\environment	comfortable/attractive ...	24/02/2007 12:11	mrutherf	91
■	31	16	physical labor\environment	privacy	24/02/2007 12:11	mrutherf	41
■	32	17	physical labor\environment	familiarity	24/02/2007 12:11	mrutherf	17
■	33	18	physical labor\environment	amenities/services	24/02/2007 12:12	mrutherf	49
■	34	22	physical labor\pain & anxiety management	anesthesia	24/02/2007 12:12	mrutherf	18
■	35	23	physical labor\pain & anxiety management	non-drug physical tech...	24/02/2007 12:12	mrutherf	78
■	36	24	physical labor\pain & anxiety management	psychological	24/02/2007 12:13	mrutherf	41
■	37	56	social labor\individual empowerment	mothers/parents as de...	24/02/2007 12:14	mrutherf	87
■	38	55	social labor\individual empowerment	encouragement of natu...	24/02/2007 12:14	mrutherf	39

Figure 8.7 Development of codes (Rutherford)

Once activated, the activated texts can be quickly turned into a set. The cursor at the bottom of Figure 8.6 is pointing to the newly created set 'urban midwives'. Below it is the set 'suburban midwives' which had been created previously in a similar way. MAXqda quickly pulled out these two sets from the attributes already assigned, supporting further analysis looking at similarities and/or differences between the way urban and suburban midwives promote their services.

Thematic framework

Rutherford and Gallo-Cruz started to develop their thematic framework by first looking at the sites and taking notes separately. They then exchanged emails and had several telephone conversations in which they developed together the initial coding themes. Rutherford started coding in MAXqda first, before Gallo-Cruz, and continued to develop the codes in an emergent way. MAXqda has two code system views. The default view shows the codes organized as a hierarchical catalogue system. The alternative view gives information on the order the codes were created, the date and time created, which team member created them and the number of coded segments (passages of text coded). This alternative view provides a log of the development of codes. Figure 8.7 shows Rutherford's initial coding process in MAXqda.

The codes have been ordered by creation date in Figure 8.6. In the first column, the *code-ID* is automatically assigned to a code in the order of creation. Some numbers are missing in this column; for example codes 1, 5, 8 and

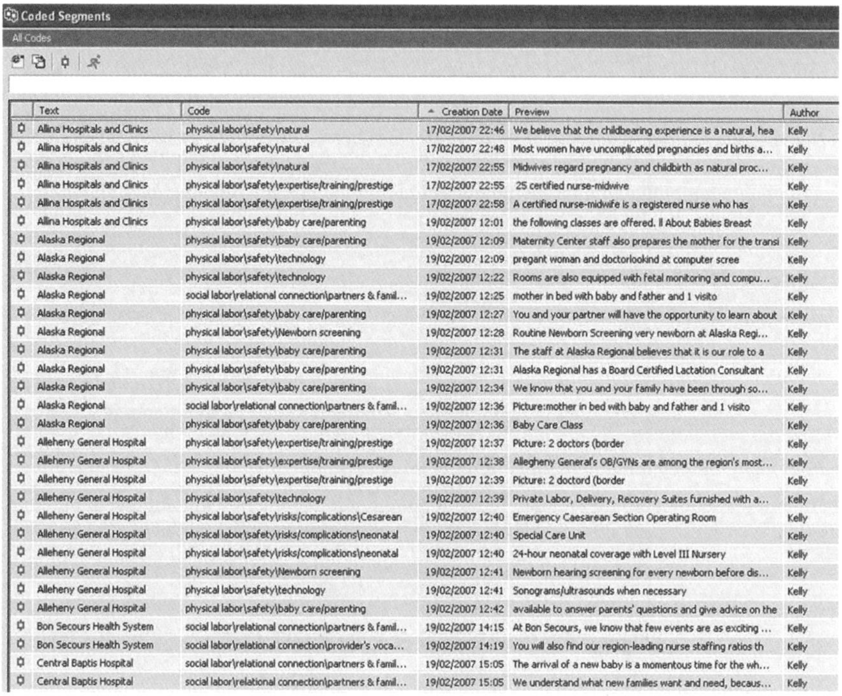

Coded Segments

All Codes

Text	Code	Creation Date	Preview	Author
Allina Hospitals and Clinics	physical labor\safety\natural	17/02/2007 22:46	We believe that the childbearing experience is a natural, hea	Kelly
Allina Hospitals and Clinics	physical labor\safety\natural	17/02/2007 22:48	Most women have uncomplicated pregnancies and births a...	Kelly
Allina Hospitals and Clinics	physical labor\safety\natural	17/02/2007 22:55	Midwives regard pregnancy and childbirth as natural proc...	Kelly
Allina Hospitals and Clinics	physical labor\safety\expertise/training/prestige	17/02/2007 22:55	25 certified nurse-midwive	Kelly
Allina Hospitals and Clinics	physical labor\safety\expertise/training/prestige	17/02/2007 22:58	A certified nurse-midwife is a registered nurse who has	Kelly
Allina Hospitals and Clinics	physical labor\safety\baby care/parenting	19/02/2007 12:01	the following classes are offered. ll About Babies Breast	Kelly
Alaska Regional	physical labor\safety\baby care/parenting	19/02/2007 12:09	Maternity Center staff also prepares the mother for the transi	Kelly
Alaska Regional	physical labor\safety\technology	19/02/2007 12:09	pregant woman and doctorlookind at computer scree	Kelly
Alaska Regional	physical labor\safety\technology	19/02/2007 12:22	Rooms are also equipped with fetal monitoring and compu...	Kelly
Alaska Regional	social labor\relational connection\partners & famil...	19/02/2007 12:25	mother in bed with baby and father and 1 visito	Kelly
Alaska Regional	physical labor\safety\baby care/parenting	19/02/2007 12:27	You and your partner will have the opportunity to learn about	Kelly
Alaska Regional	physical labor\safety\Newborn screening	19/02/2007 12:28	Routine Newborn Screening very newborn at Alaska Regi...	Kelly
Alaska Regional	physical labor\safety\baby care/parenting	19/02/2007 12:31	The staff at Alaska Regional believes that it is our role to a	Kelly
Alaska Regional	physical labor\safety\baby care/parenting	19/02/2007 12:31	Alaska Regional has a Board Certified Lactation Consultant	Kelly
Alaska Regional	physical labor\safety\baby care/parenting	19/02/2007 12:34	We know that you and your family have been through so...	Kelly
Alaska Regional	social labor\relational connection\partners & famil...	19/02/2007 12:36	Picture:mother in bed with baby and father and 1 visito	Kelly
Alaska Regional	physical labor\safety\baby care/parenting	19/02/2007 12:36	Baby Care Class	Kelly
Alleheny General Hospital	physical labor\safety\expertise/training/prestige	19/02/2007 12:37	Picture: 2 doctors (border	Kelly
Alleheny General Hospital	physical labor\safety\expertise/training/prestige	19/02/2007 12:38	Allegheny General's OB/GYNs are among the region's most...	Kelly
Alleheny General Hospital	physical labor\safety\expertise/training/prestige	19/02/2007 12:39	Picture: 2 doctord (border	Kelly
Alleheny General Hospital	physical labor\safety\technology	19/02/2007 12:39	Private Labor, Delivery, Recovery Suites furnished with a...	Kelly
Alleheny General Hospital	physical labor\safety\risks/complications\Cesarean	19/02/2007 12:40	Emergency Caesarean Section Operating Room	Kelly
Alleheny General Hospital	physical labor\safety\risks/complications\neonatal	19/02/2007 12:40	Special Care Unit	Kelly
Alleheny General Hospital	physical labor\safety\risks/complications\neonatal	19/02/2007 12:40	24-hour neonatal coverage with Level III Nursery	Kelly
Alleheny General Hospital	physical labor\safety\Newborn screening	19/02/2007 12:41	Newborn hearing screening for every newborn before dis...	Kelly
Alleheny General Hospital	physical labor\safety\technology	19/02/2007 12:41	Sonograms/ultrasounds when necessary	Kelly
Alleheny General Hospital	physical labor\safety\baby care/parenting	19/02/2007 12:42	available to answer parents' questions and give advice on the	Kelly
Bon Secours Health System	social labor\relational connection\partners & famil...	19/02/2007 14:15	At Bon Secours, we know that few events are as exciting ...	Kelly
Bon Secours Health System	social labor\relational connection\provider's voca...	19/02/2007 14:19	You will also find our region-leading nurse staffing ratios th	Kelly
Central Baptis Hospital	social labor\relational connection\partners & famil...	19/02/2007 15:05	The arrival of a new baby is a momentous time for the wh...	Kelly
Central Baptis Hospital	social labor\relational connection\partners & famil...	19/02/2007 15:05	We understand what new families want and need, becaus...	Kelly

Figure 8.8 Coding process (Rutherford)

9 are missing. These are codes that were either deleted or merged with other codes. The fourth column – *code* – in the figure, shows that Rutherford (Kelly) created the codes *natural, safety, environment, expertise/training/prestige, technology, individual empowerment, partners & family involvement, relational connection, and pain & anxiety management* all within the first few minutes of working in MAXqda (17/02/2007 22:39–22:46). MAXqda also keeps a record of the history of the *segments* (passages of text) actually coded. This record, as shown in Figure 8.8, shows that after creating these first nine codes, Rutherford started to code the text of the web site for *Allina Hospitals and Clinics* for the codes *natural* and *prestige*. Then Figure 8.7 indicates that she went back and created the code *risks/complications*. The time stamp in Figure 8.7 suggests that she had a look at the codes she had already created and reorganized them by first creating the top level codes *physical labor* and *social labor* (neither of which have any coding) and reorganized the other codes she had already created under them. Then she finished the work for that day.

From these two records, which MAXqda automatically generates, we can see that Kelly started with a few codes but worked in essentially an emergent way, reading the text of the web sites and coding them, developing new codes and reorganizing the codes as a catalogue of codes.

Gallo-Cruz began working in MAXqda about a week after Rutherford and we can see from Figure 8.9 that she began by creating all the codes Rutherford had developed at that stage. She was working on her own computer and was

☷ Code System

	Code-ID	Parent Code	Code	Creation Date	Author	All Coded Segments
■	1		Physical Labor	25/02/2007 23:19	Owner	0
■	2	Physical Labor	Safety	25/02/2007 23:23	Owner	41
■	3	Physical Labor	Environment	25/02/2007 23:24	Owner	1
■	4	Physical Labor	Pain/ Anxiety Management	25/02/2007 23:25	Owner	8
■	5		Social Labor	25/02/2007 23:25	Owner	0
■	6	Social Labor	Individual Empowerment	25/02/2007 23:25	Owner	7
■	7	Social Labor	Relational Connection	25/02/2007 23:26	Owner	0
■	8	Social Labor	Symbolic Meaning	25/02/2007 23:26	Owner	3
■	9	Physical Labor\Safety	Expertise and Accreditation	25/02/2007 23:27	Owner	278
■	10	Physical Labor\Safety	Experience	25/02/2007 23:28	Owner	86
■	11	Physical Labor\Safety	Belief in Birth as a Natural Process	25/02/2007 23:29	Owner	48
■	12	Physical Labor\Safety	Risks and Complications	25/02/2007 23:29	Owner	205
■	13	Physical Labor\Safety	Technology	25/02/2007 23:30	Owner	101
■	14	Physical Labor\Safety	Parental Education in prenatal and Baby Care	25/02/2007 23:30	Owner	237
■	15	Physical Labor\Environment	Confortable and Attractive Setting	25/02/2007 23:32	Owner	138
■	16	Physical Labor\Environment	Privacy	25/02/2007 23:33	Owner	55
■	17	Physical Labor\Environment	Familiarity	25/02/2007 23:33	Owner	22
■	18	Physical Labor\Environment	Amenities	25/02/2007 23:33	Owner	145
■	19	Physical Labor\Pain/ Anxiety Management	Anesthesia and other Medications	25/02/2007 23:33	Owner	34
■	20	Physical Labor\Pain/ Anxiety Management	Non-medical physical techniques and props	25/02/2007 23:34	Owner	59
■	21	Physical Labor\Pain/ Anxiety Management	Psych Emp/ Relax	25/02/2007 23:34	Owner	81
■	22	Social Labor\Individual Empowerment	Information/ Knowledge	25/02/2007 23:35	Owner	186
■	23	Social Labor\Individual Empowerment	Transparency of Process	25/02/2007 23:35	Owner	95
■	25	Social Labor\Individual Empowerment	Encouragement of Birthing/Parenting Abilities	25/02/2007 23:36	Owner	71
■	27	Social Labor\Relational Connection	Mother-Baby Bonding	25/02/2007 23:37	Owner	52
■	28	Social Labor\Relational Connection	Family Relationships	25/02/2007 23:38	Owner	219
■	29	Social Labor\Relational Connection	Trust and Care w/ Midwives or doulas	25/02/2007 23:38	Owner	137
■	30	Social Labor\Relational Connection	Providers' Vocation of Care	25/02/2007 23:38	Owner	73
■	31	Social Labor\Relational Connection	Visitors/ Friends	25/02/2007 23:39	Owner	22

Figure 8.9 Development of codes (Gallo-Cruz)

analysing a different group of web sites. The *code-Ids* in Figure 8.9 are in numerical order with no missing numbers. From her *coded segments* log (not shown), we can see that after she created the codes she started to do some coding. Later in the *code system* log, we can see that she started to develop new codes as she went along (cannot be seen in Figure 8.9 as the table needs to be scrolled further down).

Key aspects of the analysis process

Rutherford and Gallo-Cruz took a qualitative thematic content analysis approach. As discussed above, the coding framework they developed was emergent. They used MAXqda's code memo function to define the codes as they evolved. They also used memos linked to passages of text (segments) to directly comment on certain aspects of the web site. In addition, Rutherford was assessing each web site for dominant and secondary themes. She created these as attribute variables as they are characteristics of the web sites as a whole. Figure 8.10 shows the attributes tables sorted by the dominant themes column.

These attributes are different from the attributes based on the research design which were discussed earlier. These attributes have emerged from the analysis of the web sites. As can be seen, these attributes are also thematic codes. An assessment of dominant themes can be quickly made in MAXqda by using the *code matrix browser.*

Each column represents the coding for a particular text. You can see them named along the top row of the table in Figure 8.11. The codes are listed in the

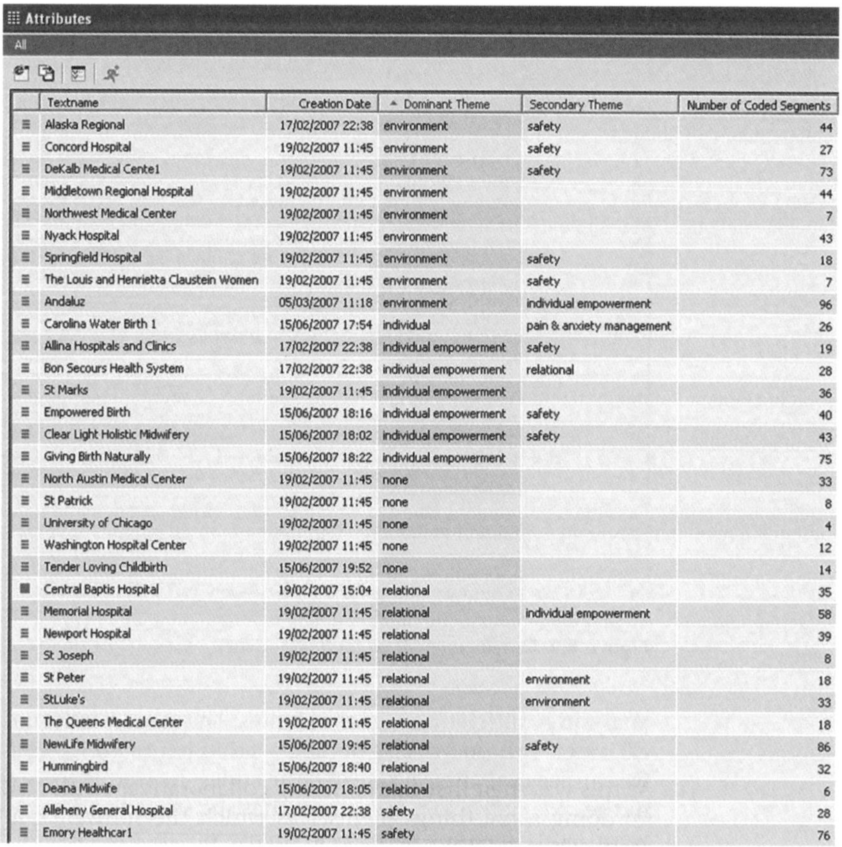

Textname	Creation Date	▲ Dominant Theme	Secondary Theme	Number of Coded Segments
Alaska Regional	17/02/2007 22:38	environment	safety	44
Concord Hospital	19/02/2007 11:45	environment	safety	27
DeKalb Medical Cente1	19/02/2007 11:45	environment	safety	73
Middletown Regional Hospital	19/02/2007 11:45	environment		44
Northwest Medical Center	19/02/2007 11:45	environment		7
Nyack Hospital	19/02/2007 11:45	environment		43
Springfield Hospital	19/02/2007 11:45	environment	safety	18
The Louis and Henrietta Claustein Women	19/02/2007 11:45	environment	safety	7
Andaluz	05/03/2007 11:18	environment	individual empowerment	96
Carolina Water Birth 1	15/06/2007 17:54	individual	pain & anxiety management	26
Allina Hospitals and Clinics	17/02/2007 22:38	individual empowerment	safety	19
Bon Secours Health System	17/02/2007 22:38	individual empowerment	relational	28
St Marks	19/02/2007 11:45	individual empowerment		36
Empowered Birth	15/06/2007 18:16	individual empowerment	safety	40
Clear Light Holistic Midwifery	15/06/2007 18:02	individual empowerment	safety	43
Giving Birth Naturally	15/06/2007 18:22	individual empowerment		75
North Austin Medical Center	19/02/2007 11:45	none		33
St Patrick	19/02/2007 11:45	none		8
University of Chicago	19/02/2007 11:45	none		4
Washington Hospital Center	19/02/2007 11:45	none		12
Tender Loving Childbirth	15/06/2007 19:52	none		14
Central Baptis Hospital	19/02/2007 15:04	relational		35
Memorial Hospital	19/02/2007 11:45	relational	individual empowerment	58
Newport Hospital	19/02/2007 11:45	relational		39
St Joseph	19/02/2007 11:45	relational		8
St Peter	19/02/2007 11:45	relational	environment	18
StLuke's	19/02/2007 11:45	relational	environment	33
The Queens Medical Center	19/02/2007 11:45	relational		18
NewLife Midwifery	15/06/2007 19:45	relational	safety	86
Hummingbird	15/06/2007 18:40	relational		32
Deana Midwife	15/06/2007 18:05	relational		6
Allegheny General Hospital	17/02/2007 22:38	safety		28
Emory Healthcar1	19/02/2007 11:45	safety		76

Figure 8.10 Display of researcher-developed attributes

first column. The codes have been collapsed to their top level codes in order to see differences in coding within and across documents on the broad themes. Dots represent where there is coding. The larger the dot, the more that code was used in a particular text. In Figure 8.11, the text representing the web site New Life has most coding for the code 'safety' and the next most used code is 'relational connection'. In this case, it would suggest that 'safety' is the dominant theme for this web site while 'relational connection' would be a secondary theme. However, the analyst would need to retrieve the actual *text segments*

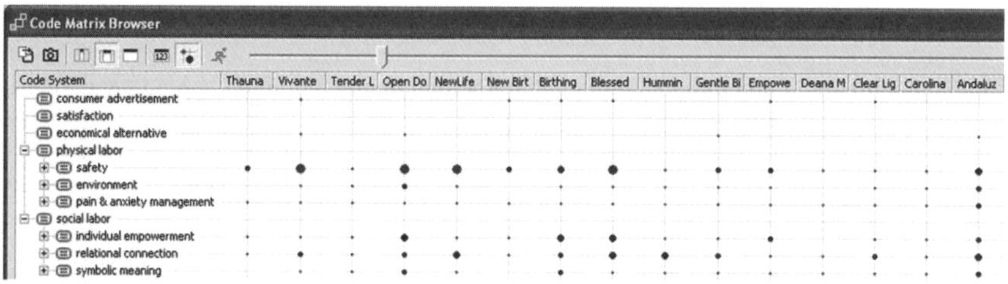

Figure 8.11 Code matrix browser – identifying dominant codes by text

coded to see how these themes were expressed as well as to assess the impact of the visual information before making a final judgement.

Teamwork in a dyad

This was the first time that both Rutherford and Gallo-Cruz had worked collaboratively and the first time they had used MAXqda. Rutherford had used ATLAS.ti on an earlier piece of research and had started to develop her codes for this project in ATLAS.ti. However, they switched to MAXqda because Gallo-Cruz's university had a licence for it and Rutherford was looking to upgrade her software. Rutherford began her work in MAXqda with the demo version which she downloaded from the MAXqda web site. When she finally purchased MAXqda, a new version – MAXqda 2007 – had just come out. So she was working with a different version than Gallo-Cruz whose university was still using MAXqda 2. This meant that they had to continue to work on their separate versions.

They collaborated by telephone and by exchanging emails with attachments of memos and summaries of work. Occasionally, they sent exported pieces of the MAXqda project. They also met together at a conference for a few days and did some work together. They worked in an iterative and emergent way; several times they revised their codes – by merging codes together and creating new codes – based on their conversations. In the end, Gallo-Cruz sent her entire MAXqda 2 project file to Rutherford who merged it with her MAXqda 2007 project.

As this was their first time working collaboratively with MAXqda, they ended up doing some things themselves which the software could have done for them. They did not use the code matrix browser (as described above) to determine dominant themes. They made a judgement call on that by reviewing the web sites and the codes. This was a learning experience for both of them and in retrospect they realize that they could have made more use of the software if they had started with more knowledge of all of the software's capabilities.

Lessons from this case

This case is a good example of how 'workarounds' can be used effectively for the analysis of materials that QDAS packages do not currently support. It is not possible to directly import or code web sites. However, Rutherford and Gallo-Cruz were able to analyse successfully web sites for their research by creating a representation of their web site in MAXqda with a hyperlink to the actual web site. One MAXqda *text* represented all the relevant pages of a web site. Each page was noted with its title within square brackets; for example [services page]. They were careful to describe the photos, graphics, videos and audios on the web page. They were able to code and comment on these descriptions within MAXqda.

This case is also a good example of how a dyad can work together on the same project. However, although this was a collaboration between the two of them, the context of their university settings determined which QDAS they would use. The fact that Gallo-Cruz's university had a licence for MAXqda was a more powerful factor in software choice than the fact that Rutherford had experience of using ATLAS.ti. In addition, they were caught up in the rapidly changing world of QDAS development. They ended up working in two different versions of the same software. However, they developed their own system of collaboration using emails, telephone conversations and occasional face-to-face meetings. They had divided up the work so that they were coding for different web sites. They were able to merge their collective work in one MAXqda project and analyse across all the web sites.

For more information on this project, see also Rutherford and Gallo-Cruz (2007, Forthcoming).

Note

1   This exemplar is based on a study carried out by researchers, Markella Rutherford, Wellesley College and Selina Gallo-Cruz, Emory University.

9 Faculty support staff in online programs[1]

The software that was used in the original project was NVivo 2.

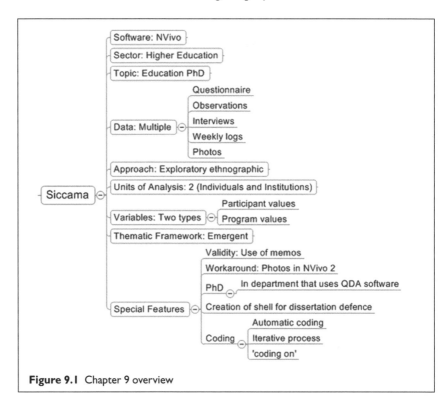

Figure 9.1 Chapter 9 overview

For the purposes of this discussion, we have converted Siccama's (2006) study into the latest version of NVivo at the time of publication – NVivo 7. In making the conversion to NVivo 7, we have also done some reorganization of the project in order to demonstrate the important features of the 7.0 version that were not available in earlier builds.

Background of project

A doctoral student in the Leadership in Schooling program of the Graduate School of Education at the University of Massachusetts Lowell, Carolyn Siccama's real world job as a faculty support staff in an online education program served as the impetus for her dissertation study. Intrigued by the way she saw her own role emerging as online education came to the fore in higher education, she wondered about the ways others in similar roles were crafting their position, the challenges they encountered, and the solutions they had devised. As she began to investigate the issue in a more formal manner, she learned that there was little in-depth information on the role professionals, like herself, played in the construction of online curriculum through their diverse interactions with higher education faculty. She realized the value a qualitative research study of this topic would have to her own field of work and the benefits it could provide to colleagues in similar positions in higher education.

Unlike many doctoral students who undertake the use of qualitative research software for their dissertation projects, Siccama had the opportunity to learn the software (NVivo 2.0) before she began her study through a doctoral level qualitative research course that integrated technology and methods training. In addition, she worked with a dissertation chair familiar with the tool, attended a dissertation discussion group of fellow software users (organized by the chair), and attended a university with a user support group for the software package.

Design of project

Siccama's project focused on two interlocking units of analysis or cases – four individuals in the role of faculty support staff for online programs *and* the institutions in which they worked. She developed a range of comparable variables (attributes) that she attached to each case (see Table 9.1). This was a complex study in that she collected multiple forms of primary and secondary data (textual and visual images) over the four-month data collection period of her study. Her study also represents a snapshot perspective as her goal was to develop a descriptive and interpretive understanding of her participants' work roles at that point in time. Table 9.1 provides a bird's-eye view of the critical features that define Siccama's work as an example of a complex project.

Data collected

1 *Demographic questionnaire*: This document would provide information on participants' characteristics and the institution's characteristics and would form the basis of her attributes (see the list of attributes in Table 9.1). It would be sent to the participants prior to the first interview.
2 *Site observation*: Siccama planned to visit each of the four participants at their place of work – once for an introductory interview and a second time for a follow-up interview. In conjunction with those visits she would observe the site.
3 *Interviews*: Siccama planned two semi-structured open-ended interviews with each participant. The first interview sought information on: 1) the work context; 2) typical work activities; 3) interactions with faculty; 4) training activities; 5) types of support provided by this position; 6) special

Table 9.1 Design framework of Siccama project

Unit of analysis	Attributes	Time frame	Data: textual (primary or secondary forms of data)	Data: non-textual (primary or secondary forms of data)
Program/institution	*Program* Age of online program No. of online degrees No. of Certificates No. of courses No. of new courses per semester	Snapshot	*Primary data* 1 Demographic questionnaire 2 Site observation 3 Interviews 4 Week in review activity log *Secondary data* Job description Program description	*Primary data* Photographs *Secondary data*
Participant within the program	*Participant* Current title Gender Yrs. in position Education background 1 Education background 2 Supervise others? How many? Supervise staff (no.) Supervise students (no.) Professional Organization Journals Published			

issues related to connecting to faculty; 7) professional development required for this position. The second interview followed up with a discussion related to the visual data collected (see below).

4 *Visual data*: Siccama planned to provide each of her four participants with a disposable camera that they would use to take photographs related to their work context. She would develop these photographs and use discussion of the photos as the basis for her second interview with the participants. In this way, she aimed to deepen insights into their insider notions of the work in which they were engaged.

5 *Week in review activity log*: Siccama had also designed a unique data collection tool in which participants would, twice during the course of the data collection period, both log activities and reflect upon work activities. In this way, she sought to find a means of gathering a detailed picture of the range of tasks and their meaning to participants.

The total scope of the data that was ultimately collected is described in Table 9.2 from her dissertation.

Table 9.2 Overview of data collection and analysis

Study Component	Case #1	Case #2	Case #3	Case #4	Total amount of data to be analyzed
Demographic Questionnaire	1	1	1	1	4 Questionnaires
Site Observation	2	1	2	2	7 Observations
Interviews	2	2	2	2	8 Interviews
Visual Data (photographs)	12	3	12	12	39 Photographs
Week in Review Activity Logs	2	2	2	2	8 Activity logs

Source: Siccama (2006: 55).

Representing the design in the software shell

The discussion of this case focuses on three distinct periods in the conduct of the project, each of which raised important issues for research design in an electronic format: 1) preplanning or proposal development; 2) data collection and ongoing analysis; and 3) final analysis and presentation of the study.

Preplanning or proposal development

In preparation for undertaking the dissertation research, Siccama, using NVivo software, created an electronic shell of the proposed project that she presented as part of the defence of her dissertation proposal. The electronic shell included cases and their attributes and placeholders for the various kind of data she would collect. Siccama also established placeholders for her prospective sources – interviews, activity logs and other kinds of data she anticipated collecting. In this sense, Siccama's data collection effort began before the proposal was approved with the thoughtful organization of the containers for the data. The screenshot below (Figure 9.2), although taken from the final version of the converted project, demonstrates the case organization. Figure 9.3 shows the casebook in which the attributes for the cases are organized.

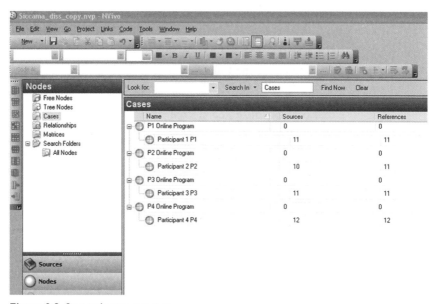

Figure 9.2 Siccama's case structure

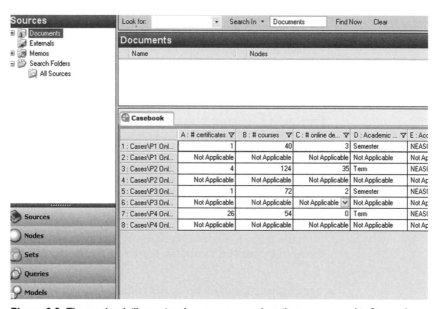

Figure 9.3 The casebook illustrating the ways cases and attributes were used in Siccama's project

Data collection and ongoing analysis

Preparing texts for efficient analysis

Siccama prepared interview transcripts and activity logs for efficient analysis through preparing them with appropriate headings that NVivo could then use for auto-coding. This allowed her to batch code large amounts of textual material. The material was then readily available in useful segments (all the answers to question 1 for instance).

Siccama chose the following method for working with the still photographs that formed a part of her data collection. In Siccama's study the second interview with participants focused on discussion of the photographic data that participants had collected. Thus, in the interview 2 transcripts there was an explanation of each photograph, and each transcript clearly notes which photographs were being described. Then the interview 2 transcripts were coded using participant descriptions of the photographs.

Coding

Initial coding of transcripts of the first interviews were done by hand and out of that emerged 60–100 possible codes. Siccama organized these initial codes into five tree nodes with multiple child nodes, and subsequently coded the transcripts electronically using this node system. Nodes were conscientiously named and renamed through the course of the study.

> Thoughout the coding process, I maintained descriptions of each code within the NVivo Node Property window. The descriptions proved to be essential to me in many ways. They served as a reminder as to my initial thoughts in creating the node, as a way to maintain consistency in my coding, as a way to track the evolution and existence of a node, and lastly as a way to build trustworthiness of my data.
>
> (Siccama 2006: 76)

Siccama followed Lyn Richards' (2005) lead in conducting analytical coding.

> I followed a systematic approach to analyzing each tree node. I would first browse the node and print out a node report that included all of the text that was coded at that specific node, which would allow me to study and reflect on the content of the node. Often at this point the data would suggest new categories or themes which required me to 'code-on' and create child nodes beneath the tree node. I would then printout a report of the newly created child nodes to see if there were possible new meanings or new categories emerging from the data. Since coding is an iterative process, initial coding from the interviews and observations gave way to more analytical coding as the Activity Logs and visual data sources began to inform the study.
>
> (Siccama 2006: 75–76)

In a retrospective comment on her coding, Siccama stated:

> My final NVivo project had 5 tree nodes which were my findings. But it didn't start this way, I went back and restored a few old NVivo backup

projects from December of 05 and it looks like the number of tree nodes changed and evolved as data was being collected, and it ranged anywhere from 3–11 tree nodes that were then merged and evolved into the final major five nodes/findings.

(Siccama: personal correspondence)

An example of Siccama's codes can be found in Figure 9.4.

Memos

Siccama discusses six different kinds of memo in the methodology chapter of her dissertation:

1 artefact memos;
2 observation memos;
3 NVivo methodology unfolding memos;
4 transcription memos;
5 chapter update memos;
6 theme memos.

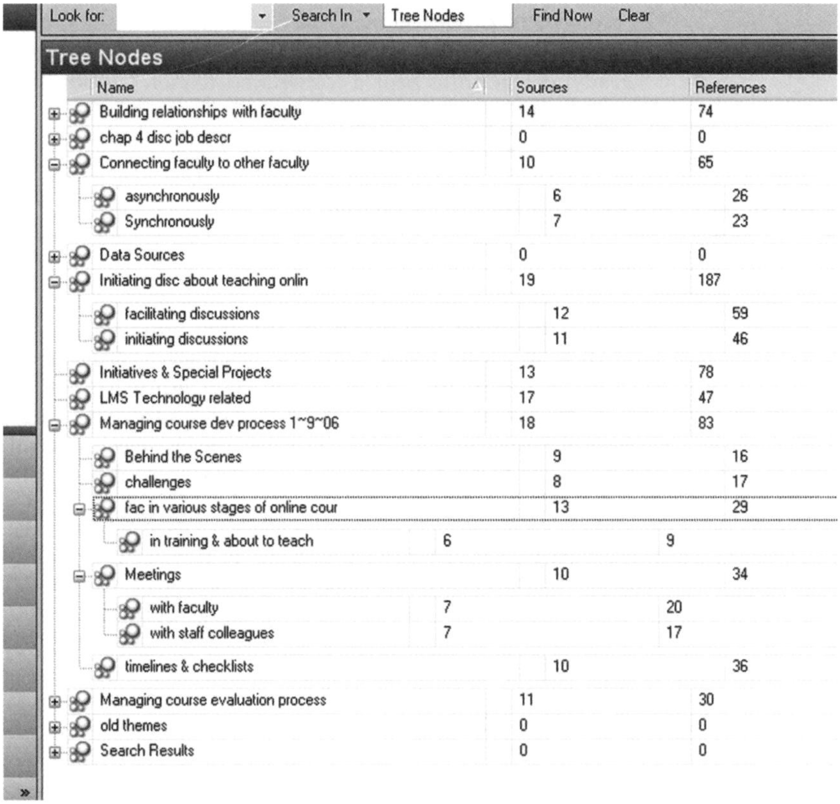

Figure 9.4 Siccama's codes

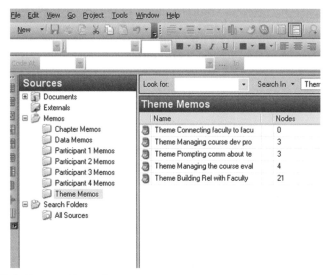

Figure 9.5 A glimpse at Siccama's memos

In NVivo 7.0, her memos can be organized in folders, providing an efficient means of retrieving and working with them (Figure 9.5). As suggested by her adviser, Siccama kept a log related to her methodology as it related, in particular, to her use of the software.

Final analysis and presentation of the study

Validity

Siccama discussed validity from the traditional standpoint (sans software) and then in more depth from the nouveau standpoint (validity as integral to software use). In her discussion of validity from the traditional standpoint, she discussed issues related to data collection (completeness and transcription), measures used to ensure the greatest penetration of the topic, member checking, triangulation based upon multiple data sources and peer debriefing.

In discussing validity from the nouveau standpoint – validity enhanced with QDAS – Siccama turned to Richards' (2004) work for guidelines. This led her to consider the ways she strengthened her claims for validity through:

- maintaining audit and log trails;
- interrogating interpretations;
- scoping data;
- establishing saturation.

In each section, she walks the reader through the ways the software was used and how its use helped her to support the interpretations she reached.

Representing the role of the software package in the conduct of the study

In helping her committee to understand the role NVivo played in the conduct of her study, Siccama created a graphic image that became a quick favourite among her graduate school colleagues (Figure 9.6). The image provided a visual means of understanding how data collection, analysis and the search for validity are integrated through the use of the software package.

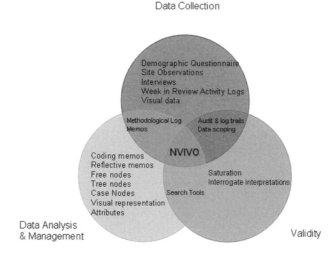

Figure 9.6 'Figure 1: NVivo integration into research study' (Siccama 2006: 54)

Lessons from this case

This case presents an interesting contrast to Mandel (Chapter 11), demonstrating the very different kinds of institutional support for QDAS use graduate students may have available to them as they undertake their dissertation research. In Siccama's case, multiple kinds of support related to the use of the software package were available before and during the conduct of the study. Because use of the tool was valued within the institutional culture, Siccama could feel greater emotional security in the choice to use the tool and assurance that her committee would give heed to the substance of the final product – the dissertation – rather than being led astray by concerns about the presence of technology.

This case provides a nice view of a small but complex study in which multiple kinds of data (interviews, activity logs, observations, visual data, job descriptions, etc.) are integrated to provide a comprehensive understanding of the phenomenon under study – faculty support staff working in online programs. In contrast to Mandel's (ATLAS.ti) use of families to organize the units of analysis for the research design, Siccama's project demonstrates the ways NVivo's cases do a similar job. By making appropriate use of cases and attributes, Siccama established a foundation from which searches could be efficiently conducted. Through her reflective discussion of the ways software use enhances validity in qualitative research, Siccama sheds new light on a challenging topic. Finally, through modelling her understanding of software's contribution to the overall project, she provided graduate students and faculty with new awareness of the role of QDAS in qualitative research.

Note

1   This exemplar is based on a EdD dissertation, 'Work activities of professionals who occupy the role of faculty support staff in online education programs', by Carolyn Siccama, Leadership in Schooling, Graduate School of Education, University of Massachusetts Lowell.

10 Beyond planning a field trip[1]

The software that was used in the original project was NVivo 7.

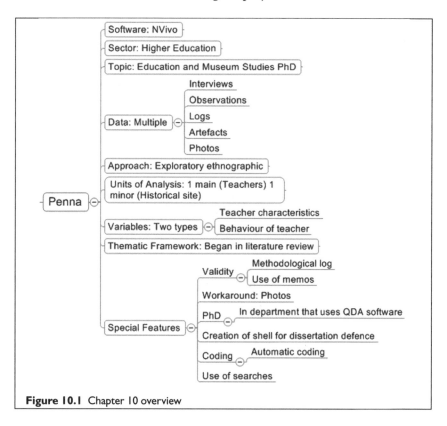

Figure 10.1 Chapter 10 overview

Background of project

As a middle-grade social studies teacher, Stacy Penna was highly appreciative of the value historical museums brought to students' learning. As a doctoral student in the University of Massachusetts Graduate School of Education, she began to wonder about the ways field trip experiences to historical museums served as teachers' in-service professional learning and the ways field trips to these institutions influenced teachers' practices. A review of the literature revealed that museum education researchers had paid scant attention to this critical area of museum learning, despite the numbers of teachers visiting historical museums on an annual basis with classes of students. This was the genesis of Penna's dissertation study examining the question: How are the educational practices of four urban eighth grade social studies teachers affected by the educational resources of a historical site? (Penna 2007)

Penna began working with qualitative research software well before she undertook her dissertation. She was first introduced to these tools in a class on qualitative research methods in which NVivo 2.0 was used throughout the course. Using the knowledge gleaned from this course, she developed the literature review for her doctoral qualifying paper (a paper used to initiate the literature review for her dissertation study) in NVivo 2.0. NVivo 7.0 was released as she began her dissertation study, and she switched over to the new version of the product for the conduct of the dissertation.

Penna's dissertation chair was comfortable with the software, and throughout the process Penna participated in a dissertation advisory group in which all members were also conducting qualitative research dissertations using NVivo 7.0. Penna also participated in the campus-wide Qualitative Research Network's NVivo user's group. After graduation, Penna's experience with NVivo led to her being hired by QSR International (developer of NVivo) to oversee the East Coast sales market in the USA.

Design of project

A historical museum in the town of Mylen, the pseudonym for an urban area in northeastern Massachusetts, served as the focus for this study. With support from a federally funded grant, the historical museum in Mylen had entered into a partnership with the Mylen school district to 'improve the teaching of U.S. history in the eighth grade' (Penna 2007: 69). Central to this school improvement effort was the participation of eighth grade social studies teachers in field trips to the historical site. Penna studied four teachers enrolled in this programme, examining their pre- during- and post-field trip experiences, as well as reviewing the materials shared with teachers and other experiences relevant to teachers' learning in the programme. Penna asked teachers to capture their experiences in logs created during the field trip and through teacher-generated photographs that captured issues important to their learning. Penna, herself, took photographs of the historical site, schools and field trips to assist her in remembering and identifying important elements of the experience.

While the main emphasis of the study was the four participating eighth grade teachers, Penna also included in her investigation an examination of the historical site, its components and the perspectives of key members of this staff, particularly Jane, the historical site's school liaison coordinator.

Penna's study, like Siccama's (Chapter 9), is representative of a complex case design (see Table 10.1).

Table 10.1 Design framework of Penna's project

Units of analysis	Variables	Time frame	Data: textual (primary or secondary forms of data)	Data: non-textual (primary or secondary forms of data)
1. Historical site	*	Snapshot	*Primary data*	*Primary data*
2. Teachers	Attend summer institutes		1. Pre-field trip interview (w/demographic questionnaire embedded)	1. Photographs by teachers
Case 1	Centre experience		2. Field trip observation	
Case 2	Field trip experience at centre		3. Teacher logs from field trip	
Case 3	Field trip per year		4. Post-field trip interview	
Case 4	Gender			
	Graduate Education		*Secondary data*	*Secondary data*
	Major		1. Teacher artefacts	1. Photographs by researcher
	Middle school		2. Observation of teacher workshop	
	Minor		3. Site informant interview	
	Primary sources from Centre		4. Site artefacts	
	Social Studies Pedagogy			
	Student Structure			
	Teacher Certification			
	Teaching social studies at current M.S.			
	Teaching social studies over career			
	Teams			
	Use centre's resources			
	Workshops at centre			
	Years Teaching			

Note: * Penna chose not to use attributes for the characteristics of the historical museum site.

Representing the design in the software shell

Data organization

Penna's experience with QDAS prior to undertaking the dissertation had instilled in her the importance of building the software shell in advance of conducting the research. Her shell, built with care and intentionality, was developed in tandem with the development of the dissertation proposal and was available for review at the time of her proposal defence. Penna's shell provided her with the backbone for structuring the dissertation project. By constructing the software shell, she demonstrated her knowledge of the scope and organization of the project, as well as the ways project organization would contribute to the final products.

Key features of her data organization within NVivo 7.0 included the establishment of:

- units of analysis (cases);
- fixed characteristics of variables she would track in relationship to the units of analysis (attributes);
- identification of data to be collected;
- process tracking documents (journals and memos).

Because she was using NVivo 7.0, the way she established these features needed to be consistent with the particular affordances and restrictions of the software. Thus, for example, units of analysis were represented as cases (not families as they might have been in ATLAS.ti). As mentioned earlier, each QDAS package has its own unique features and possibilities, but to use any QDAS package effectively the researcher must come to it with a meta-understanding of how qualitative research projects can be most effectively represented in the E-Project.

Units of analysis

There were several ways Penna might have elected to develop her units of analysis or cases, as they would be represented in NVivo 7. Each choice emphasizes different possibilities for the ways the E-Project can support the researcher's interpretive process. (See Table 10.2)

In Figure 10.2 you can see the node area for Penna's E-Project with the case area highlighted. On the right you can see the five cases she created for the project.

Carefully thinking through the issues related to establishment of the unit(s) of analysis was the beginning place for outlining Penna's interpretive strategy.

Attribute variables

In developing her attribute variables, Penna turned to a tool developed by fellow dissertation group member Carolyn Siccama. Siccama had created a table, which she included in her dissertation proposal, demonstrating the way

Table 10.2 Case development matrix

Possible approaches to case development	Discussion
1. Four Cases; one for each participating teacher	This is the simplest method. It would allow her to track each teacher as a separate case and attributes would be attached only to teacher cases
2. A case for each school from which the teachers are drawn; teachers represented as sub-cases under the school case	This method would provide Penna with a way to explore how the school setting might be a factor in relationship to teacher practice. However, because Penna's interest was primarily on the teacher participant, while this might be interesting information, it was not essential to answering her research question
3. A combination of (1) above with the addition of a case for the historical site (optional to have a sub-case for the informant from the historical site)	This is the way Penna chose to develop the cases for her shell. Each teacher had a separate case and there was a case for the historical site
4. A combination of (2) above with the addition of a case for the historical site (optional to have a sub-case for the informant from the historical site)	This would have been the more complex way to set up the cases, allowing Penna to track teacher in relationship to school, as well as providing a means of analysing her data in relationship to fixed characteristics of the historical site. However, this method would have given her more than she needed

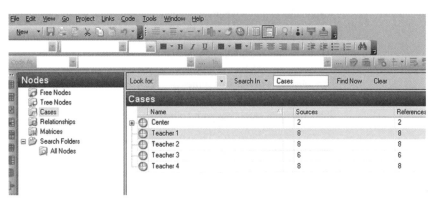

Figure 10.2 Penna's case nodes

she set up attribute variables. Penna's attribute variable table is shown in Table 10.3.

With this information she was quickly able to set up her attributes within the classification section of her NVivo 7 E-project, as shown in Figure 10.3.

The attributes were populated with the values described in Penna's organizational table and applied to each case. Figure 10.4 shows an illustration of a portion of the properties of one of Penna's teacher cases, illustrating the ways the values were applied to the case.

Table 10.3 Appendix J from Penna's dissertation: 'Visual representation of how attribute variables will be set up in NVivo'

Attribute	Value type	Value(s)
Gender	String	Female Male
Middle school	String	Eight middle school in district
Middle school structure	String	Junior high model Academic team
Undergraduate educational background	String	BA BS
Graduate educational background	String	MS MEd MAT PhD EdD
Teaching social studies over career	Number	Populate after first interview
Teaching social studies at current middle school	Number	Populate after first interview
Social studies pedagogy	String	Populate after first interview
Field trip experience	Number	Populate after first interview
Field trip experience (historical museum)	Number	Populate after first interview
Use historical museum's educational resources	String	Yes No
Attend museum's teacher workshops	Number	Populate after first interview
Attend museum's summer institutes	Number	Populate after first interview
Use lesson plans from museum	String	Yes No
Use museum's primary documents	String	Yes No
Share museum resources with colleagues	String	Yes No

Source: Penna (2007: 219).

Units of analysis (cases) working in synchronization with fixed characteristics (attributes and their values) were the cornerstone of Penna's E-Project, allowing her to develop an interpretive strategy for in-case and cross-case analysis of the four participating teachers.

An important note! Penna chose not to attach attributes to her case for the historical site, as there was only one site involved. Thus, the case for the historical site is used exclusively as a bin to hold all documents and scraps of information related to the historical site. If her study had been larger and included more than one historical site, it would have been important to create attributes and values for the various sites, but given the scope and focus of this study that was not necessary.

As a result of having created attributes and values for her cases, in her

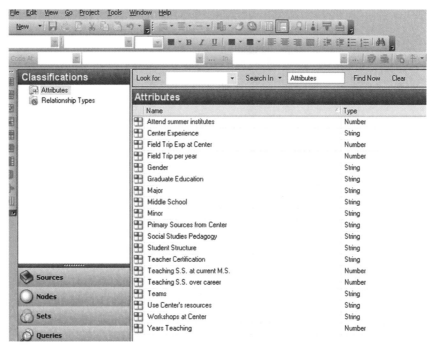

Figure 10.3 Penna's E-Project showing attributes in the classification section

	A : Attend sum... ▽	B : Center Exp... ▽	C : Field Trip ... ▽	D : Field Trip ... ▽	E : Gender ▽	F : Graduate E... ▽	G : Major ▽	H : Middle Sch... ▽	I : Minor
18 : Cases\Cent...	Unassigned	Unassigned	Unassigned	Unassigned	Unassigned	Unassigned	Unassigned	Unassigned	Unassigned
19 : Cases\Cent...	Unassigned	Unassigned	Unassigned	Unassigned	Unassigned	Unassigned	Unassigned	Unassigned	Unassigned
Cases\Teac...	1	Interim	2	4	Male	M.Ed	Social Science	Not Applicable	not related
21 : Cases\Teac...	1	Interim	6	2	Female	CAGS	History/US	Not Applicable	Sociology
22 : Cases\Teac...	0	Experienced	17 ✓	2	Female	MAT	History	Not Applicable	Political Science
23 : Cases\Teac	0	Novice	1	1	Female	MATriculating MA	Criminal Justice	Not Applicable	Psychology

Figure 10.4 Properties of one of Penna's teacher cases

dissertation Penna was able to provide readers with a clear and concise understanding of who the participants were and how their experiences and perspectives might vary. Table 10.4 is drawn from Penna's dissertation (Penna 2007: 72).

In the section below on the power of searches, we discuss the ways the proper establishment of cases and attributes allowed Penna to interrogate the data in ways that added great depth to her interpretation. This analytic capacity would have been strongly curtailed if she had not used the case and attribute features of the QDAS program.

Data collection

In her dissertation proposal, Penna outlined the various forms of data she would collect. Table 10.5, taken from her dissertation, illustrates the full range of data she included in her E-Project data base (Penna 2007: 77).

Table 10.4 Table comparing participants in Penna's study

	John	Karen	Sue	Amy
Highest degree	MA in elementary education	CAGS reading and language	MA in curriculum	BS criminal justice
Undergraduate major	Social studies	US history	History	Criminal justice
Teaching certification	MS social studies	Elementary and middle school SS	Social studies 7th–12th grades	General middle school
Years Teaching	10	7	20	3
Years teaching eighth grade Social studies in Mylen	3	6	14	1
Middle school	Washington	Hamilton	Washington	Jefferson
MS team	Heterogeneous	Heterogeneous	Heterogeneous	Heterogeneous
Eighth grade students on team	Special needs	Special needs	Heterogeneous	Special needs
Years experience with site	2	6	18	1
Professional Development at Site	1	1	0	0
Summer institute workshops	4 (2005–2006)	4 (2005–2006)	2 (2005–2006)	3 (2005–2006)
SS in-service professional development besides site	None	None	Yes – a few classes	None
Site field trip attended	Immigrants	Mill Power	Immigrants	Inventions

Table 10.5 Penna's overview of data collection

Type of Data	Case 1	Case 2	Case 3	Case 4	Total amount of data
Teacher pre-field trip interview	1	1	1	1	4 interviews
Site field trip observation	1	1	1	1	4 observations
Teacher–participant log	1	1	1	1	4 logs
Teacher post-field trip interview	1	1	1	1	4 interviews
Visual data Historical site	12	12	12	12	48 photographs
Visual data Teacher	20	12	12	8	52 photographs
Teacher artefacts	8	19	8	4	39 artefacts
Data from historical site					
Observation of teacher workshop					1 observation
Site informant interview site artefacts					1 interview 35 artefacts

The screenshot in Figure 10.5 illustrates the ways folders were set up in the source section to contain these various kinds of data. Penna chose to create folders for the kind of data. Due to the fact that she had set up cases to represent each participant, it would have been redundant to create folders for each case in the source area. Note also the labelling system that Penna used for specific documents, carefully identifying the Case # and the document type. Such labelling procedures, while seemingly mundane, allow her to make quick visual identification of materials.

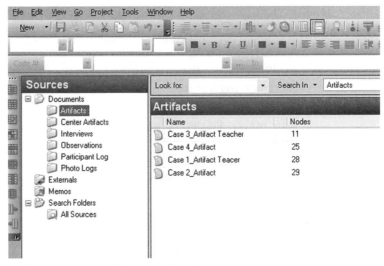

Figure 10.5 Source area within Penna's E-project open on artefacts

Visual data

Two forms of visual data were included in this project. The primary form was still photographs taken by the four participating teachers. The teachers were asked to take photos that would represent their experience working with the historical site. The developed photos were used as prompts for the follow-up interview. This kind of data required Penna to develop a special strategy for integrating the materials into the E-Project so that they could be used effectively to support the interpretive process. Penna chose not to import the photos, but rather to create a photo log for each participants' visual data contributions. She did this for two reasons: 1) she had begun the study in NVivo 2.0, which did not support images; and 2) although she shifted the project midway into NVivo 7.0, the first version of NVivo 7.0 was still shaky with regard to supporting use of photographic data (slow-downs and crashes did occur as users got used to the new capacities and developers created new patches to solve internal problems). As a result, she stored the photographs elsewhere, but the logs were available to be coded, allowing them to be integrated with other data in the E-Project.

Journals and memos

The coding journal, methodological log and memos represent three critical tools Penna made use of for documentation of the interpretive process.

Coding journal

From the beginning, Penna established a coding journal in which she recorded decisions and changes made to the E-Project in relationship to coding and related development of the software shell. 'While NVivo 7 allows for in-depth coding of data, it was important that I did not develop tunnel vision with these coding tools', stated Penna (2007: 100).

This segment from her coding journal provides insight into the ways the tool supported her thinking by capturing critical developments in the development of her interpretive scheme.

> 7/12/2006 10:06 PM
>
> Printed out Coding reports for Case 1, finding some nodes more relevant than others. Reading through reports, finding key words, connections, writing these on the back of the coding report
>
> Code the same way for next Case, though spend less time on certain nodes – FT/teachers actions, FT/MT actions. Look for collaboration.
>
> Not sure how to handle Center node has a lot of info.

Methodological log

In a parallel manner to the coding journal, Penna also set up a methodological log in which she documented issues related to larger methodological issues that unfolded over the course of the project. This segment from that log shows how this tool functioned for Penna.

9/7/2005 – 10:27:31 PM

Meeting with Freida

– good meeting got a lot of background about Mylen and Center
– Freida can find teachers willing to be in study.

Can she ask them informally? How do I get info about them to put in my proposal?

– Need to find a prof dev model that fits for lit review, look at partnerships and museum curriculum for teachers.
– Mylen uses a model where museum is the expert with teachers being introduced to hands on activities and instructional techniques modeled

What are teachers learning from museum workshops, on site visit and post visit reflection

Areas of learning: content, instructional tech, personal learning,

How does prior knowledge affect experience?

Social learning with museum staff at workshops and site visit affect teacher learning?

Learning within group at museum – from students

Do teachers feel they have input into museum curr or mus has input in their's (reciprical relationship)

Is it a partnership with all parties?

Are partnerships relevant to learning

The ability to code the coding journal and the methodological log provided Penna with the opportunity to track issues related to methodology as they pertained to the larger project and the E-Project in a consistent and efficient manner. This information could then be woven into the narrative of the dissertation and the discussion of the methodological elements.

Memos

Equally important to her interpretive process was the use of memos, which she developed over the course of the project to capture emerging notions.

For this study I created a variety of memos in NVIVO$_7$ with title headings and entries that are dated and timed stamped. During the data collection phase of the study, I wrote memos of my reactions, surprises and concerns about observations, interviews and visual data. My memo writing process for my collected data followed this pattern: 1) after an interview or observation I wrote a memo on the event in a notebook; and 2) transferred my comments into an NVIVO$_7$ memo that held all the collected data memos for each participant. Having one memo for each participant made analysis and coding more organized. Within these participant memos, I wrote about my subjectivity. These subjectivity comments were copied or linked to my NVIVO₇ subjectivity memo to track my role as researcher, my assumptions, ethics and access issues during the study. I created a case history memo for each participant which allowed me to analyze each case in depth, which strengthened my with-in case analysis.

(Penna 2007: 101–102)

Figure 10.6 shows how this strategy was translated into the E-Project. Here you can also see that the memos have been coded at a variety of nodes, further information on the ways memos are being integrated into the researcher's interpretive strategies.

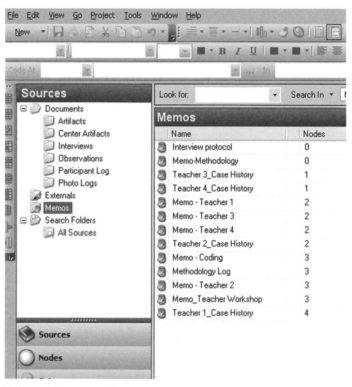

Figure 10.6 Penna's memo section

Thematic framework

By thematic framework, we refer to the full range of interpretive structures developed by the researcher to break up the data from documents (textual and non-textual) into interpreted fragments for recomposition as larger elements of meaning. Coding is a primary concern when considering the thematic framework, but by no means the only concern. Other issues that fall under this umbrella heading include comprehensive consideration of data to be integrated through coding, preparation of data for efficient coding and strategies for specialized forms of data. Several features related to the development of the thematic framework of Penna's project demonstrate the robustness of her NVivo use, including the use of QDAS for her literature review and attention to the preparation of data for efficient coding.

Literature review

The development of the thematic framework actually began in the literature review phase (see Figure 10.7). In setting up the E-Project for her dissertation, Penna immediately translated the NVivo 2 literature review into the new NVivo 7 shell. This allowed her to connect the items from the literature review to the hands-on research project.

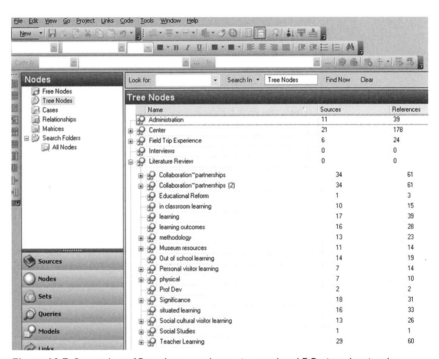

Figure 10.7 Screenshot of Penna's tree node area in completed E-Project showing the top-level child nodes established under her literature review parent node

Data preparation in anticipation of coding

Through careful planning before she undertook data collection, Penna was able to maximize efficient use of NVivo 7. For instance, Penna designed her interview protocols with an eye to: 1) provide her with information needed to populate the attribute values (discussed in an earlier section); and 2) to use NVivo's quick coding features through pre-assigning thematic bins. By using the Microsoft Word heading feature, Penna was able to 'tell' NVivo how to code by section, allowing her to conduct broad brush coding for whole interview transcripts with a single keystroke. Developing the template for section coding as part of the development of the interview protocol meant that Penna was one step ahead of the game. The first page of Penna's interview protocol demonstrates how this was achieved (Penna 2007, 2008) (see Table 10.6).

Table 10.6 Appendix B: Pre-Field Trip Interview Protocol

Appendix B

Pre-Field Trip Interview Protocol

Inquiry Category A: Demographic Info

1. Educational Background:
   - Degrees?
   - Major
   - Minor
2. Teacher Certification:
3. Are you involved with any professional organizations that pertain to social studies?
4. Name of middle school:
5. How does your middle school organize students?

Inquiry Category B. Social Studies Experience

6. How long have you taught social studies in your career? In this school?
7. How would you describe how you teach social studies to your students?
8. Define Social Studies: What areas do you need to teach?
9. What do you consider to be best practices for teaching social studies?

Inquiry Category C: Experience with Museum Resources/Professional Development

10. How long have you worked with the museum or brought students to the museum?
11. Have you used any of the museum's resources? Workshops, institutes, lesson plans, primary documents, activities guides?
12. Which resources have been most helpful to you in your practice as a social studies teacher? Why?
13. How do you use the museum's resources in your classroom?
14. Will you be able to use the ideas from workshops and institutes in your own teaching?
15. By working with the museum, have your attitudes or beliefs about social studies been affected?

The power of searches

Early users of QDAS, while captivated by its capacities for organization of data, made inadequate use of its search capacities. The search capacities cannot be made good use of without good research design oriented towards the unique affordances of QDAS. If, however, the user has developed a strong structure for the software shell through establishment of the units of analysis, accompanying variables, units of observation and thematic framework, then the search feature can be an extremely powerful tool for refining the thematic framework and interrogating the data.

Penna set herself the task of using the dissertation project to better understand NVivo 7 search capacities. The following screen capture shows a range of searches (see Figure 10.8). For instance, she tried out several text searches on the term 'hands-on', as well as using matrix searches for considering how collaboration was occurring between participants and the historical site.

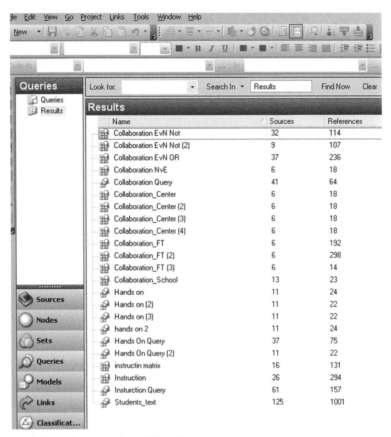

Figure 10.8 Results section from NVivo 7

Lessons from this case

Dissertations serve two important purposes: 1) they allow novice researchers to practise the skills they have learned in class in real world environments. In this sense they are instructional playgrounds; 2) dissertations, however, are also arenas in which new knowledge is created by the rising generation of researchers. Some of that knowledge may be methodological. As older scholars, we need to be challenged by the methodological questions and new leanings of rising researchers. The use of QDAS can be an area where new scholars can question old practices and bring new insight into the use of tools that can expand our methodological reach.

Features of this case that bear consideration are the workmanlike way that units of analysis, variables, units of observation and data collected were established with the software shell. With a well-constructed shell, the researcher was able to build interpretations with confidence that the foundation was solid.

Another strong feature of this project was the development of the literature review and its careful integration within the E-Project as the work unfolded. E-Projects make it possible to work literature into the fibre of the entire project, enriching the theoretical depth of the project in new and exciting ways.

Note

1   This exemplar is based on a EdD dissertation, 'A case study of the effect a historical site's educational resources have on the practices of four urban eighth grade social studies teachers', by Stacy L. Penna, Leadership in Schooling, Graduate School of Education, University of Massachusetts Lowell.

11 Doing what it takes: the impact of organizational issues on Massachusetts School-Based Health Center success[1]

The software that was used in the original project was ATLAS.ti 5.

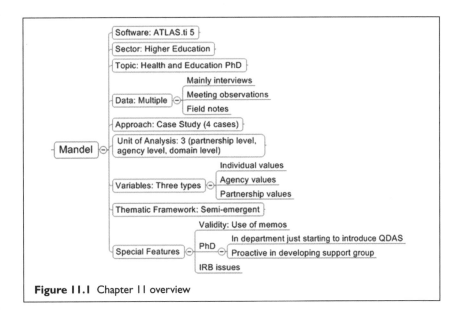

Figure 11.1 Chapter 11 overview

Background of project

School-Based Health Centers (SBHCs) are inter-agency partnerships between school departments, schools and community health systems. They are designed to deliver school-based health services that can include primary, acute and chronic medical care, mental health services, and other ancillary services such as dental and nutrition services. They function in concert with the school staff. SBHCs are a demonstrated effective venue for delivering primary care to medically underserved youth so they experience fewer learning barriers. The philosophy behind them is that there is a strong link between students' health and their ability to learn. Neither health care nor public education systems have been able to tackle this issue alone, so SBHCs are seen by some as one solution.

Despite evidence-based benefits, SBHCs have encountered challenges that limit growth and threaten long-term sustainability. While research exists on visible SBHC concerns such as financing, ideological opposition and politics, a paucity of literature exists on organizational dissimilarities in professional orientation and institutional mandates among health and school systems potentially causing partnership barriers. Notwithstanding inter-organizational challenges, some SBHCs are high-performing, while others are not.

The purpose of this research was to examine how and why organizational issues of health and educational systems impact the development, implementation and ultimate SBHC success.

The main research question this study addresses is:

- How do organizational issues of health systems and school systems make a difference in how SBHCs in Massachusetts achieve success as measured by a state rating system?

Secondary questions that were also explored are:

- Does the manner in which SBHC partnerships between schools and health systems were developed and maintained make a difference in how SBHCs achieve success?
- Are there variations in the ways that particular SBHCs and their sponsoring agencies align key organizational elements, manage conflict, and promote understanding and cooperation across institutional boundaries?

To assess specific organizational strengths and weaknesses, the study developed and employed a conceptual model based on: (1) the congruence model of organizational behaviour; (2) domain theory; and (3) social network theory.[2]

Design of project

This research looked at four SBHCs in Massachusetts middle schools. All four sites shared similar characteristics but two were rated as 'excellent' and two were rated as 'needs improvement' based on a state-based past performance rating scale. To protect confidentiality each SBHC site was referred to by a colour rather than actual name. The red and blue sites were the more successful (excellent) sites and green and yellow were the less successful (needs improvement) sites.

There were a number of units of analysis. The basic unit of analysis is the SBHC partnership (4). Another unit of analysis is the agency – education or health (2). A third unit of analysis is professional affiliation/domain – management, policy or service (3).

Four data collection techniques were employed:

- semi-structured interviews;
- meeting observation;

- document review;
- a short survey.

The semi-structured interviews were conducted with SBHC key stakeholders from both the health and education arena and from various professional domains including direct service, management and policy. People who were interviewed were asked a series of questions that included their understanding of (1) SBHC operations; (2) the history of the partnership between the school and health system; (3) how differences between the school and health system are addressed; and (4) their suggestions and recommendations for the future. Fifty-two interviews were conducted (see Table 11.1).

In addition, meetings between the various stakeholders were observed in order to gather information regarding the procedures for information sharing, decision-making, leadership, frequency of communication and interaction between and within organizations that sponsor SBHCs. Mandel wrote up detailed field notes after visits to the sites.

Documents relating to how agencies describe themselves, their collaborating partners and SBHCs were also reviewed to determine if they corroborated other data collection methods. Documents included annual reports from schools and health systems, mission statements, organizational charts, memoranda of agreement, grant proposals, policies and minutes of meetings. In addition, available public documents such as newspaper articles and assessments were examined. Finally, schools, health systems and/or SBHCs web sites (where available) were viewed.

The in-depth interviews followed an interview guide but they did not follow a set structure that would be useful for automatic coding. The observations also followed an observation guide, as did the analysis of the written documents. However, field notes did not have any fixed structure.

The original design called for a 12-item Leadership Effectiveness and Adaptability Description (LEAD) survey to be administered to each school principal who directs the school in which the selected SBHCs are located and each SBHC clinical and/or administrative director. A companion survey was also supposed to be administered to all other interview subjects including each leader's superiors, associates and subordinates. These surveys, developed by the Center for Leadership Studies (1993), are validated instruments that measure 'self' and 'other' perception of leadership-style profile and leadership-style adaptability. However, only 21 out of 52 were completed.

A summary of the design is shown in Table 11.2.

Constraints on the design

Originally, Mandel wanted to interview students participating in each SBHC partnership. Any proposal involving children would have to go to her university's full IRB committee even though ordinarily her type of research design would qualify for a expedited review. To satisfy her university's IRB, she modified her proposal so that she would only observe children who were members of a public group or committee within the school. The university IRB

Table 11.1 Interviewees in each site by domain and agency

Site	State[4] rating	Total interviews	Policy/ education[1]	Management/ education[1]	Service/ education[1]	Policy/health[1]	Management/ health[1]	Service/health[1]
Red	E	13	0[2]	2	4	3	6	3
Green	NI	12[3]	4	3	2	2	3	1
Blue	E	12[3]	2	3	4	3	4	2
Yellow	NI	15	2	3	4	5	3	3
Total		**52**	**8**	**11**	**14**	**13**	**16**	**9**

Notes:

1 Some persons considered themselves part of more than one domain.

2 The Red and Green sites are in the same city. Therefore, all education policy interviews were recorded on the green site, but pertain to both red and green.

3 Nursing supervisors at both the Green and Blue sites asked to be interviewed in a group. Thus, they were technically counted as one interview each but actually had three people in the Green site and two in the Blue.

4 E = Excellent, NI = Needs Improvement.

Table 11.2 Design framework of the Doing What it Takes project

Unit(s) of analysis (UA) Unit(s) of observation (UO)	Attributes	Time frame	Data: textual (primary or secondary forms of data)	Data: non-textual (primary or secondary forms of data)
The SBHC partnership (UA) The Agency (UA) Domain (UA) Individuals (UO)	State rating Excellent Needs Improvement Agency Education Health Domain Policy Management Service	Snapshot	Semi-structured interviews (52) Meeting observations (6) Field notes (12) Documentation (44) LEAD survey (21 out of 52 completed)	No non-textual data

provisionally approved her design but required that before she could begin data collection, she needed a letter from each participating agency that demonstrated that all agreed to participate in the research and agreed to adhere to the participant protections required by the university.

This whole process took several months because: (a) it often required a lot of correspondence back and forth to find the right person to approach and to get a response; (b) the procedures and approval mechanisms varied from site to site; and (c) it was often necessary to reassure system managers that the study would not disrupt or alter programme schedules. The Yellow school system had a formal IRB process as did the Green and Red school systems. The Blue school system had no formal research protocol but she needed the superintendent's approval in writing. This letter took several months to obtain due to other challenges that were preoccupying the superintendent. The Yellow health agency did not have its own IRB and Mandel had to go through the hospital/medical centre's IRB with which the agency was affiliated.

This proved to be a long process and required Mandel to pass the Human Participants Protection Education for Research Teams Online Course, sponsored by the National Institutes of Health. Ultimately, she discovered that the medical centre would waive consent if she had already obtained IRB consent from a reputable medical centre or university. As she already had consent from her university, the medical centre entered into a collaborative agreement with them. However, this was after she had jumped through many hoops and had completed a long application. The Red health agency had a formal system for approving research that was relatively straightforward. The Green and Blue health agencies had no formal or informal IRB and provided a letter granting permission. The school systems from all four sites would not even accept her IRB application if students were included. In the end, after consulting her dissertation chairperson, Mandel decided not to pursue students as subjects for her study. The order in which she collected the data from each site was determined by the order in which permission was granted from each site. This process delayed the start of her data collection by about six months.

Project supervision

Leslie Mandel conducted this study as her PhD dissertation at the Heller School for Social Policy and Management, Brandeis University. She was supervised by a dissertation committee of five members who included very experienced qualitative analysts but few of whom had any personal experience using ATLAS.ti which is the software she used in the study. This is not an atypical situation among graduate students as QDAS is still not used by the majority of academics. In fact, it is spreading from the bottom up – the early adopters tend to be graduate students and junior researchers.

Mandel had limited prior exposure to any qualitative software. She had briefly used NUD.IST in 2000 as part of an advanced qualitative research class at the Heller School. Several years later, she tried to teach herself ATLAS.ti before attending an intensive introduction to ATLAS.ti run by di Gregorio. She followed that up a few months later by inviting di Gregorio to run a master class in ATLAS.ti at Brandeis. Mandel's study was one of the projects discussed at the class. She followed this up with another master class at Brandeis the following year and a few private consulting sessions. The Heller School faculty were very supportive of the workshops at Brandeis. At that time the School was looking into adopting ATLAS.ti for their qualitative researchers and their doctoral students. Mandel herself was part of a network of qualitative research students at Brandeis who formed a very effective self-help group. However, her experience is very different from that of the University of Massachusetts Lowell students discussed elsewhere in this book. QDAS use had been introduced earlier at their university. They had the benefit of a faculty member experienced in NVivo who integrated their training of qualitative analysis with the use of the software tool. At the time, faculty at Heller were using traditional qualitative analysis methods and had no resident expert in the use of qualitative software. Mandel had to be proactive and bring in help externally.

Representing the design in the software shell

Units of analysis and attribute variables

In ATLAS.ti units of analysis and attribute variables are represented by *primary document families*. The notion of 'families' is the same as the notion of sets. Similar documents or raw data can be grouped together. The families are not exclusive, so documents can be assigned to more than one family. This enables the researcher to restrict the analysis to a particular family of documents or a particular combination of document families. In this study, there were four SHBC partnerships that were being studied. They are represented in ATLAS.ti as Case: Red, Case: Blue, Case: Green and Case: Yellow. This enables each partnership to be looked at separately. In addition, comparisons needed to be made between the two agencies in the partnership – Education and Health. They are also represented by families. Comparisons also needed to be made between those partnerships which were rated 'excellent' and those that were rated 'needs improvements'. Comparisons also needed to be made between the type of staff involved in the partnership – policy-makers, management and service provider. In addition, during analysis it was necessary to distinguish the raw data which were from interview, observations of meetings or field notes. Hence, families were used to represent all these aspects. Families could have been used to represent the different scores respondents received from the LEAD survey. Then the documents from those respondents would have been assigned accordingly. Figure 11.2 illustrates the families used in this study.

These could have been created beforehand because all this information was in Mandel's proposal before she started to collect the data. In fact, the families were created after Mandel received training in the software.

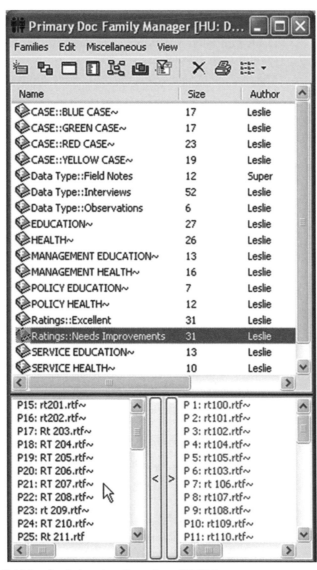

Figure 11.2 Units of analysis and attributes from ATLAS.ti

Thematic framework

Mandel initially followed Miles and Huberman's advice and developed pre-codes before starting the analysis. These were based on her research questions, hypotheses and theory. They were created first in ATLAS.ti in the *code manager*. At the same time, she created broader categories in the *code family manager* in which to group similar codes together. The *code family manager* is similar to the *document family manager* mentioned previously. It is a way to group together similar codes. Figure 11.3 shows the *code family manager*. It has been arranged in the order in which the code families have been created.

The code families – Social Networks, Leadership, Understanding, Communication, Stakeholder, SBHC History, Demographics and Human Resources were created initially. Additional code families were created as the coding process became more refined.

The *code family manager* is the area where similar codes are grouped together.

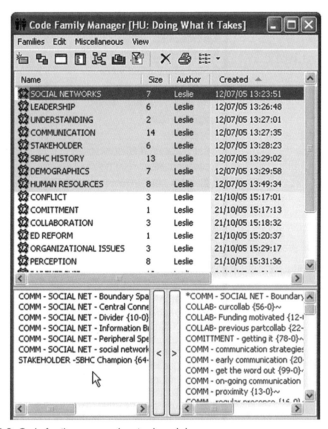

Figure 11.3 Code family manager showing broad themes

Note: The shaded area indicates the initial broad themes that were created (on 12 July 2005) 'Social networks' is highlighted darker and the codes assigned to that code family are listed in the lower left-hand window where the cursor is pointing.

When setting up the shell of an ATLAS.ti project, it can be a starting place to create the broad themes that you are going to code. Mandel did that in this project. The codes themselves are created in the *code manager*. Figure 11.4 shows some of the codes in this project in the order in which they were created. However, they had been refined during the course of the project while reading and interpreting the data. The comment box at the bottom of the Figure 11.4 records how the code 'ORG STRUCTURE – formal org elements' has developed during analysis. It has been merged with two other codes and the definitions of all the codes can be seen in the comment box.

If some of the broad areas you need to code are clear at the outset, they can be created as code families in ATLAS.ti. If some of the codes themselves are known

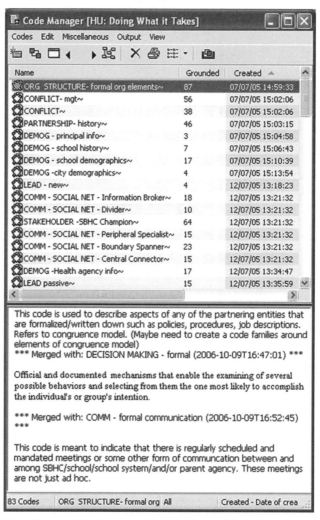

Figure 11.4 List of codes in code manager in the order in which they were created

in advance, they can also be created at the outset in the *code manager*. These can later be merged, refined, deleted and added to during the analysis process.

Journals and memos

Mandel initially created memo families for the types of memo she anticipated she would write. She thought she would write about each site from the perspective of the two agencies. Hence, she developed memo families for Red Education, Red Health, and so on. However, her memos evolved in a different way. As you can see in Figure 11.5, no memos were written for those initial

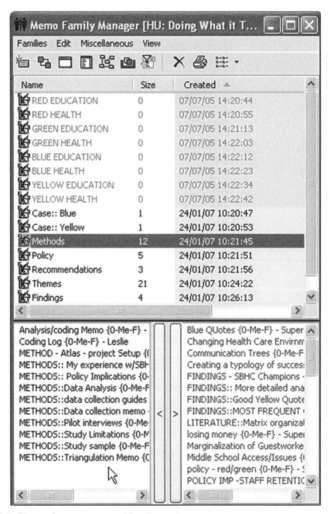

Figure 11.5 Types of memos created for the project

Note: The shaded area shows the initial type of memos Mandel thought she would create. Below the shaded area are the types of memo she actually created. 'Methods' is shaded darker and the methods memos are listed in the lower left-hand window where the cursor is pointing.

families she created. Instead, memos were written about methods (12), policy (5), recommendations (3), themes (21) and findings (4).

The way the memos actually developed can be seen in Figure 11.6. The Methods memos were created first. However, Mandel also started to record some themes she started to see emerge early on. The bottom window in Figure 11.5 shows part of her memo on the theme – us – them mentality.

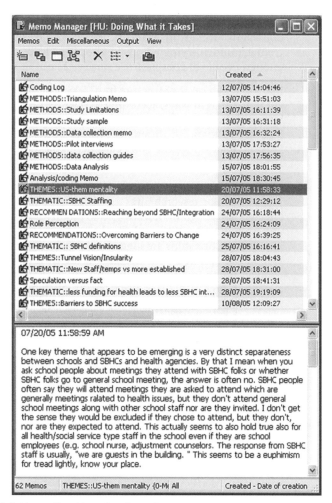

Figure 11.6 Memos listed in order of creation

Key aspects of the research process

With the support of the ATLAS.ti software package and a robust E-Project design, Mandel was able to effectively juggle the various demands of her qualitative research project – reading the transcripts, writing up her observations, coding and reflecting in her memos. With the visual clarity that a software package provides, she also spent a lot of time reflecting on the codes she developed, defining them, merging codes when necessary and refining them. The structure she set up in ATLAS.ti to reflect the design of the project served her well.

Certain aspects in her original design are not included in the ATLAS.ti setup. She chose not to include the documentation she collected about the four partnerships in the ATLAS.ti project. She also did not include the LEAD scores as document families in ATLAS.ti. Part of the reason for this was that she had trouble (a) identifying who were the SBHC leaders in each site and (b) getting enough people to complete the survey (21 out of 52 completed the survey).

Mandel relied on the structure in ATLAS.ti to help her manage her data and to cut it in different ways, according to the unit of analysis she wanted to explore. She used the query tool in ATLAS.ti to cut the data by site, agency and domain in order to map out differences in perception among different providers of SBHCs. In addition, the co-occurrence explorer could have been used to look at how themes were related – restricted to different types of provider.

Mandel had to get permission from all four health agencies and four school systems in her research sites as well as IRB approval from her university. It affected her design in that she had to modify it so that she would not interview any students. In addition, she had to carefully anonymize her data in ATLAS.ti. The four partnerships are identified by colour; for example Red Site, Blue Site, and so on. The names of documents are by an alphanumeric code. The code enabled her to identify the site. She had a paper master copy of the key to the codes, so she could assign the relevant attribute variables in ATLAS.ti. Within the text the names of schools, health centres, and so on were identified by the colour code; for example Green School or Yellow Health Centre as are the names of informants; for example Green Principal, and so on. Her E-Project had to be password-protected and paper copies of the data have to be kept in a locked file cabinet. She also is required to archive the data for five years after the final reporting after which it will be permanently destroyed.

Lessons from this case

This project is a good example of the issues facing a doctoral student using QDAS where the expertise in the software is just starting to be developed in the university. Mandel was very proactive in seeking support externally. In doing so, she was also proactive on behalf of other students at her university – organizing both introductory and advanced training by bringing in an external consultant (di Gregorio). During Mandel's time at Heller, the Director of the PhD Program together with qualitative researchers at Heller and the Sociology department researched a number of QDAS packages and decided to purchase ATLAS.ti in the spring of 2004. Heller introduced the software in their applied qualitative methods course at that time. There is now growing expertise in the software with several faculty members using the software. Finally, Mandel has been asked to teach class sessions in other programs at the university on the use of QDAS.

As mentioned earlier, early adopters of QDAS tend to be graduate students and junior research staff. Usually they will have little support from their institution on QDAS – often due to a lack of knowledge on the part of staff on the amount of support that is necessary. Often QDAS is seen simply as a piece of software whereby the student can pick up knowledge on their own. The fact that use of QDAS requires rethinking on how to approach an analysis is not widely recognized. Nor is it appreciated that QDAS can be used as a thinking tool in the early stages of research design and can be used to help students to keep organized and on target with their analysis. However, supervisors need to be proficient in QDAS in order to help students.

This case is also a good example of how a complex study with multiple units of analysis can be managed in ATLAS.ti. The use of families is key. Mandel used the full repertoire of families: document families in order to be able to restrict her analysis to different units of analysis; coding families in order to manage her codes, first by identifying broad themes, later as an aid to refine those themes and restrict analysis to them; and memo families to organize the variety of memos she created for the study. Because of the organization of the document families she was able to use the query tool effectively to look for trends and variations among the different SBHCs and agencies.

For more information on this project, see Mandel (2007).

Notes

1   This exemplar is based on a PhD dissertation by Leslie A. Mandel, Heller School for Social Policy and Management, Brandeis University.
2   A more detailed description and references for these theoretical perspectives are offered in Chapter 2.

12 | Follow-along study[1]

The software that was used in the original project was ATLAS.ti 5.

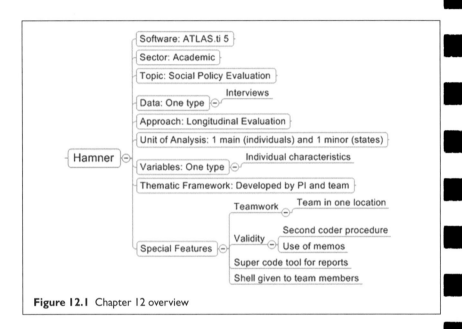

Figure 12.1 Chapter 12 overview

Background of the project

The follow-along study is a three-year qualitative study of people with disabilities that will evaluate the effect of systems change initiatives on their lives. It is part of the Disability and Rehabilitation Research Project on Emerging Disability and System Change funded by the National Institute on Disability and Rehabilitation Research (US). This research is being conducted by the Institute for Community Inclusion at the University of Massachusetts, Boston. The goal of the follow-along study (the FAS) is to seek a greater understanding of the experience of individuals with diabetes in their search for employment and/or receiving supports.

The main research questions for this study are:

1 What are the labour market experiences of people with emerging disabilities from disadvantaged populations? Looking at:

   (a) their labour market histories and change over time;
   (b) effect of disability and any stigma associated on employers;

(c) disclosure issues surrounding the disability in finding and keeping a job.

2 What is the nature of the interactions between people with emerging disabilities from vulnerable populations and various service systems as they relate to employment (VR, SSI/DI, Ticket, OS, TANF)? Looking at:

(a) history of these interactions and change over time;

(b) factors that affect how people's interactions with generic service systems change over time;

(c) whether use of supports is contingent upon how the disability is currently affecting the individual, or whether environmental factors (family, local labour market, transportation) compound the stigma of disability and channel people into the service system.

3 At what point and how do various environmental and personal factors interact in the decision to seek public assistance and rely on the state for various supports as opposed to attempting to subsist in the labor market? Looking at:

(a) factors (family situation, local economy, economic need, symptoms of disability, etc.) that constrain and/or influence this choice and change over time;

(b) the range of experience of people with emerging disabilities in negotiating the various options for meeting their needs.

4 What role does employment play in the lives of people with a disability or health condition defined as an emergent disability? Looking at:

(a) variations by other demographic characteristics such as gender, age, race, ethnicity, socio-economic status;

(b) how they maintain employment.

Design of project

This is a longitudinal study following 45 people with diabetes from four states (Massachusetts, Maine, New Hampshire and New Jersey) over three years. Each participant will be interviewed three times a year, so there will be a total of nine interviews per respondent. Information has been collected on their age, gender, ethnicity, marital status, employment status, diabetes type and receiving SSDI/SSI.

The unit of analysis is the individual, as the focus is on the individual's experience over time. However, another unit of analysis could be the state, allowing for the comparison of experiences by state. The individual is also the unit of observation (see Table 12.1).

Table 12.1 Design framework of the Follow-along project

Unit(s) of analysis/ units of observation	Attributes	Time frame	Data: textual (primary or secondary forms of data)	Data: non-textual (primary or secondary forms of data)
Individuals (UA and UO) (45) The State (UA) (4)	Demographic Gender Age Marital status Ethnicity Employment Diabetes type SSDI/SSI State	Longitudinal Prospective at nine time periods over three years	In-depth interviews – some telephone, some face to face (45 × 9)	No non-textual data

Representing the design in the software shell

Units of analysis, units of observation and variables

In ATLAS.ti imported documents can be organized by *primary document families* which are the same idea as sets. *Primary document families* are not mutually exclusive, so a document can be in as many families as is relevant. As the unit of observation and analysis is the individual over time, there needs to be a *primary document family* for each respondent. In this *family*, all the interviews for a particular individual (a maximum of nine in this study) will be assigned. This will allow for restricting the analysis to that individual over time. It will enable the analysis of changes experienced by that individual over the three years of the study. Figure 12.2 illustrates some of the 45 respondent *document families* in the study. In the figure, *size* refers to the number of documents that have been assigned to the family. As this screenshot was taken when the project was halfway through the study, not all of the interviews had been conducted and of those conducted not all had been transcribed and assigned to the ATLAS.ti project. In addition, there was some attrition over the three years.

In Figure 12.2, the respondent Andy has been selected (Resp::Andy is highlighted). In the lower left-hand box of the *primary document family manager* (where the cursor is pointing) you can see Andy's six interviews which have been assigned to this family. Double clicking on *Resp::Andy* will filter the ATLAS.ti project so only Andy's interviews will be available for analysis.

In addition to the respondent *families*, a *document family* was created for each time point in the study (nine in all). This would enable analysis *across* all the interviews at a particular point in time. Figure 12.3 shows the time-point *families*. As mentioned above, the screenshot of the study was taken halfway through the study before all the data was collected and assigned in ATLAS.ti. That is why there are no documents assigned to time points 7–9.

Primary document families were also used to represent the variables in the study – age, gender, marital status, race, employment, diabetes type, location

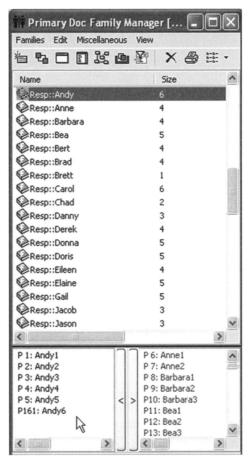

Figure 12.2 Document family manager showing respondent families

and on SSI. In addition, there are *document families* on data type – telephone interview or face-to-face interview; and interviewer. These latter two families can be used for quality control checks. Figure 12.4 illustrates these families.

Primary document families can be combined into what are called *super families*. So it is possible to combine, for example, the *family* 'type II diabetes' with the *family* 'full-time employed' and save it as a new *super family*. Then by double clicking on this *super family*, it is possible to restrict analysis to just the transcripts of those respondents with type II diabetes who are in full employment.

Thematic framework

The thematic framework was derived from the research questions which were operationalized in the interview protocols for the study. The main topic areas covered in the first three protocols were:

• Employment and disability

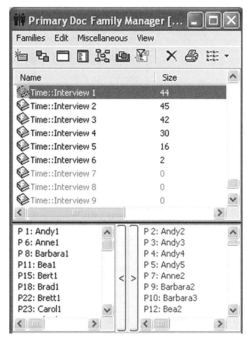

Figure 12.3 Document family manager showing time-point families

- Government services
- Diabetes
- Context
  ○ Financial
  ○ Social capital
- Changes since last interview

Figure 12.5 shows the codes used in this study in the order in which they were developed. The shaded area shows the codes developed during the coding of the first transcript assigned to ATLAS.ti. More codes were developed initially but during the analysis process codes were refined, merged into other codes or expanded. This can be seen in the comment box (at the bottom of the code manager) for the code *finance* – it had been merged later on with a code for *money*. ATLAS.ti keeps a record of these changes in the comment box for each code. The comment box is also used for recording the definition of a code.

In Figure 12.5, the column labelled *grounded* refers to the number of *quotations* (or separate passages) linked to that code.

By looking at the dates the codes were created and the dates the documents were coded (coding started on the first document on 28/06/05 and on the second document on 17/08/05), it can be seen that the coding scheme was pretty well established by the end of coding the second document. As coding was shared between team members, it was essential that a coding frame should be agreed early on in the study. The whole team was involved in the initial

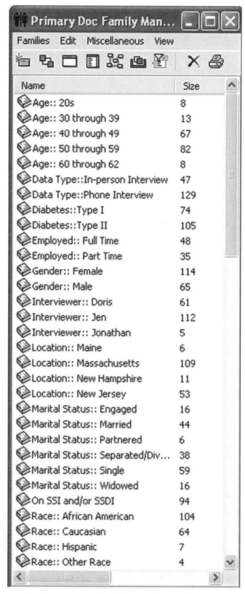

Figure 12.4 Document family manager showing attribute and quality control families

coding process as they individually coded the document and then met to reconcile the codes. However, coders were allowed the scope to continue to develop and/or modify codes by meeting regularly. di Gregorio suggested that they have a *code family* called 'emergent codes' where coders can assign new codes for discussion with the team.

Towards the end of the first year of analysis, the team decided to create *super codes* for the key information that they would need to extract for reports.

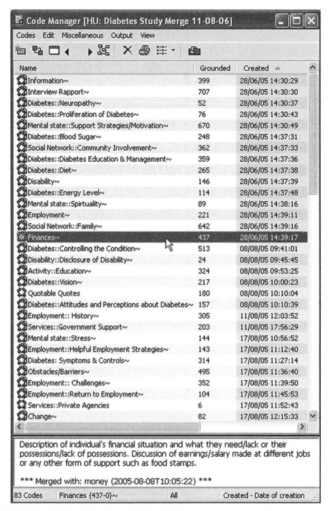

Figure 12.5 Codes displayed in the order in which they were created

Super codes are saved search expressions or queries. In this case, it was a series of codes which co-occur with the code *employment*. Codes which co-occur are codes that are linked to the exact same *quotation* (passage of text) or are linked to *quotations* that overlap or are linked to *quotations* where one *quotation* is inside another *quotation*. Once a *super code* (or saved search expression) has been created, it will automatically retrieve the latest coding that pertain to that search expression. They are listed with the codes in the code manager. The symbol 🔅 indicates a *super code*. Figure 12.6 illustrates them.

The query itself is displayed in the *comment* box at the bottom of the *code manager*. In Figure 12.6 the *super code* Employment & Disclosure of Disability has been selected. In the *comment* box the saved search expression is recorded – "Disclosure of Disability" COOCCUR "Employment". The team

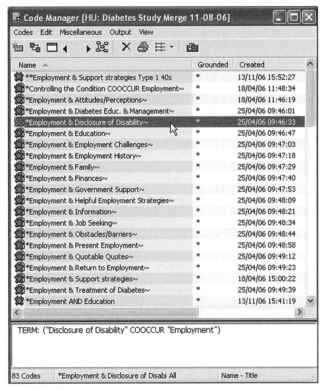

Figure 12.6 Code manager showing super codes

found that setting up these queries in advance enabled them to quickly retrieve the information they needed to produce interim reports. The information could be retrieved across the whole database or restricted by *document families*; for example for a particular respondent or for respondents with particular characteristics (females with type II diabetes, etc.).

Memos

Memos are key to the analysis process and ATLAS.ti has good tools for memoing. The team started to use memos early in the project to record their initial ideas and impressions. Figure 12.7 list the initial memos in the order in which they were created.

In Figure 12.7 *size* indicates the number of characters (letters and spaces) in the memo. These early memos were short in length. However, in Figure 12.7 *density* indicates the number of *quotations* (passages of text) that are linked to the memo. Many of the memos have several *quotations* linked to them; eight have over 20 *quotations* linked, while one memo – problems with government support – has 50 *quotations* linked to it. In this early phase of memoing, initial ideas were supported by linking to the evidence in the text that supported those ideas. In ATLAS.ti, memos can be printed out or exported to Word where

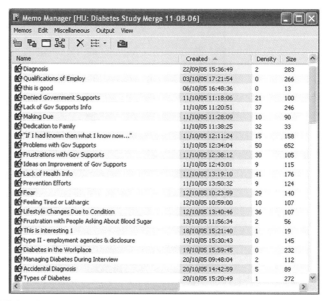

Figure 12.7 Initial memos in the order in which they were created

the linked quotations can appear in full under the text of the memo – complete with the reference to which document it came from. Alternatively, the memo can be opened in the *network view* in ATLAS.ti and each quotation can be retrieved in context see (Figure 12.8.)

Figure 12.8 shows the memo – accidental diagnosis – in the *network view*. It is a short memo reflecting one of the team's insight that a number of people did

not recognize that their symptoms were those of diabetes. This memo was created early on in the project and five quotations have been linked to it. In Figure 12.8, one of the *quotations* (143:9) has been selected and loaded in the *primary document pane* in the left (the *quotation* is highlighted). The text of the *quotation* can now be read in the context of the transcript.

Following this initial period of memoing, Doris Hamner, the principal investigator, reviewed the analysis so far (21 October 2005) and wrote up her reflections in a series of much longer memos. (See the list of these memos in Figure 12.9.)

Doris begins her memo on 'Return to Work':

10/21/2005

DH – today I am looking through our coding to do some preliminary analysis and to also check out how everyone has coded. This is a commentary memo because I am going to include some notes I have on the overall analysis of the project.

She continues by identifying the few codes which have a lot of coding and indicating the areas where she would like to see overlaps. She then looks in

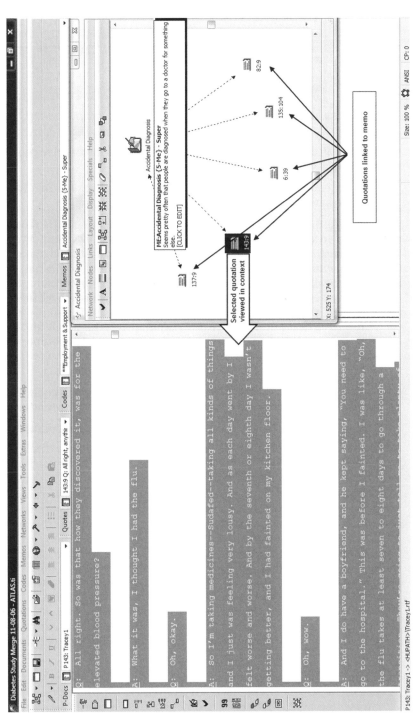

Figure 12.8 Memo accidental diagnosis displayed in network view showing linked quotations and showing selected quotation viewed in transcript

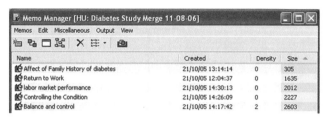

Figure 12.9 List of 'consolidating memos'

more detail around the issues that have emerged so far for these people return-
ing to work or finding another path in life.

In the memo on 'balance and control', Doris summarizes the literature on
how these two concepts relate to people with diabetes.

> Balance. I have read one article that is a meta-ethnography that goes over
> many articles on diabetes. This Paterson article 1998, Journal of Nursing
> Scholarship indicates that those who refer to control the disease are also
> those who were cheating or not following diet tips, medication, etc. Those
> who speak of balance are those who are following protocol. . . . So far I am
> thinking about what we mean by CONTROL as opposed to what we mean by
> BALANCE. Obviously, the jargon that patients use is also the jargon that
> they have heard from the medical community. (This article also points out
> the importance of demographics such as if person lives alone, supportive
> allies the person may have . . .)

She continues by discussing coding dilemmas the team has had in interpreting
these codes. She discusses the pros and cons of creating new codes yet keeping
the coding frame 'lean'.

I have called these kinds of memo 'consolidating memos' because they are a
review of work done so far with recommendations on how to move the analysis forward. Doris has used these memos both to consolidate her own thinking
and to communicate to the team the next steps.

Team members continued to write memos on insights as they coded. Towards
the end of January 2006, two relatively long 'key issue' memos were written.
One on the experience of the Social Security system and the other on information – sources of information, dissemination of information, needs, and so
on. These two memos pull out the analysis of these two topics from what had
been done up to that point in ATLAS.ti. The memoing feature in ATLAS.ti
should be seen as a place to start to write up the analysis. Memos on 'key
issues' are the building blocks for a report or article. As this is a longitudinal
study, memos on changes in the experience of the individuals in the study
over time were also written. The *network tool* in ATLAS.ti can be used both
as a tool to pull out this information and as a visual memo of an individual's
experience.

Figure 12.10 tracks respondent Andy's community involvement over two
years. The six interviews that were conducted with him over two years are
represented at the bottom of the network. Each one is represented by the
document icon –   . The code for community involvement is at the top of

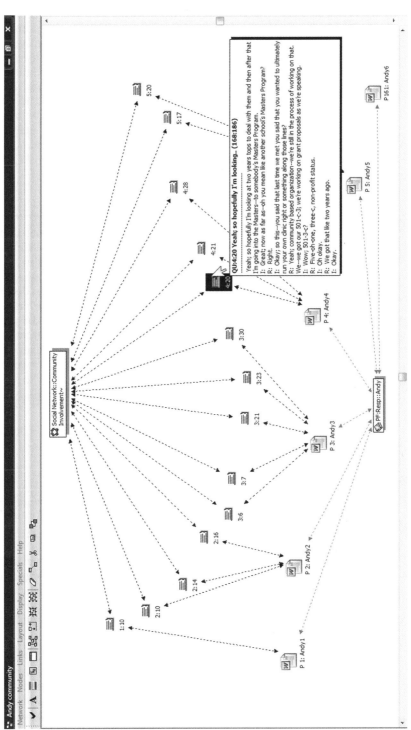

Figure 12.10 Network view showing respondent Andy's community involvement over time

the *network view*. Between the documents and the code are the *quotations* (passages of text) from each of Andy's interviews which have been linked to the code (or coded to) Community Involvement. In the *network view* you can also see from which transcript each *quotation* comes. Each one of these *quotations* can be viewed in turn. Quotation 4:20 has been selected in Figure 12.10 to show the full text for that *quotation*. The visual representation in the *network view* gives an immediate assessment of where most of the talk about community involvement is concentrated. The actual talk can be accessed immediately from the *network view* allowing for an immediate analysis of – in this case – the respondent's community involvement over time. A memo can now be written up and linked to this network view.

Teamwork

This project has a team of four people – Doris Hamner, the principal investigator, Soheila Lopopolo, the ATLAS.ti supremo, Jennifer Bose and Julisa Cully. All four worked with ATLAS.ti, although Jennifer Bose, who is visually impaired, could only work partially in ATLAS.ti as she experienced problems with ATLAS.ti interfacing with her screen reader. The team decided that because this was a longitudinal study where they would be interviewing people at nine different time points, each team member would be responsible for interviewing the same people (as far as this was possible) at each time point. For continuity purposes, the team also decided that each team member would be the primary coder for the people they interviewed. So team members coded and analysed the interviews they did in ATLAS.ti in order to take advantage of the knowledge they were accumulating about individuals as they went back and interviewed them again and again.

Quality control was ensured by having the team members secondary code each other's work. A spreadsheet is kept by Soheila to keep track of the coding process (see Table 12.2).

Table 12.2 Spreadsheet column headers for tracking coding process

Transcript Name (PD no.)	Primary coder	Date coded	Secondary coder	Date coded

Each team member works on their own computer with their own copy of the ATLAS.ti project. Soheila, as coordinator of the project, is in charge of merging the different versions of the project together. Merging is done when a number of transcripts have been coded by their primary coder and need to be secondary coded, and when new transcripts arrive from the transcriber and need to be added to the project.

Figure 12.11 is a flowchart of the ATLAS.ti teamwork process coordinated by Soheila. The transcriber sends the interview transcripts to Soheila – the ATLAS.ti supremo – who assigns them to the ATLAS.ti project. ATLAS.ti is different from other QDAS packages because documents are not imported into an internal database in the program. Instead, they remain external to the program. When a document is assigned to ATLAS.ti, the program records the path

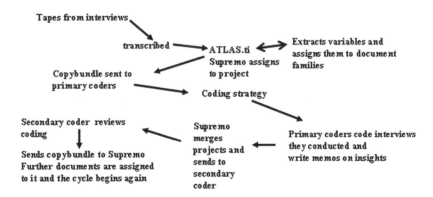

Figure 12.11 Teamwork flowchart for study

to where the document is located (on a hard drive or network drive) and automatically assigns it a unique identifier (the *P* number) which is how the program recognizes a document. This feature of ATLAS.ti has two implications when managing teamwork with the software:

• The documents need to be in the same location in each team member's computer *(otherwise ATLAS.ti will not be able to find the document when the researcher wants to work with it).*
• The *P* number of each document has to be the same in each team member's version of the project *(otherwise the merge procedure will not be able to merge different team members versions of the project if, for example, P1 is James in one project and Jill in another project).*

The simplest solution in keeping to the first criteria is to have all the documents for a project in one folder and save the ATLAS.ti project in that folder. This is a default location – the program will automatically look for a document in the same folder where the ATLAS.ti project is located. In addition, when moving a project from one computer to another in order to merge the projects, a procedure called *copybundling* should be used. This procedure zips up the ATLAS.ti project and all its documents in one flat file which can be transferred to another computer by first saving it onto a memory stick or emailing it to another computer. Once copied onto the other computer, it can be *unbundled* and the project and associated folder and documents will be recreated on the target computer, ready to be merged.

In order to keep to the second criteria – each document in each team member's project having the same unique identifier (the *P* number) – it is easiest to have one person who assigns the documents to the ATLAS.ti project and then makes an identical version for each member of the team. This is the method Soheila adopted for this project.

As you can see in Figure 12.11, the ATLAS.ti coordinator or supremo – who is Soheila in this project – assigns the newly transcribed documents to the project. She then extracts the information about the variables relevant to each document and assigns the documents to the appropriate document families.

She then makes a copy of the project for each team member, *copybundles* the projects and sends them to the team members to primary code. After each team member has primary coded their documents, they copybundle their projects and send them to Soheila who merges their work together in one new overall project. She then sends that project to be secondary coded. After the secondary coding is done, the projects are copybundled and sent back to Soheila to be merged again. The cycle then begins again with newly transcribed documents being assigned to the project.

The way to design how the teamwork is managed needs to take account of two factors:

1   the requirements of the research design *(in this case, the longitudinal design where each respondent is interviewed nine times led the research team to decide that for continuity purposes the work should be divided, so that each team member interviewed the same respondents at each time point and then primary coded those respondents)*;
2   the requirements of the software package *(documents remain external to the ATLAS.ti project and need to be managed in a particular way)*.

As has already been shown in the section on memos, each team member was also writing memos on their insights as they were coding. Doris, as principal investigator, was also using memos as a way to consolidate her thinking on the work so far and as a way to communicate with other team members on the way forward. As the analysis progressed, team members started to write lengthier memos on the key issues that were emerging. All members of the team were physically located in the same building so they could have regular face-to-face meetings to discuss the analysis.

Lessons from this case

This case is a good example of how to set up a longitudinal design in ATLAS.ti. *Document families* need to be set up for each respondent and all the transcripts for that respondent need to be assigned to their *document family*. This will enable the analyst to restrict the analysis of each respondent's case as a whole and to track changes in that respondent over time. The *network view*, as illustrated in Figure 12.10, can be used to track changes over time for a particular respondent. Memos for each respondent can be used to record changes over time.

In addition, in order to track changes across the database at a particular point in time, *document families* need to be created for each time point. In this study, there were a maximum of nine time points over the three years of the study.

This case is also a good example of how the *super code* feature was used effectively in order to retrieve issues core to the project during the analysis. In a longitudinal study, this not only facilitates the production of interim reports but also aids in reviewing what has been covered in previous interviews in order to plan what needs to be addressed or followed up in the next interview.

Finally, this case illustrates a successful way to organize teamwork in an ATLAS.ti project. The use of a central coordinator responsible for setting up the project, distributing copies for each team member, merging their work and tracking the quality control process enabled the team to work in a consistent manner. If problems arose with working with the software, team members could consult the coordinator. In addition, the coordinator was in a good position to spot problems. Memos were also used as an effective communication tool among team members.

For more information on this project, see Disability and Rehabilitation Research Project on Emerging Disability and Systems Change (2007).

Note

1 This exemplar is based on a study by the Institute for Community Inclusion, University of Massachusetts, Boston, led by principal investigator, Doris Hamner.

13 | Microbicides Development Programme case study[1]

The software that was used in the original project was NVivo 2.

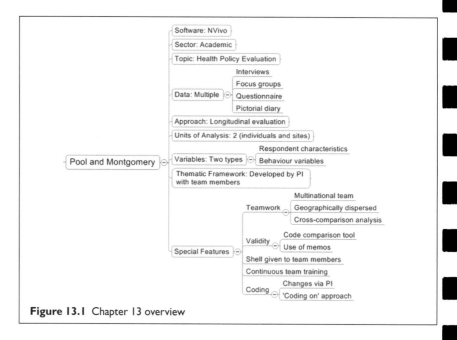

Figure 13.1 Chapter 13 overview

For the purposes of this discussion, we have converted the MDP study into the latest version of NVivo currently – NVivo 7. In making the conversion to NVivo 7, we have also done some reorganization of the project in order to demonstrate the important features of the 7 version that were not available in earlier versions.

Background of project

The Microbicides Development Programme is an international partnership[2] set up to evaluate and test vaginal microbicides (a gel that is inserted into the vagina) to prevent HIV transmission. It is funded by the UK Department for International Development and administered by the Medical Research Council Clinical Trials Unit and Imperial College London.

This case study is from Phase III of the project where a multinational randomized, double-blind, placebo-controlled trial of one type of microbicide is being tested in two strengths. Integrated into the clinical trials, there is a social science component involving a random subsample of trial participants. This case concerns the social science behavioural response to the microbicide PRO 2000. The social science component concerns various issues, including women's (and men's) response to the gel. Other concerns are to assess the accuracy of key data collected in the clinic and to assess understanding of the informed consent procedure

Design of project

There are six sites where the social science evaluation is being conducted. Three of the sites are in South Africa – the Africa Centre in KwaZulu Natal, Durban and Johannesburg. The other sites are in Mwanza, Tanzania; Masaka, Uganda; and Mazabuka, Zambia. Robert Pool, at the Barcelona Centre for International Health Research and Catherine Montgomery, London School of Hygiene and Tropical Medicine are responsible for the overall design, planning and coordination of the work of these sites. A variety of data collection techniques are being used in order to triangulate data on acceptability, adherence to product and sexual behaviour. The participants keep a pictorial coital diary where they record their sexual activity and use or non-use of the gel. During visits to the clinic a health worker uses a Case Record Form (CRF) – a closed-ended questionnaire – to record sexual activity and gel use during the previous week. In addition, the women are interviewed in depth at three points during the trial. Some of the women's partners are also interviewed as an additional dimension to the triangulation. In addition, focus groups are conducted at each site to understand community perspectives on sexual practices and the acceptability of gel.

At each site, women are randomized to one of three arms: PRO 2000 at 0.5 per cent, PRO 2000 at 2 per cent or a placebo (control group). The units of observation are the participants and the community. The units of analysis are both the participants for within-site analysis and the trial sites for across-trial analysis.

This is a longitudinal study. Women remain in the trial for 52 weeks, or for up to 104 weeks in Uganda. The trial is recruiting women over a 30-month period, so as some women leave the trial, others are continuing or being newly enrolled. Women are followed up at the clinic monthly, but a long behavioural CRF is only administered at weeks 4, 24, 40 and 52. The in-depth interviews with women and partners and the coital diaries are linked to these long clinic visits.

Variables include demographic variables such as age, gender, occupation, type of sexual partner; and behaviour variables such as gel-only use, gel and condom use, anal sex, vaginal washing, and so on.

The design framework in Table 13.1 summarizes the design of this project.

Table 13.1 Design framework of the MDP project

Unit(s) of analysis	Attributes	Time frame	Data: textual (primary or secondary forms of data)	Data: non-textual (primary or secondary forms of data)
Trial sites (UA) Africa Centre Durban Johannesburg Mwanza Masaka Mazabuka Individuals (UO) (UA) Women using gel Partners Community (UO) Women in community not in trial Men in community	Respondent • Age • Gender • Occupation • Partner type Behaviour • sex frequency • use of gel and/or condom • anal sex • symptoms • involve partner	Longitudinal (52 weeks)	In-depth interviews Focus groups Questionnaire (case record form) – numeric data	Pictorial coital diaries – numeric data

Representing the design in the software shell

Data organization

Each site works only on its dataset. However, all the sites' work is merged monthly into one overall project in order to enable cross-site comparisons. In NVivo 7, data can be organized into folders. There is a folder for each of the site's documents. Within that folder there are sub-folders for the different kinds of data each site is collecting. Figure 13.2 shows the sub-folders for the Johannesburg site. There are folders for the three types of data they are importing into NVivo – focus groups, home visit reports (observations) and in-depth interviews. The in-depth interviews folder has sub-folders for the three different time periods when the women on the study are interviewed.

Note that a decision was made not to include the pictorial coital diaries and the case records forms in NVivo 7 although it was possible to do so. To include them would have required a bigger investment in time for document preparation. However, information from them was extracted prior to each in-depth interview and reference is made to the information in them during the interview. So the information from them is captured in both the interview data and in the attribute variables (discussed below).

Memos can also be organized in folders in NVivo 7. Each site has its own folder for memos. In addition, there is a folder for communications to all sites. Figure 13.3 shows the sub-folders for memos for Johannesburg. There are separate folders for the research journals kept by each member of the Johannesburg team. In addition, there are memos on specific interviews. These are

Figure 13.2 Document folders in NVivo 7

linked to the relevant interviews (see Figure 13.4). In addition, there is a folder for the quality control (QC) reports that team members have made on particular interviews in terms of both interview questioning and coding.

Figure 13.4 shows how the memos on interviews are linked in NVivo 7 to interviews. The cursor is hovering over one of the memo link icons in order to display which interview the memo is linked to. The document can also be accessed in this view by right clicking over the memo in the list view and selecting 'open linked item'.

Figure 13.3 Memo organization in NVivo 7

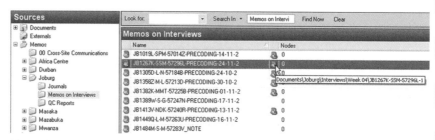

Figure 13.4 Memos linked to documents in NVivo 7

Units of analysis, units of observation and attribute variables

Case nodes

The units of analysis are the trial site (six sites) and the study participants. The units of observation are the study participants, some of their partners and the community where the trial takes place. In NVivo 7, both units of analysis and units of observation are represented by case nodes.

Figure 13.5 illustrates the organization of the units of analysis and units of observation in NVivo 7. There is a case node for each of the six trial sites (Africa Centre, Durban, Joburg, etc.) in order for cross-comparisons to be made. The case nodes for the Johannesburg site have been expanded in Figure 13.5 to

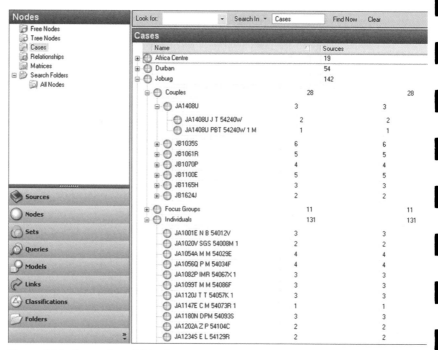

Figure 13.5 Case nodes in NVivo 7

show how the units of observation are organized. There are case nodes for the individual in-depth interviews of the women and for the focus groups. These are both units of observation for the trial site. In addition, the interviews of the sample of women whose partners have also been interviewed have been organized under a separate case node for couples. Organizing couples together in case nodes facilitates comparisons made for triangulation purposes.

Figure 13.5 also shows how each case node contains all the material for that individual or couple or site. In this project, for individual women, that would include their in-depth interviews at three time periods during the study as well as any home visits that may have been made. Look at the column titled *source* at the top of Figure 13.5 and you will see the number of source materials coded at each case node. For Durban there are 54 source materials; for Johannesburg there are 142 source materials coded. Comparisons between Durban and Johannesburg can be made with those case nodes. Under the Johannesburg node you can see the three kinds of source material listed. Under *couples*, the first couple *JA1408U* contains 3 source materials – the two interviews conducted so far with the woman *JA1408U J T 54240W* and the one interview conducted with her partner *JA1408U J T 54240W 1 M*. The individual case nodes for each woman and her partner enable them to be analysed separately. The couple case node enables the couples to be analysed as a unit.

Attributes, time variables and values changing over time

In NVivo 7, setting up the case nodes correctly is important because it is only at case nodes that you can attach attributes (variables). In this study there are two basic types of variables – respondent variables (demographic information such as age, gender, etc.) and behaviour variables (such as use of condom/gel; symptoms; frequency of sex, etc.). Look back at the design framework – Table 13.1. The behaviour variables could change over the three time points that the women have been interviewed. As the attributes can only be attached to the case nodes which contain all the material from a particular respondent, each variable that could change over time needs to be created three times. For example, the behaviour attribute, *acceptability of the gel*, needs to be created three times to represent the three time points the women are interviewed – *acceptability T1, acceptability T2* and *acceptability T3*.

Figure 13.6 shows how the variables have been set up in NVivo 7 for this project including those variables which could vary over time. Figure 13.7 shows how the case nodes have been assigned attributes. The casebook is filtered so you can just see the values for Johannesburg. At the time of writing the Week 52 interviews (T3) had not been imported into NVIVO. However, we can see in Figure 13.7 how values have been assigned for the *acceptability* (of the gel) at Week 04 (T1) and at Week 24 (T2).

With this setup it is possible to compare the six sites for similarities or differences in the acceptability of the gel over time. This can be done by creating a matrix table for the site case nodes and the values for acceptability of the gel for the three time periods. It also enables you to select those cases where initially

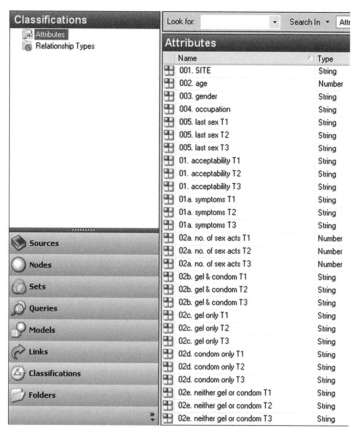

Figure 13.6 Setup of attributes in NVivo 7

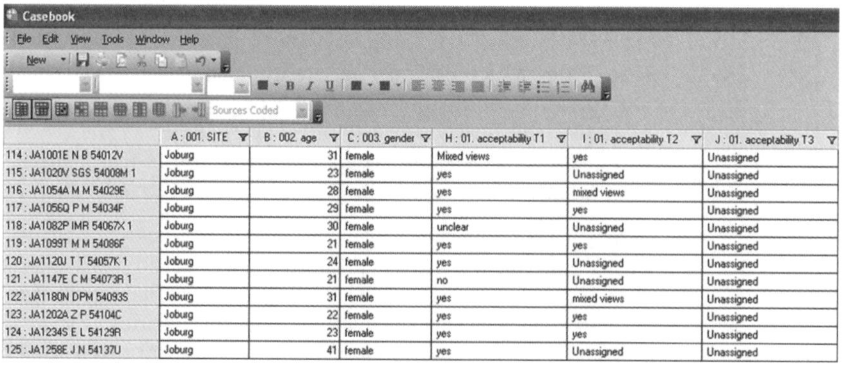

	A : 001. SITE ▽	B : 002. age ▽	C : 003. gender ▽	H : 01. acceptability T1 ▽	I : 01. acceptability T2 ▽	J : 01. acceptability T3 ▽
114 : JA1001E N B 54012V	Joburg	31	female	Mixed views	yes	Unassigned
115 : JA1020V SGS 54009M 1	Joburg	23	female	yes	Unassigned	Unassigned
116 : JA1054A M M 54029E	Joburg	28	female	yes	mixed views	Unassigned
117 : JA1056Q P M 54034F	Joburg	29	female	yes	yes	Unassigned
118 : JA1082P IMR 54067X 1	Joburg	30	female	unclear	Unassigned	Unassigned
119 : JA1099T M M 54086F	Joburg	21	female	yes	yes	Unassigned
120 : JA1120J T T 54057K 1	Joburg	24	female	yes	Unassigned	Unassigned
121 : JA1147E C M 54073R 1	Joburg	21	female	no	Unassigned	Unassigned
122 : JA1180N DPM 54093S	Joburg	31	female	yes	mixed views	Unassigned
123 : JA1202A Z P 54104C	Joburg	22	female	yes	yes	Unassigned
124 : JA1234S E L 54129R	Joburg	23	female	yes	yes	Unassigned
125 : JA1258E J N 54137U	Joburg	41	female	yes	Unassigned	Unassigned

Figure 13.7 NVivo 7 casebook showing assignment of attribute values to case nodes

there were mixed feelings about the gel but later on in the trial they became happy with it. There are endless possibilities for analysing the data longitudinally now that the case nodes and attributes have been set up as described above.

In this study it has been necessary to code at all the levels of the case node hierarchy so that it is possible to compare trial sites in matrices or to look at couples with particular characteristics or at a particular individual's group of material. However, when using matrix tables it is not advisable to use the number of cases as an option as (at least in NVivo 7 SP 4); it will count a case at every level of the hierarchy that is coded for it. Depending on what kind of matrix you are creating you need to think through how NVivo is counting. For some kinds of question involving matrices, it may be better to use Sets.

Use of Sets

Sets are used for a variety of purposes in NVivo 7. They are more flexible than source folders as an item can be in more than one set. It is also possible to group documents and nodes in the same set. In this project it is useful to use sets for the three different time periods in matrix tables. The source material has already been organized in folders according to the type of data and the point in time – as discussed above (see Figure 13.2). This was done in order to manage the large amount of data in this project. For certain operations it is useful to restrict the scope of an analysis to a document folder, such as all Masaka interviews at week 24. However, for other operations it is necessary to have the time periods organized in sets. This is the case if you want to create a matrix table comparing attitudes at, for example, Week 04 and Week 24. If the matrix is used with the document folders for Week 04 and Week 24, it will include every single document as a row in the matrix table. There may be times when you may want to compare document by document. However, often you want to have a summary count of attitudes at time 1 compared to attitudes at time 2. For that kind of question, sets are used, as sets are treated as one whole, not as separate components of the items that are in it.

For example, sets were made for Johannesburg interviews at Week 04 and at Week 24. (This can be easily done from the respective document folders already set up.) Then a matrix table was run to compare attitudes to the gel at Week 24 compared to Week 04. Figure 13.8 shows this matrix table. The

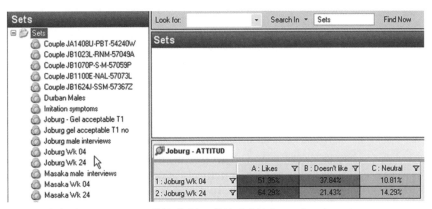

Figure 13.8 Matrix using sets of Week 04 and Week 24 Johannesburg interviews

numbers are row percentages of the number of documents in each cell. (In this case a document represents one individual.)

As shown in Figure 13.8, we can see that there was an increase in the percentage of women who liked the gel at Week 24 compared to Week 04.

It is not unusual in NVivo 7 to have the same item represented as a document folder, as a set and even as an attribute. It gives you a lot of flexibility in handling the dataset. While some sets such as the sets for the time periods in longitudinal studies should be set up beforehand, others will only be created when you have a particular query to run that requires sets or as an analytical tool to group similar items together to reflect on during the analysis process.

Thematic framework

It was important that all six sites code for the same things in order that a cross-comparison analysis would be possible. To that end, Robert Pool and Catherine Montgomery in collaboration with the six site teams devised a basic coding scheme for all teams to follow. This coding scheme evolved during an initial pilot stage of the project. It was later modified after the teams had some experience of using it. They adopted a strategy of coding broadly for topic areas and going back in each broad node and coding more finely. This means that the analysts would be going over and over the transcripts coding for different things. They would also refine their codes by coding directly in the broad code. This technique, called 'coding on' was coined by Lyn Richards, NVivo's co-developer, and is an effective way of working in NVivo. It is particularly effective when working with teams as they are more likely to be consistent in their coding and less likely to miss out text which should be coded when they use this method.

The broad TOPIC areas are: condom, disclosure/communication/involvement, gel, family planning, illness, menstruation, partner, pregnancy, risk, sex, trial and vaginal practices. A second broad area was PRACTICAL aspects of using the gel in the trial. These included (gel) applicator, availability (of gel), storage (of gel), and timing/frequency (of gel use). Cross-cutting these broad codes were codes for ATTITUDES – doesn't like, likes and neutral – and codes for CHARACTERISTICS – causes symptoms, cleanses, convenient, cures, difficult, easy, enjoyment, inconvenient, no change, protects and wet/dry. MOTIVES were also cross-cutting categories and were broken down into reasons for NOT doing something (enrolling in the trial, using the gel, using condoms, etc.) and reasons for doing something. The teams were also coding for INCONSISTENCIES in the interviews; this was broken down into internal inconsistencies within an individual interviewee and couple inconsistencies where couples had contradictory interviews.

Figure 13.9 shows the organization of these themes in NVivo 7. Tree nodes in NVivo 7 are a hierarchical catalogue of codes. They are to be used with the queries to produce finer level coding. So you would use a query to look at instances of what was said about liking the gel (a coding query combining Gel AND Likes). Likewise, you could use a coding query to pull out what was said

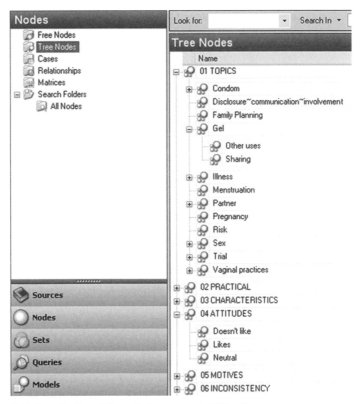

Figure 13.9 Organization of thematic framework in NVivo 7

about liking condoms (Condoms AND Likes). These queries can be saved as nodes or codes, so NVivo does the finer level coding for you.

It is also possible to restrict the scope of any query by documents, document folders, case nodes, any other nodes, sets and attributes. So it is possible to do a simple coding search on Gels AND Likes restricted to Johannesburg and compare that with Gels AND Likes restricted to Durban. This simplifies the coding task so that the team is coding at broad or general areas.

In this project the teams were instructed to stick to the above framework so cross-comparison could be made across the trial sites. However, the teams were also encouraged to develop their own questions relevant to their sites and use NVivo's queries to do so. If this required additional coding, this could be done with a copy of the project which is just for the site.

Journals and memos

In each site, each team member using NVivo kept a pre-coding journal where they recorded their reflections about the interview and the interviewee just after the interview. They also kept a Coding Journal where they recorded both housekeeping items such as coding completed and insights about the interviews. Some of the teams also had more in-depth memos on particular interviews. Others also kept their quality checking memos in the software. (See Figures 13.3 and 13.4 on the organization of the memos.) These journals and memos are important in the analysis. There is information about the perceived reliability of the respondent's report as well as insights on main themes that are emerging. The journals also play an important role in communicating to other members of the site team as well as to the overall coordinators of the project – Pool and Montgomery.

In addition, there is a folder for cross-site communication. Instructions from Pool and Montgomery are included in here. So through the journals and memos there is a two-way communication system set up between each site and the coordinators. In addition, the insights recorded will help with the cross-comparison of the six sites.

Teamwork

This project is a good example of a large-scale research project with multiple teams. Robert Pool, the principal investigator, set up the 'shell' of the NVivo project which included the thematic framework, as discussed above, and the attributes. This shell was duplicated and a copy sent to each team (six teams in all). Pool's colleague, Catherine Montgomery, was the NVivo 'overall supremo' in this project – coordinating the communication between each team. Each team's project was named with an identifier so the various site projects could be identified. At each site, each team had its own NVivo 'site supremo' who coordinated the work with the software at that site. Each site worked only with their own data. The NVivo site supremo was responsible for ensuring that the documents to be imported in NVivo were prepared according to the template designed by the coordinating team. In addition, each supremo decided how the coding work was to be divided up among team members. Some sites (such as the Durban site) had only one person working with the software but most of them had at least two people working with the software and the site supremo was responsible for merging the work of the site into one overall project before emailing it to the coordinating team. The site supremo was also responsible for quality control checking of the transcripts and the coding.

Site supremos emailed the project on a monthly basis to the coordinating team where they were merged into one overall project. In order to ensure that the sites could be cross-analysed, the sites were not allowed to make changes to the coding framework. They were encouraged to report back any problems with the codes and suggestions for changes to the codes. Another quality control check was done by the coordinating team.

A generous budget for capacity building was included in the grant for this project. All the researchers needed initial training in NVivo. The principal investigator was an experienced QDAS user having used the Ethnograph, ATLAS.ti, NUD*IST and NVivo. He realized that all the teams required not only initial training but also continued support. di Gregorio was brought in for the initial training and subsequent support in NVivo. London was the venue for the initial training. Subsequent continued support was in Africa. A five-day-training was organized in Durban, South Africa which focused on coding strategy and memo writing. It was also an opportunity for members of the teams to meet and discuss common issues and themes that were emerging from the study. The coding framework was revised at this meeting. Six months later another five-day-training for the teams was held in Maputo, Mozambique. The objective of that meeting was to enhance their qualitative analysis skills. A medical sociologist came in for the first half of the week to focus on analysis techniques and di Gregorio ran the second half of the week which built on the questions and approaches of analysis they developed in the first half of the week but this time using NVivo's tools for exploring them. Further group meetings are planned.

Figure 13.10 illustrates the overall coordination of the teams as described above. Not all the members of each team could join in the capacity-building meetings. It was the responsibility of the members who attended to feedback their learning to their team members.

At the first capacity-building meeting the teams were asked to record their workflow using NVivo at their site. Figure 13.11 shows the Johannesburg team's flowchart. The other sites had a similar process. The audio files are saved on the server. On Wednesdays the audio files are allocated by the NVivo supremo for transcribing and translation into English (the interviews are done in the respondents' own language). The transcribing and translation is sometimes done within the team and sometimes it is outsourced. The translated files are imported into NVivo where initial broad coding is done. The broad coding is then quality checked before it is fine coded. (Fine coding is done by more experienced members of the team.) Both pre-coding memos (interviewer's reflections on the interview) and memos during the coding process are recorded in NVivo. Finally, attributes are imported via an Excel spreadsheet

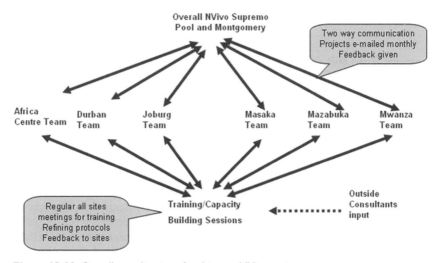

Figure 13.10 Overall coordination of multi-team NVivo project

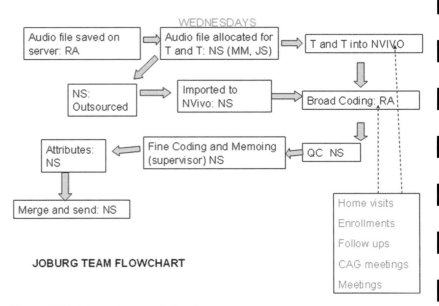

JOBURG TEAM FLOWCHART

Figure 13.11 Johannesburg team's flowchart

before the various team members' projects are merged and emailed to the coordinating team.

Managing such a large team requires careful coordination and communication. Support is required for the initial setup for such a complex design. Team members need to be trained in the software and in the approach to the analysis, so that everyone is working in a consistent manner. Training needs to be ongoing in such a project. Regular retreats with members of all the teams not only increase their skills and ensure consistency across the projects but also increase their enthusiasm and commitment to the project.

Lessons from this case

This project is a good example of a large-scale longitudinal design. The key is to identify the units of analysis and units of observation and represent them in the case nodes. In NVivo 7 a case node holds all the material that is relevant to a particular unit of analysis or unit of observation. In addition, with such a large project the data needs to be organized in an easily accessible way. The use of document folders is crucial in order to separate out data from the different sites and to identify the different types of data collected and (for the in-depth interviews) the three time points at which they were collected. The three time points are also represented by sets. Different operations you may wish to do in NVivo require the use of the document folders while others require sets. It does not take long to set both up and gives you a very flexible dataset to use. Finally, variables which could change over time need to be created as attributes three times (in this instance – or as how many time points you are collecting data).

In NVivo 7 attribute values can only be assigned to case nodes so this is the best solution for changing variable values.

This project is also a good example of a multi-team project. It illustrates the importance of a strong coordinating supremo who sets up the 'shell' of the project for each team with clear instructions on how to proceed. It also shows the importance of budgeting for training and capacity building and providing ongoing support for the teams during the life of the project.

For more information on this project, see Pool (2005).

Notes

1   This exemplar is based on the work of principal investigator, Robert Pool, Barcelona Centre for International Health Research (CRESIB), University of Barcelona and Social Science Coordinator, Catherine Montgomery, Health Policy Unit, London School of Hygiene and Tropical Medicine.

2   **Africa:** AMREF/NIMR, Mwanza, Tanzania; Medical Research Council (South Africa), Durban, South Africa; Reproductive Health and HIV Research Unit, University of the Witwatersrand, Johannesburg, South Africa; The Africa Centre for Health and Population Studies, South Africa; MRC/Uganda Virus Research Institute, Entebbe, Uganda; University Teaching Hospital, Lusaka, Zambia; **Europe:** Imperial College, London; London School of Hygiene and Tropical Medicine; MRC Social and Health Public Services Unit, University of Glasgow; St George's Hospital Medical School; University of Southampton; Population Services International, Europe; Barcelona Centre for International Health Research (CRESIB), University of Barcelona; University of York; Oxford University.

PART III

Implications and practical guidelines

14 Implications of using Qualitative Data Analysis Software

This book has focused on the fundamentals of designing research in the E-Project and using E-Projects in research settings. We would be remiss, however, if we did not devote some attention to the wider implications the technology raises for the practice of qualitative research. In particular, we are concerned with three issues: 1) the role of the E-Project as a genre; 2) the representation of research design in the E-Project; and 3) the issue of scaling up QDAS use in organizations and professions.

The role of the E-Project

Recognizing the E-Project as a genre represented a critical step in our evolution as QDAS users. Our identification of this idea was long in coming. It took many years of experience with different kinds of project and user and in a variety of contexts for the notion to make itself felt. Similar to Luria's notion of the reorganization of higher cortical functions, we suddenly realized that our understanding and approach to QDAS had shifted in some fundamental way. It was in exploring the meaning of this shift that we were able to conceive our QDAS-based work as reflecting the principles of a 'genre'.

Here are some of the bits and pieces of evidence that helped us to find our way to this idea:

- We realized that there is a vast difference between the knowledge and skills of beginning and advanced users of QDAS. We tried to understand those differences and the various processes by which users developed their skills.
- We realized that advanced users can look at the bare bones of an E-Project and quickly identify its strengths and weaknesses.
- We saw conventions or standards developing as soon as we tried to use E-Projects with others.
- We had experience conducting 'master classes' in which we would examine, trim, pare and reshape E-Projects presented to us. We tried to access the knowledge we were using to do this.
- We had to grade E-Project use, and that required us to say what was novice versus sophisticated use and why. This meant many hours wandering through E-Projects developed without fixed standards, which was also very instructive.
- We began to visualize our qualitative research work with the visual interface of the QDAS we were using – our projects were seen as an identifiable container rather than existing as papers in numerous files and notebooks.

- In discussing a qualitative research project, we were frustrated if we did not have the level of access that QDAS would make possible. Having learned to look at qualitative research with these tools, we felt unduly restricted when these tools were not in use. It almost felt like a hearing loss, as if we were communicating without the full range of sounds.

Through many conversations that drew on these discrepant but related pieces of evidence, we began to realize we were watching a new research genre in formation. Just as the research paper, dissertation or annotated bibliography were once new forms with debatable criteria, so, too, the E-Project was feeling its way into existence. Through our QDAS experiences we were participating in the process of defining and solidifying the E-Project's genre characteristics. Unable to see the forest for the trees, we had been focusing on technical details of the tools, unable to take in the bigger picture that the E-Project represented for qualitative research practice.

It is the E-Project, not QDAS *per se*, that raises the greatest challenge to qualitative research as it is currently practised. The E-Project is a challenge because of its potential to become a central research genre, one through which all forms of research practice will intersect. Thus, how you plan your project and collect your data, as well as the ways you interpret and present your findings – all will be represented and developed within the E-Project. To return to the lessons of Chapter 1, the E-Project's key features of portability and transparency coupled with the ensuing need for standards, changes business as usual for qualitative researchers. The E-Project allows us to 'see into' the researchers' process, throwing light into the darkest corners of data collection and interpretation.

The notion of the E-Project represents a technological shift in the practice of qualitative research that is unlike anything qualitative researchers have faced before. Moving from pen and paper to computer did not change qualitative research practice significantly, but moving to QDAS can significantly alter practice once users move beyond the elementary stages of store and retrieve.

We do not raise this issue to threaten or bully our readers, but to help them to see what the stakes are as qualitative research moves into this new era. We think the E-Project represents an exciting new development in the field of qualitative research, but making sense of this new genre will raise tensions in academic and non-academic settings.

In making a case for the E-Project, it is important to iterate that the E-Project is a notion that spans different brands of QDAS. This is a dynamic field of software development, characterized by rapid change. While we cannot predict what a particular QDAS package may resemble five years from now or whether or not it will still be in existence, we can assume that the characteristics of the E-Project as we have described them will still have relevance. The notion of the E-Project will have relevance, we believe, because it provides a means of understanding how to enact good research design in a digital environment.

The representation of the research design in the E-Project

The conceptualization of the E-Project as a genre highlights the fact that QDAS is much more than a container of the research materials and a coding tool. The research design itself should be developed, modified and represented within the QDAS. This has implications for teaching QDAS and for the way to approach setting up a project in QDAS. Teaching QDAS should be integrated with teaching qualitative data analysis. QDAS training should not be seen as a separate standalone component of instruction, somehow divorced from wider methodological considerations. Starting points should be identifying the features of the software which should be used to represent the different elements of the research design. Teaching by using examplars of different research designs in QDAS is one way of developing knowledge of reading an E-Project. Likewise, students (or any analyst for that matter) can start with their own research questions and develop their research design in QDAS – using it as a thinking tool.

Working in QDAS has put back in the forefront issues dealing with the organization of research materials. As discussed in Chapter 2, the way researchers organize their materials – both data and ideas/themes – affects what they can access for analysis. QDAS's strength is the ability to quickly access relevant data for reflection and then access that same data, perhaps restricted in scope to a particular sub-group within the study for comparison. However, the research design needs to be represented accurately in the E-Project in order to be able to use the tools in this way. At the same time QDAS allows for flexibility as well as organization. The E-Project can grow with the analyst; the research design can be modified as needs be within the QDAS.

The critical components of design that need to be represented in QDAS (discussed fully in Chapter 2) are:

- the unit(s) of analysis (the 'what' or 'who' being analysed, i.e. individuals, organizations, programmes, etc.)
- the unit(s) of observation (the components that make up a unit of analysis);
- variables (including demographic information, survey responses, time periods);
- data types (textual – structured, semi-structured, unstructured; graphics; audio; video; combined graphic and text, e.g. web sites, newspapers);
- thematic framework (a priori, semi-emergent, emergent).

As mentioned above, these components can change over time due to unexpected contraints on the research or new insights about the subject matter. However, they should be brought into the E-Project right from the beginning of a study. Within the E-Project the design can be viewed and revised. In addition, the analyst can feel secure that they will be able to use QDAS to support the analysis they require.

Scaling up QDAS use

However, the use of QDAS in qualitative research does not take place in a vacuum. These tools and the researchers who use them are embedded in various institutional contexts – universities, non-profit agencies, businesses or other government offices – and it is critical we understand the ways these contexts support, or fail to support, researchers in their quest to master these tools and integrate them into their practice. Moreover, these tools are used within specific disciplines, contributing to the professional discourse of these communities, as well as the wider world of qualitative research in general. QDAS is not an isolated activity. Particularly, as use widens within and across institutions, it becomes more and more a community endeavour. As with the introduction of any new technology and/or significant institutional reform, integration into practice comes through a series of developmental stages in organizational growth.

The questions we ask in this section are: What are the implications of using QDAS for the conduct of QR research to the organizations and institutions in which researchers are located? To the practice of their discipline? And to the field of qualitative research? In answering these questions, we focus on two major areas: 1) organizational practices; and 2) professional contexts.

Organizational practices

Whether you are speaking of academia, the business world or a non-profit organization, robust or skilled use of the E-Project at the organizational level requires organizational commitment of resources and will. There are two critical areas organizations must address in order to provide adequate support to their QDAS users: 1) access, maintenance, and technical support; and 2) the community of learners.

Access, maintenance and technical support

Until very recently, researchers (and their parent organizations) have approached the use of QDAS as an individual or small group effort. One purchased a licence and then tried to figure out how to use the software product either independently – just clicking around or relying on the tutorials provided by the developer – or sought out help from an independent consultant. There were no user groups organized within organizations, and there were limited opportunities to meet or speak with other users. Although academic and research organizations are aware of the challenges of implementing technologies in other realms, few thought of their QDAS dilemma as an issue of technologically scaling up. Perhaps we thought of QDAS as being about qualitative research, not technology. We were wrong.

In a few sheltered settings, QDAS is now being addressed as an issue of scaling up in the classical sense that this term has been used with software and/or Internet technologies. The first step in this process is the recognition of the need of a site licence in order to provide users with easy access to the tools they need. Software developers, themselves caught within the prevailing paradigm, have had to scramble to develop new pricing schemes and embed new software securities, and so on for the protection of their software under these new circumstances.

Unfortunately, in many cases, the recognition of the need for broad access proceeds recognition of a comprehensive plan for internal distribution and monitoring of licences and a plan for maintenance and technical support. A site licence may be purchased at the behest of a savvy user or group of users, but then it is allowed to languish in the technological backwater of the organization until it atrophies and disappears. Users may be surprised to learn that their organization holds a licence and may have difficulty learning how it can be accessed.

We have both had the opportunity to work on the crafting of policies for QDAS organizational use and support. We know that there is no one-size-fits-all answer for such policies as every organization presents unique circumstances with regard to its structure and resources. We are also aware that academic and non-academic settings will present considerable differences that must be taken into account. However, we can offer these broad guidelines for thinking about the development of policies and support structures for QDAS organizational use.

1 Plan to locate your site licence at the highest/broadest possible level of the organization. By this we mean, the higher or broader the location of the site licence the better the leverage in terms of cost and users. For instance, if you can locate it at the university level, this will be better financially in the long run than at a department level. However, you must balance this consideration against the importance of having a supportive administrative group behind your plan to purchase and support the product you elect to use. Remember, too, that you can move the site licence up to a higher level as your user base and organizational needs expand.

2 Establish a cross-cutting group of interested users and technology leaders who will be responsible for policy oversight. Make sure you get the right representation in the group – it cannot just be social scientists and it cannot just be techies – you need both.

3 Survey the organization's needs in this arena. Seek knowledge on the kinds of user that will desire access to QDAS and the ways they would want to use QDAS.

4 Review QDAS products and make a selection for your organization. In addition to the software capacities, compare the licence policies and the adequacy of the developer's capacity to provide technical assistance to an organization of your size, remembering also that you are not the only organization asking for technical assistance from the developer. How will upgrades be handled?

5 Focus on one software package initially. If you are going to build a sophisticated mass of QDAS users within your organization, you need to establish a group that will have a common base of understanding. QDAS users need to speak a similar language, such as develops around the use of a similar tool. Moreover, internal technical support will be stretched too thin if you are trying to address the needs of users of multiple products. Once the use of one tool is well grounded, it would be safe to branch out, but start with one! QDAS is complex software; do one package well and you will be in a strong position to think about other possibilities.

6 Establish categories of users, including the privileges and responsibilities associated with each category of use. In an academic organization, you

might distinguish between the kinds of licence privilege that you offer to individual faculty, research teams and graduate students. In some organizations, there will be divisions among those who can receive 'free' licences and those who will need to pay a nominal fee for a licence leveraged from the price of the site licence. These decisions will be dependent on the kinds of user you have and the structure of the licence offered by the QDAS of your choice.

7   Determine the number of seats you will need for your licence. Always ask for more than you think you will need as once wider access is available the requests for access to the software will snowball.

8   Create an application form and process that describes the policies and defines the kinds of user. Imagine every possible scenario you might encounter with regard to who might ask you for a seat and how that request should be handled.

9   Identify an individual who will be responsible for handling requests for the software, keeping records of users, troubleshooting access concerns and identifying access issues that must be addressed by a policy body.

10   Recognize that time, effort and resources have to be dedicated to not only the acquirement of the licence, but also its oversight and appropriate use. Just as in the early years of QDAS use, many imagined the software would actually analyse the data . . . in the early years of QDAS scaling up, users often imagine the systemic piece will be magically absorbed by the organization. Do not believe it for a minute! Getting the site licence is only one piece of the puzzle; overseeing the licence takes work.

11   Set regular opportunities to report on successes and challenges to the policy-making group overseeing the licence. These are your allies and they can offer wonderful support for ensuring that the resource is well used by the organization.

12   Technical support will cover a wide gamut of issues from the simple and easy to solve in a technical manner (I can't download the software; my licence key isn't working) to the middling level (How do I open a project? How do you code? What is a case?) to the most complex (How do I use this tool with 5 research teams located in 10 different countries? How do I construct searches that will help me to answer this question?). As you can see, the technical questions are the simple ones . . . the hard ones are the questions that take you directly to the heart of qualitative data analysis. You will need to identify a person or process that will allow users to get directed to the resources that can best help them to solve their problems.

Building a community of learners

Providing QDAS support from within an organization to organizational users presents a unique set of opportunities and challenges. What works with QDAS, not surprisingly, is what works with technology scaling up in many realms. The best environment for robust QDAS use will support a network of resources distributed across a community of learners in which all can participate, selecting the level of assistance or involvement that makes best sense to their needs.

The ideal location for the QDAS network is within the network of qualitative researchers at the organization. If you have not already done so, we urge you to consider banding together formally to support qualitative research *and* QDAS use within that context. You will find many ways to support each other and your research goals, and, as a formal group, you will be able to speak to your administration with a louder voice.

Our experience demonstrates that a strong QDAS community of learners will provide multiple learning opportunities that, in turn, support the ongoing process of building internal resources and leadership for QDAS use. These opportunities will include one-on-one, formal training, and user group experiences.

On demand

For users of all levels there are questions that need a quick direct response. Sometimes the question can be answered by using the software's Help feature; sometimes a developer's web site FAQ section will have the answers or a web-based tutorial. In other cases, the response will come from a troubleshooter located at the software developer's firm. If the organizational contact person has experience with the software they may field the response. As new users are brought into the organizational base of QDAS use, efficiency will be gained by helping them to understand how they can help themselves. This means disseminating information about the supports and services they can access and how to do so.

Formal technical training

Formal training in the software is a necessity for almost all users. This may not be so in the future when QDAS is deeply integrated within qualitative research practice. At this juncture, however, when there are a mixture of users and non-users within organizations, it is advisable to provide formal training opportunities. Not to put too fine a point on it, QDAS is complex software requiring understanding of the ways the research design can be represented within the E-Project. Non-users may assume that as proficient software users, they will be able to make their way on their own, applying knowledge of other packages to the QDAS software they are adopting. They may not under-stand how their early decisions may affect their ability to use the more sophisticated features of the QDAS package at a later point in the research. Those who are not knowledgeable of qualitative data analysis may not recog-nize where they are making poor decisions in the set up of their E-Project in QDAS.

For all of these reasons and many more we could offer, we strongly urge organ-izations to provide new users with sound formal technical training. This train-ing can be provided by insiders and outsiders. It is essential, however, that trainers be well versed in a QDAS-based research design perspective.

User's group

Once the user base for the QDAS package is established, the formation of a user group is an easy way to provide a self-supporting way for organizational members to learn and grow in the software use. Again, this is another reason why you should start with one software package, as it will be difficult for users of multiple software packages to connect in this way. Going with one package will give the user group immediate 'umph'.

Topics can be selected by members. The informal and trusting atmosphere of a user's group allows all members – beginners or experienced users – to find a place in the group and contribute in meaningful ways. How often the group should meet will depend on the schedules of members, their needs and other organizational issues. Create a schedule that works for your group.

Opportunities for QDAS project analysis

An exceptional way for you to learn about good research design in QDAS is to share your E-Project with others as you design and conduct your study. This can happen in many ways through oversight from your supervisor or in consultation with your research colleagues. Your user's group may create opportunities for E-Project review. Also, outside consultants may offer 'master classes' in which E-Project review is the focus.

Through participation in such opportunities where you can share your E-Project at various stages of development and/or examine the E-Projects of others, you will have the opportunity to learn hands-on about what works in QDAS-based research design, what does not work and why. There is no place else that you can learn about E-Projects in quite the same way. The cases in this book are an attempt to provide you with just such a lens on project development. Through looking at many kinds of E-Project you can continue this same kind of learning in other venues.

It is critical that in sharing your E-Project, you attend to the issues of confidentiality that will be raised. This is not a barrier to public review of E-Projects, if appropriately addressed. The benefits of critique are many, and so it is important that researchers find ways to make it possible to engage in this way.

Workshops on related topics of interest

If you have taken our suggestion for creating a network of qualitative researchers who are using QDAS, you will find that every time you talk about qualitative research you are also talking about QDAS. You will not be able to separate the two. Thus, when you attend a workshop on ethics and qualitative research, you will naturally hear talk about the implications for QDAS. When you hear a presentation about a qualitative research study on a health issue, you will ask questions about the research design as it pertains to QDAS. Once it is grounded in you – everything about qualitative research is about QDAS – and, vice versa, everything about QDAS is about qualitative research. So the more you explore qualitative research, the richer your cache of knowledge about QDAS becomes.

Professional practices

Qualitative researchers are scattered across many disciplines and represented within many organizations and institutions. Despite this seeming distance among us, we also recognize ourselves as belonging to a single unique inter-disciplinary grouping of individuals committed to supporting the practice of qualitative research methodology at the most sophisticated and challenging level. In the coming years, practising our skills as qualitative researchers will require that we become fluent in the authoring and reading of the E-Project, which means that we must understand how to represent excellent qualitative research design within QDAS. Researchers who do not possess these skills will soon be considered unskilled or poorly trained. Just as we now assume that white-collar workers will be able to use word-processing programs, so, too, in the qualitative research world, QDAS will be considered essential. What are the implications of this development for the ways we oversee and police our disciplines and professional organizations? How can professional organizations support organizations and institutions to adopt responsible use of QDAS?

These general questions lead to questions of a more specific nature.

- Do we discuss these tools in professional settings? How do we have these discussions?
- Do we have standards for the use of these tools within professional practice?
- Have we developed standards for the presentation of research that uses these tools?
- Do we help institutions with whom our professional community interacts to understand why these tools are important, how they should be used and what constitutes best practices?
- Have we addressed the critical ethical questions that QDAS raises for our professional community? Have we communicated our findings to others?

As a field, we have only begun to enter into the possibilities of these conversations. We look forward to participating in these discussions, which promise to be rich in intellectual challenges.

The future of QDAS

In the early years of development, QDAS construction flourished in many Mom and Pop micro-businesses. As time has gone by and the need to keep up with the developments in operating systems, those micro-businesses that could scale up into small company status survived and others fell to the wayside. This story of development parallels software development narratives in a range of other areas (word processing and learning management systems are two good examples). It remains to be seen if one package will ultimately become dominant.

However, the tasks for which QDAS was developed – careful and deep analysis of textual and visual documents – is one that is required in many different fields. Indeed, this is the skill that is at the heart of advanced reading skills; that is the ability to interpret text and graphic documents. In this sense,

QDAS belongs to a class of software or software capacities dedicated to textual or visual analysis that runs the gamut from search engines to geographical information systems to various database systems. While we think of QDAS as unique to qualitative research, many of its features or capacities can be found in a variety of kinds of software. Many of the functions that could benefit QDAS (e.g. voice recognition software, coding tools for video, transcribing capacities, media-sharing strategies) are under development in a wide development of areas. As these new software possibilities move to the fore and are packaged in tools that can be made use of by qualitative researchers, they expand, reshape and challenge the landscape of QDAS.

We do not have a crystal ball that will tell us what the future of QDAS will hold, but we have lived with these new technologies long enough to know that we would be safe to say: Everything changes. Rather than attach oneself to a specific software or other tool, the more important thing is to understand the principles by which research design is represented with these new media. With these principles in mind one will be able to weather technological change, adapting to new tool possibilities as they emerge.

Appendix 1: Getting started in Qualitative Data Analysis Software

The range of software available

The Qualitative Data Analysis Software (QDAS) packages discussed in this book are all what are called 'theory building software'. This is the most common type of tool used to support qualitative data analysis. They combine code and retrieve functions with very sophisticated searches (both lexical and code-based searches) as well as network or diagram functions, visual displays of data, memoing and annotation facilities, some quantitative content analysis tools and possibilities for mixed methods analysis. We are not happy with the label – theory building – as there is an implication that the software itself builds the theory. In reality, they are theory-building support tools. The analyst(s) do(es) the theory building.

Other types of package to support qualitative data analysis are *code-and-retrieve* software (these packages were the first kind of software support tool for qualitative data analysis; they have mostly evolved into theory-building packages); *concordance* software (for quantitative content analysis on a corpus of text for the analysis of language use); and *text retrievers/content analysis* software (for finding data in very large databases but not coding them). There are also specific packages designed to support the analysis of audio and video data. However, many theory-building software packages also support audio and video analysis; e.g. ATLAS.ti and HyperResearch already support the analysis of audio and video while NVivo 8 will also support in a very sophisticated way the analysis of video, audio and graphics. More details about these various kinds of software tool can be found on the online QDA web site – http://onlineqda.-hud.ac.uk. The development of this web site was funded by the UK Economic and Social Research Council (ESRC) as part of its Research Methods Programme.

Making decisions about software

I (di Gregorio) am often asked which QDAS is the best. There is no one best software package. In reading through the cases in this book, it is evident that there are common issues researchers need to address regardless of the package. All the researchers whose QDAS projects have featured in this book have been working successfully in their chosen package. However, I sympathize with the new user trying to decide which of the wide range of QDAS they should adopt. This is a very dynamic field. The packages featured in this book are among the most popular packages and are available world-wide. They are being constantly developed so any statements comparing packages will rapidly go out of date. Yesterday's 'workarounds' are available as standard features today. In addition, it is difficult to judge a package by simply downloading it and playing with it. These are all complex packages and if you have never used such a package before, you will not have a clear idea of what to look for. A good guide for comparing packages has been produced by the CAQDAS project at the University of Surrey (Lewins and Silver 2007). They update their guide from time to time so it is best to check on their web site – http://caqdas.surrey.ac.uk for an up-to-date version. I will not attempt to duplicate their feature-by-feature description of each package. Instead, in tune with the approach of this book, I will raise the more general questions you need to address when choosing QDAS.

Context issue 1: Where will the researcher be located?

In Chapter 4 we looked at different kinds of setting where a researcher can be located. The researcher can be part of an organization such as a university or research institute; the researcher can be part of a network of researchers across the same organization or across different organizations; or, the researcher could be part of a more informal collaboration with another researcher or researchers. If you are located in an organization, you need to check whether that organization already has a site licence for any QDAS package. If it does have a licence there could be a community of users that you could tap into for support. This is an important criterion in determining which package to adopt. The existence of some users means that you could set up a support group, organize QDAS seminars, and so on if none already exist. QDAS licences may not be held centrally, so you may need to do some detective work to find users. You should look beyond your own department; in universities, qualitative analysts can be found in most social science departments as well as some of the arts departments, law departments and medical schools.

It is possible that your university or organization supports more than one QDAS. In which case, it is worth finding users of each QDAS and talking to them about their experience of using QDAS. If one package has a stronger group of users it is worth joining that group. It is important to check that your university or organization is using the most recent version of the software. Most QDAS companies issue service packs from time to time which fix bugs that may exist in the software and often adds additional functionality. If a central IT department is in charge of the purchase and management of the software, they may not be aware of these updates which have to be downloaded. It is also possible that they may be aware of them but not give them much importance. It is important to insist that the latest version is distributed in your organization; in particular, in this current phase when these packages are being improved very rapidly. In addition, when talking to current users about their experience of a package, check out which version they are using. If it is not the current version, their experience will be outdated. You can check which version is current by going to the developers' web sites (details in Appendix 5).

If your university or organization does not support any QDAS, then you will have to decide whether to go it alone and buy a personal copy for your own use or whether to try to get your institution to purchase a package. Purchasing your own copy of a package may be the quickest way to get a package in the short term. However, there may be longer-term benefits if you first identify other people who analyse qualitative data in your institution who may be interested in using QDAS. Together you could make a case for the purchase of QDAS on an organization-wide basis. The added benefit is that you will have identified a group of people who could function as a support group in your institution. You may also discover when trying to identify people who may be interested in using QDAS that a few people have already decided to go it alone and have purchased their own QDAS package and have already started to use software. Chapter 14 discusses in detail the issues that need to be considered when introducing QDAS in an organization.

Context issue 2: Is the researcher part of a team?

If you are part of a team it is best to check whether any members of the team have experience of using QDAS. It is best to build on any existing knowledge of QDAS use. However, a member of a team may have experience of one package, yet the institution where the team project is located only supports another package. The team may be forced to use the package the institution supports. The good news is that it is easier to learn another QDAS package once you have mastered one package. However, it is very important to get training as each package is structured differently. It is important not to be complacent about using a different package. As can be seen in this book, terminology varies from package to package as do the tools to use to represent the different elements of a research design, such as units of analysis, variables, and so on. You will have to rethink how to represent the research design in the new package.

Context issue 3: What are the researcher's skills and knowledge base?

Using a QDAS packages requires two separate skill sets – knowledge of qualitative data analysis and computer literacy. If you are new to analysing qualitative data it is important to take courses in qualitative research methods before attempting to learn QDAS. There are many approaches to analysing qualitative data and it is important you have a clear understanding of research methodology. Likewise, you need to feel comfortable using computers. All QDAS packages are complex pieces of software. While they are becoming much more user-friendly, they require basic computer skills such as fine mouse control, use of context menus, file management, backing up files, short cut keys, and so on. If you are not confident working with computers, it would be a good idea to study for the European Computer Driving Licence or the International Computer Driving Licence before starting to learn QDAS. Further information about the syllabus and where you can register for courses can be found on the European Computer Driving Licence Foundation web site – www.ecdl.com.

Design-related issues when choosing QDAS

The cases featured in this book could have been analysed in any QDAS package. It is true that the packages have different strengths and weaknesses but these strengths and weaknesses keep changing as new versions of each package are launched. Currently, any statements we make here comparing packages could well be out of date by the time of publication. Instead, we are listing a series of questions related to your research design you should consider if you have a choice of QDAS packages.

What kind of qualitative data am I collecting?

You should check what kind of files can be used with the various QDAS packages you are considering. Most QDAS are now able to import Word documents with most of their formatting features. Most are currently working on .pdf file importation and NVivo 8 is the first package to accept .pdf files. If you will be using multimedia data, you need to check which ones support videos, audio files and graphics. When downloading demo versions of the software, import a few of the various types of file you will want to use to check how they look in the software package. See how flexible they are in terms of resizing them once in the software and if there are alternative ways they can be viewed. Remember, you will be staring at the screen for a long time working on your data. How the data looks in the software is not a trivial issue.

If you have any data that is structured – such as a structured interview schedule or a focus group transcript – would it benefit from automatically coding for its structure? If so, you should check how the auto-coding features of each package work.

If you have a lot of data, you might want to check the facilities each package has for organizing that data.

How will my units of observation and units of analysis be represented?

For projects where there are more than one unit of analysis, you should look at how they can be represented in the software. You should look at the features that enable you to restrict the scope of the analysis to the various levels you will need.

How will my variables be represented?

You should check how variables are represented in the software. Can they be organized? Can they be combined? You should check the features that enable you to restrict analysis to certain variables and/or compare responses/themes by different variables. If you have a lot of variables, you should check how easy it is to create them and link them to your units of observation. Check whether they can be set up in Excel and imported into the software package. This could be a quick way to set them up, particularly if your project is being analysed by a team. Setting up the variables could be allocated to one team member who could set them up in Excel.

Am I using a mixed methods approach?

If you have quantitative data that relates to your unit(s) of observation, check to see how they can be represented in the software package. Usually, this would be the same way as how variables are represented in the software. The ability for the package to produce matrix tables would be useful for making comparisons.

Do I have a longitudinal study?

How can time be represented in the software? How can variables that change over time be handled? Can a timeline be generated? At the moment, handling longitudinal data in QDAS is a bit awkward but can be done (see Chapters 12 and 13). However, this is an area that could be developed in the future.

Am I working in a team?

How can teamwork be organized in the software? At the moment, teamwork can only be organized by each team member having a version of the project which then can be merged into one overall project. However, in the future that may change with the possibility of a project being located on a server and allowing access to multiple users. In the meantime, you should check how the merge process works in each package. You should also check the software's capacity to track inputs and changes made by different team members. If inter-coder reliability is important, does the software have tools to facilitate inter-coder reliability?

What kind of analysis support will I need?

All QDAS have powerful search tools that will retrieve combinations of codes across all the data or restricted to parts of the data. They vary in how the results are displayed so you should check the various display options. At the moment, only NVivo produces results that can be automatically added to the thematic database as new coding and which can be used to do further fine coding. All the packages allow for creating networks or diagrams but these vary in how they work and you should try them out to see what suits your style of analysis best. ATLAS.ti is the only package where the database is structured as a 'spider-web' of links. Its network tool can be used to see how parts of the data are linked, as well as adding new links to the data. Packages are now offering more visualization tools as different ways to see the data.

Balancing design issues with context issues

The above questions are the ones you should ask when you have a choice of QDAS packages. It is best to download demos of these packages and experiment with setting up the design of your project in them. However, often the context issues discussed earlier in this chapter may take precedence over the design issues – given the circumstances of your research. However, through the use of 'workarounds' it is possible to compensate for any weaknesses in the package you eventually adopt. At the time Rutherford and Gallo-Cruz (Chapter 8) were doing their research, ATLAS.ti 5 might have been the best choice for their project (a) because it supported graphics, and screenshots of the web sites could have been imported and coded in the project and (b) because Rutherford had previously used ATLAS.ti 5. However, given that the university Gallo-Cruz was in supported MAXqda, they decided to work in MAXqda. Through the use of a 'workaround' to represent the web sites together with MAXqda's strong analysis tools, they were able to do a very effective analysis of the data.

Commercial-related issues when choosing QDAS

Buying a QDAS package is an investment and the package should be seen as an essential tool for a qualitative analyst. We would recommend that professional qualitative analysts purchase their own package. However, universities need to invest in QDAS for their students and to support their staff. Research organizations, whether in the government, not-for-profit, or commercial sectors, need to invest in these tools to support their staff. Buying a site licence for a large number of users is a major investment. Commercial factors that need to be considered are the technical support arrangements the software companies provide and the long-term viability of the company. Before purchasing a package, it is worth investigating whether the company has a dedicated technical support office. It may be an idea to check the responsiveness of that office by sending a few technical questions based on the demo version of the software. If large amounts of licences are being purchased, it is worth seeing how flexible the company is in tailoring prices and usage terms to reflect your institution's particular needs. Finally, it is important to check how financially viable the company is. How many programmers do they employ? Will they be able to keep up with the competition in producing more user-friendly and technically enhanced software? Will they still be around in five years time?

We do not have all the answers but we encourage you to pose the questions. The software packages featured in this book are current viable options. However, we are aware that QDAS is in a very dynamic phase of development and changes are happening very quickly. These commercial issues should be given equal weight with the other issues we have discussed.

Getting expert help

Finally, do not attempt either to learn QDAS or implement its adoption in your organization without expert help. QDAS are complex packages and requires training by someone who not only is an expert in the package in question but who is also an experienced qualitative analyst. You need to understand not only how the software works but how it can be applied to your research. In addition, implementing the software in a team or for instructional purposes or across a research organization requires careful planning. It is best to bring in a consultant who has experience not only in the software but also in using it with teams or for instruction, and so on. Most of the QDAS companies have a web page which lists trainers and consultants but they currently do not take responsibility for the quality of those trainers. You do not want a PhD student to advise you on a complex research design or approach in which they have no experience. Check the credentials and experience of any expert you consider using. Ask for references.

Appendix 2: Checklist for representing the research design in the software featured in this book

Introduction

We have emphasized that the research design needs to be considered first when starting a project using QDAS. The same questions need to be addressed regardless of which software package you use. However, QDAS are structured differently and use different terminology. In addition, as a package is further developed, the terminology may change slightly. This is usually a response by the developers to make the software more user-friendly but it may be a bit confusing if you already know an earlier version. However, as you become more expert at reading E-Projects you will be able to recognize quickly such changes.

The research design questions

The following design questions are relevant for any piece of research. They are the core research design issues discussed in Chapter 2. The questions are written in a grid format so you can copy these grids from the book and fill in your answers to these questions.

Research topic/problem

Table A2.1 Research topic worksheet

State the research topic	
Motivation for topic choice (intellectual, personal, political, practical, theoretical, etc.)	
Research task: Reflect on motivations	
Research task: Challenge your key ideas about this topic	
Research task: Refine topic area	

Research questions

Table A2.2 Research questions worksheet

What kinds of question are you asking? (What? Why? How?)	
What is the best methodological approach to answer your questions? (e.g. an ethnographic study, grounded theory study, an evaluation, etc.)	
What theoretical frameworks can inform your study?	
What data collection methods can help you answer your questions?	
Research task: Identify the literature that is relevant for your research (Start literature review analysis in QDAS)	
Research task: Reflect on your research questions – modify them and your approach if necessary (Use any experiential knowledge you have of the topic and any new knowledge from the literature)	

Data collection

Table A2.3 Data collection worksheet

What kind of data are you going to use? (Primary data: interviews, focus groups, videos, photos, etc.) (Secondary data: data collected for other purposes; e.g. records on individuals, etc.) (Tertiary: data collected and analysed by others; e.g. census reports, etc.)	
What is the scope of your research? (Units of analysis; e.g. individuals, organizations, programmes, etc.; units of observation)	
What is your sampling strategy? (Census, probability, snowball, convenience, theoretical, etc.)	
Where is the research setting? (Natural setting, researcher setting, neutral setting)	
What is the time dimension for the research? (Snapshot, prospective longitudinal, retrospective longitudinal, historical)	

Research task: What ethical issues do the research question and data collection methods raise?
(Consider how you will address these issues to gain IRB approval)

Research task: What resources are required to conduct the research?
(Budget, staffing, training, equipment, software, etc.)

Research task: How will you negotiate access to research sites and/or study respondents?

Research task: Reflect on answers to above questions? Do you need to revise data collection strategy? Do you need to revise research questions?

Data handling and analysis

The way data is organized and handled varies among the different types of QDAS. The tables below are organized according to how to proceed with the four packages featured in this book. However, the same questions need to be addressed regardless of the package. These checklists are designed for those who have had some training in the software or can be used in conjunction with a training programme. They are not a substitute for training in QDAS.

ATLAS.ti 5 checklist

Table A2.4 ATLAS.ti 5 data handling and analysis checklist

Topic	Research design question	What you do in the software
Data organization	What kind of data am I collecting?	Create *document families* for the different kinds of data you will have
Data organization	Where will I store my data? (Note: ATLAS.ti is the only QDAS where data are not imported in an internal database. The data remain external to the program and the program records the path to where the data are located)	(a) Create a folder in Windows Explorer where you will save all the data files for your project (b) The simplest path option is the HU path – so make sure you save your HU in the folder where the documents are stored
Data format	Do my textual data have any structure to them? If so, will they benefit from automatic coding of that structure? (e.g. answers to open-ended questions from a survey)	Prepare the text in Word with unique identifiers for each section and a blank line (two hard returns) to separate out sections

(Continued overleaf)

Table A2.4 continued.

Topic	Research design question	What you do in the software
Scope of the research	What are my unit(s) of analysis and unit(s) of observation?	Create *document families* for your unit(s) of analysis and unit(s) of observation
Variables	What variables are relevant to my study? (e.g. demographic information, characteristics of organizations, etc.)	(a) For data where one document equals one person, use *document families* to represent variable values (b) For data where more than one person's data is in a document, use codes to represent variable values – you may be able to automatically code for these variables if you prepare the transcript as described for structured data under 'Data format' (above)
Mixed methods	Am I doing a mixed methods study? (combining quantitative and qualitative data)	The quantitative variables (such as the answers to closed-ended questions) are represented by variables – therefore either *document families* or codes as per variables above
Time frame	Do I have a longitudinal study?	Create *document families* for each time period
Thematic framework	Do I know in advance any of the broad topic areas I will be coding?	Create *code families* for broad topic areas and codes for any codes you know you will use in advance
Audit trail	How do I document the decisions I make as I develop the E-Project?	Create a memo called 'research journal' and record your research process. You can date/time stamp it to keep an audit trail
Analysis	As I analyse the data, how will I connect ideas and capture emergent questions?	Use *co-occurrence explorer* to check for relations in the data; you can filter for different parts of the data Write *memos* on your emergent thoughts on key issues. *Link* them to relevant codes or text Use *network tool* to explore existing links within data and to create new links
Analysis	How do I interrogate the data, to test the propositions I am forming and to ensure saturation of a concept?	Use of *query tool* to retrieve combinations of codes which can be restricted by filtering to different units of analysis or variables for comparison purposes Use of codes – primary – documents – table for code patterns – can be restricted to just certain documents and certain codes

MAXqda 2007 checklist

Table A2.5 MAXqda 2007 data handling and analysis checklist

Topic	Research design question	What you do in the software
Data organization	What kind of data am I collecting?	Create *text groups* for the different kinds of data you will have
Data organization	Will I have any *externals*? (Data which are relevant to the study but you decide not to import into the internal database – either because they are in a format not supported by the software or because you are going to analyse only part of them and it is not worth importing the whole document; e.g. long government reports)	(a) Create a folder in Windows Explorer where you will save any external files for your project (b) Create a new text in the MAXqda project and type your notes about that data. Create an external link to that data. MAXqda records the path to that file
Data format	Do my textual data have any structure to them? If so, will they benefit from automatic coding of that structure (e.g. answers to open-ended questions from a survey)?	Prepare all the texts in one Word document with a unique identifier which must be in the form of: #TEXTtextname. #CODEcodename Type text here #ENDCODE Etc.
Scope of the research	What are my unit(s) of analysis and unit(s) of observation?	Use *text groups* to represent the unit of analysis. For complex designs, *sets* can also be used to represent units of analysis. The *texts* themselves can represent the units of observation
Variables	What variables are relevant to my study? (e.g. demographic information, characteristics of organizations, etc.)	Create *attributes* to represent variables. Values are attached to *texts* which are assigned in a spreadsheet format
Mixed methods	Am I doing a mixed methods study (combining quantitative and qualitative data)?	The quantitative variables (such as the answers to closed-ended questions) are represented by *attributes*. Set up as for variables (see above)
Time frame	Do I have a longitudinal study?	Create *sets* for each time period
Thematic framework	Do I know in advance any of the broad topic areas I will be coding?	Create *codes* in *code system* for them

(Continued overleaf)

Table A2.5 continued.

Topic	Research design question	What you do in the software
Audit trail	How do I document the decisions I make as I develop the E-Project?	Use the logbook feature to document your research decisions. They will automatically be date/time stamped
Analysis	As I analyse the data, how will I connect ideas and capture emergent questions?	Write *code memos* on key codes Use *text memos* to comment on the text Use *MAXmaps* to explore existing relations in the data and to create new ones. You can check out co-occurring codes. Use *code matrix browser* for a quick visual overview of documents by codes Use *code relations browser* for a quick visual overview of codes by codes
Analysis	How do I interrogate the data, to test the propositions I am forming and to ensure saturation of a concept?	Use the *text retrieval* to retrieve combinations of codes which can be restricted by *activating* different units of analysis or variables for comparison purposes Use *code relations browser activated* for selected codes to look at patterns across the dataset Use *MAXdictio* for quantitative content analysis of text

NVivo 7/8 checklist

Table A2.6 NVivo 7/8 data handling and analysis checklist

Topic	Research design question	What you do in the software
Data organization	What kind of data am I collecting?	Create *document folders* for the different kinds of data you will have
Data organization	Will I have any *externals*? (Data which are relevant to the study but you decide not to import into the internal database – either because they are in a format not supported by the software or because you are going to analyse only part of them and it is not worth importing the whole document; e.g. long government reports)	(a) Create a folder in Windows Explorer for them (best in C drive or a network drive if you will always have access to the network) (b) Set your options in NVivo 7/8 to that folder so NVivo will find them automatically

Data format	Do my textual data have any structure to them? If so, will they benefit from automatic coding of that structure (e.g. answers to open-ended questions from a survey)? (In NVivo 8, you will be able to automatically code for speakers in videos; e.g. focus group videos)	Prepare the text in Word with a unique identifier using the 'styles' feature (Heading 1, Heading 2) to identify each section
Scope of the research	What are my unit(s) of analysis and unit(s) of observation?	Create *case nodes* to represent these units
Variables	What variables are relevant to my study (e.g. demographic information, characteristics of organizations, etc.)?	Set up *attributes* in *classifications* area. Assign values in the *casebook*
Mixed methods	Am I doing a mixed methods study (combining quantitative and qualitative data)?	The quantitative variables (such as the answers to closed-ended questions) are represented by *attributes*. Set up as for variables (see above)
Time frame	Do I have a longitudinal study?	(a) Create *document folders* for each time period (b) Create *sets* for each time period
Thematic framework	Do I know in advance any of the broad topic areas I will be coding?	Create *Tree Nodes* or *Free Nodes* for them
Audit trail	How do I document the decisions I make as I develop the E-Project?	Create a memo called 'research journal' and record your research process. You can date/time stamp it to keep an audit trail
Analysis	As I analyse the data, how will I connect ideas and capture emergent questions?	Write *memos* on key issues and use *see also links* to link them to relevant parts of the data In NVivo 8, use the various *charts* to visualize the data and to spot patterns Use *annotations* to comment on the text Use the *modeller* to explore existing relations in the data and to create new ones
Analysis	How do I interrogate the data, to test the propositions I am forming and to ensure saturation of a concept?	Use the *queries* to retrieve combinations of codes which can be restricted by filtering to different units of analysis or variables for comparison purposes Use *matrix queries* to look at patterns across the dataset

XSight 2 checklist

Table A2.7 XSight 2 data handling and analysis checklist

Topic	Research design question	What you do in the software
Data organization	What kind of data am I collecting?	You can import textual *documents* or textual project *artefacts* (e.g. client proposals, discussion guides, stimulus material). Use an alphanumeric naming convention to organize them in your preferred order
Data organization	Are you not going to transcribe audio or videotapes?	You can extract *verbatims, articulations* (summary statements) or *ideas* (your interpretations) and type them directly into the *analysis frameworks* (see 'Thematic framework' below)
Data format	Do my textual data have any structure to them? If so, will they benefit from automatic coding of that structure? (e.g. answers to open-ended questions from a survey)	Currently XSight does not have an automatic coding feature
Scope of the research	What are my unit(s) of analysis and unit(s) of observation?	Create *respondents* to represent these units of observation and analysis. *Subsamples* can also be used as units of analysis
Variables	What variables are relevant to my study (e.g. demographic information, characteristics of organizations, etc.)?	Set up *sample characteristics* to represent variables
Mixed methods	Am I doing a mixed methods study (combining quantitative and qualitative data)?	The quantitative variables (such as the answers to closed-ended questions) are represented by *sample characteristics*. Set up as for 'Variables' (see above)
Time frame	Do I have a longitudinal study?	(a) Create *tags* for each time period (b) Assign appropriate time *tag* for each commentary
Thematic framework	Do I know in advance any of the broad topic areas I will be coding?	Create *analysis frameworks* for them
Audit trail	How do I document the decisions I make as I develop the E-Project?	Create 'research journal' in the *reports* and record your research process

Analysis	As I analyse the data, how will I connect ideas and capture emergent questions?	Write memos on key issues in the *reports* area In *analysis frameworks* filter by topic area (*headings*) or by unit of observation (*samples*) to get a quick overview of the data Use *maps* to organize ideas and *link* them to the data
Analysis	How do I interrogate the data, to test the propositions I am forming and to ensure saturation of a concept?	Use the *queries* to retrieve *verbatims* and *articulations* which can be restricted by filtering to different units of analysis or variables for comparison purposes Split matrix tables for further comparisons

Your design framework

Copy the table and fill in the columns about your research.

Table A2.8 Your design framework worksheet

Unit(s) of analysis/units of observation (e.g. individuals, organizations, programmes, etc., i.e. what you want to compare)	Variables (e.g. region, position, etc.)	Time frame (e.g. snapshot, retrospective, longitudinal)	Data type(s) (e.g. interviews, focus groups, etc. – include numbers and length in time)	Thematic framework (e.g. major themes, codes, etc. if known in advance)	Purpose (e.g. evaluation, exploratory, policy development, etc.)

Terminology comparison across the software

A glossary is included as a separate appendix. Table A2.9 provides a quick reference guide for those who need to read an E-Project in a software package they do not know.

Table A2.9 Quick design terminology comparison across four packages

	ATLAS.ti	MAXqda	NVivo	XSight
Unit(s) of analysis	Document families or codes	Text or text groups or sets	Case nodes	Respondents or subsamples
Attributes	Document families or codes	Attributes table	Attributes Casebook	Sample characteristics
Data organization	Document families	Text groups	Document folders	Use alphanumeric workaround
Thematic frame	Code manager Code family manager	Code system	Free nodes Tree nodes	Analysis frameworks and headings

Appendix 3: Checklist for teams using Qualitative Data Analysis Software

Introduction

Chapter 4 discusses at length issues for teams using QDAS. This appendix pulls together as checklists and worksheets issues that teams using QDAS need to consider. Every team project is different so these checklists should be used as guides. For projects where there is little experience of QDAS, it is recommended that you bring in a consultant to help you set up team processes.

Managing teamwork – the QDAS supremo

Every QDAS team project needs to appoint one person who is knowledgeable of both qualitative analysis and the particular QDAS package to manage the teamwork in the QDAS. That person is responsible for setting up the E-Project to represent the design of the research (as discussed in Chapter 2 and Appendix 2), to write instructions on data preparation, to divide up the teamwork, to be responsible for quality control systems, and to bring together or merge the combined teamwork into one project. Table A3.1 is a checklist of the supremo's responsibility as well as tasks that can be delegated.

Know your team

Decisions about the composition of team members may be beyond the control of the QDAS supremo. Decisions could have been made for specialist knowledge reasons or for pragmatic reasons. However, the supremo needs to know the strengths and weaknesses of the team, particularly when deciding how to divide up the work in the E-Project. Table A3.2 is a checklist of possible combination of skills that can be found in a team. A third dimension to the table should be considered – experience of using QDAS. The table also recommends ways of matching skill to the division of the work in the E-Project.

One combination that should be avoided is to allocate all the work in the E-Project to novice analysts. Important analytical decisions are being made through coding and/or memoing in the E-Project and experienced analysts need to be involved in working in the E-Project. Also do not be tempted to wait until all the data has been collected to start the analysis in the E-Project. Team members could become overwhelmed. Start with a small amount of data. Copy Table A3.3 and map out your teams' skill set.

Table A3.1 Supremo checklist

Task	Supremo's responsibility	Tasks that can be delegated
Data preparation	Set up template for transcriptions; decide file formats for multimedia; decide if any data to remain external to internal database; quality control transcriptions	Transcription work itself
Design in QDAS	Set up project in QDAS following design framework	Bring in external consultant if necessary
Training in QDAS	Assess team members' QDAS skills	Bring in external consultant to train team. Training can be restricted to just the tasks team members will do
Division of work in team	Write instructions for each team member Send out to each team member their version of the E-Project	If supremo is not the principal investigator, will need to involve PI in this decision Involve team in discussion about division of work based on strengths and weaknesses (see Table A3.2 below)
Communication	Create flowchart of the communication process with team (see Figure A3.1) Decide on communication tools Contact point for requests for changes in E-Project by team members	Use IT support about range of communication tools available to team (e.g. common servers, email, WebEx, conference call systems, etc.)
Security	(a) Develop system for anonymizing respondents (b) Develop system for keeping databases secure (c) Develop secure modes for transporting databases	Use IT support about database system
Quality control	Create flowchart of quality control process	This could be delegated to more experienced team members (e.g. doing inter-coder reliability on selected codes)
Combining collective work	Contact point for receiving team members' E-Projects. Merging team members' E-Projects into one overall project	

Table A3.2 Team skill set checklist and recommended division of work

Qualitative analysis	Subject area specialist	Subject area generalist
Experienced	Experienced analyst Subject specialist **Assignment:** *code specialist area*	Experienced analyst Subject generalist **Assignment:** *code for more general topic areas; can code for specialist areas but should consult a subject specialist*
Novice	Novice analyst Subject specialist **Assignment:** *code specialist area – should be paired with or supervised by an experienced analyst*	Novice analyst Subject generalist **Assignment:** *code for broad topic areas only – should be paired with or supervised by an experienced analyst*

Table A3.3 Your team's skill set worksheet

Qualitative analysis	Subject area specialist	Subject area generalist
Experienced		
Novice		

The research process

The supremo should map out two flowcharts to manage the teamwork flow process. The first is the supremo's own flowchart which maps out their responsibilities and how they interact with the team. The second is an overview of the whole team process.

Figure A3.1 is an example flowchart for a QDAS supremo. Every project is different so supremos will have different flowcharts but Figure A3.1 gives you an idea of the kinds of thing you should include in a flowchart.

Figure A3.2 is an example of a team flowchart. Again, every team project will have different requirements and team flowcharts will vary. However, it is important to be clear about how team members will coordinate their work. Create your own flowcharts.

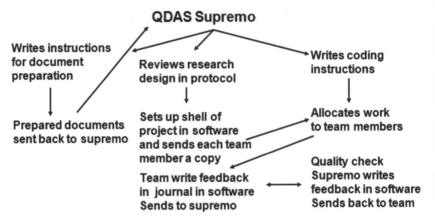

Figure A3.1 QDAS supremo example flowchart

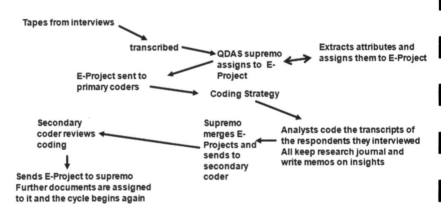

Figure A3.2 Research team example flowchart

Appendix 4: Glossary

Methodological terms

abduction A type of reasoning that involves looking at data and considering all possible explanations. Based on these considerations, the researcher forms hypotheses to confirm or disconfirm until they come up with the most plausible explanation.

CAQDAS An acronym for Computer-Assisted Qualitative Data Analysis Software.

coding The process of defining, chunking or dividing data into units with identifying tags. Codes can be a priori or emergent.

data, primary New data that the researcher collects specifically for their study.

data, secondary Data that had been collected for other purposes.

data, tertiary Data analysed by another research (e.g. summary reports).

deductive A type of reasoning that starts with general principles and moves to conclusions about specific instances.

E-Project Our term for the Electronic Project – a qualitative research project conducted within QDAS.

epistemology The branch of philosophy concerned with the nature and criteria of knowledge; what criteria knowledge must meet in order to be classifed as knowledge rather than belief.

ethics The branch of philosophy concerned with evaluating human action.

ethnography A method of research that describes social or cultural life based on direct and systematic observations.

experiential knowledge Knowledge based on an individual's own experience.

grounded theory A method of conducting qualitative research that relies on inductive analysis to build conceptual frameworks or theories. The researcher starts analysis while still collecting data so that initial analysis can inform further data collection.

hypothesis A testable statement about the relationships among variables which, if confirmed, will support a particular theory.

induction A type of reasoning that begins from studying a range of individual cases and from them develops patterns to form a conceptual category.

Institutional Review Boards (IRBs) A committee that is given responsibility by an institution to review research projects involving human subjects. The purpose is to ensure the protection, safety, rights and welfare of research participants.

longitudinal study Research that is conducted over a timespan – either retrospectively or prospectively – to examine changes over time.

matrix A rectangular display of data in rows and columns.

memo writing A process used in qualitative analysis to develop a researcher's thinking about their research and reflect on their ideas about their codes and their interrelationships. It helps the researcher to move into more abstract ways of conceptualizing their data.

method Method refers to the actual techniques used in collecting and analysing data (e.g. interviews, observations, examining documentation, etc.).

methodological congruence The consistency in logic from research question, methodological approach, research design, data collection techniques and approach to analysis.

methodology The study of how research should proceed (e.g what kind of logic is used, what criteria they have to satisfy, etc.).

models Models can be used in qualitative analysis as visual memos about relationships you think may be in the data. It is also a way to display existing relationships in data.

ontology The branch of philosophy about the assumptions a particular approach to social enquiry makes about the nature of social reality.

phenomenology A research approach where explanation must be grounded in the first order constructions (or the subjective perspectives) of respondents. These constructions are then related to the second order constructions of the social scientist.

QDAS An acronym for Qualitative Data Analysis Software and the preferred acronym used in this book.

reflexivity The researcher's examination of their research process in a way that enables others to assess whether the researcher's stance, assumptions, and so on influenced the outcome of their analysis.

representation The form in which the results of research can be presented. The E-Project offers a new way of presenting qualitative research.

research design The planning procedure for conducting a piece of research.

research nexus A term coined by Hesse-Biber and Leavy (2006: 20) to refer to the relationship between epistemology, theory and method.

sampling, theoretical Sampling used in a grounded theory approach where the purpose is to sample in order to develop theoretical categories. The purpose is not to generalize to particular populations. Hence, the researcher seeks data that will illuminate the developing categories until they reach the point where gathering more data will not reveal any more theoretical insights (theoretical saturation).

shell Our term that refers to the representation of the research design in QDAS.

supremo The QDAS coordinator in team research.

theory An organized system of knowledge.

trustworthiness The credibility, dependability and confirmability of qualitative research.

unit of analysis The basic entity which is the object of research. This can be individuals, organizations, programmes, and so on.

unit of observation The components of the unit of analysis. If your unit of analysis is the individual and you are interviewing these individuals, the unit of observation and the unit of analysis are one and the same. If your unit of analysis is organizations and you are interviewing individuals in the organizations, then the unit of observation is the individual.

validity The extent to which an analysis is accurate, correct or credible.

variable Any characteristic that can change or can be expressed as more than one value.

workarounds Our term for finding ways to work around what is possible with the existing technology to achieve our objectives for analysis.

QDAS specific terms

ATLAS.ti 5

absolute paths Absolute paths are full file names indicating where a file is located on a computer or server; for example C:\Project X\Project Data\Interview1.doc. ATLAS.ti does not have an internal database for the importation of data. Instead, the data remains where it is located on a computer or server and ATLAS.ti records the path to that data.

audio files ATLAS.ti supports most common audio formats (like WAV, MP3, WMA, SND, etc.) unless appropriate MCI drivers are not installed.

author More than one author can work on a project and by logging in ATLAS.ti keeps track of each author's work.

auto-coding The auto-coding tool finds text passages, selects a specified amount of text (e.g. the exact match, or spread to the surrounding word, sentence, or paragraph), and then codes the passages with a previously selected code. Auto-coding is useful when coding structural information like speaker turns in group interviews, or other sections that can easily be identified by a text search.

auto-colour mode The 'auto-colour' mode colours nodes along two dimensions according to their groundedness (i.e. the number of quotations to which they are linked) and their density (i.e. the number of other codes connected). Groundedness increases the red component, while density increases the blue component of the node colour. Auto-colour is restricted to nodes representing codes.

boolean operators Four boolean operators are available with the query tool: OR, XOR, AND and NOT.

codes Codes are typically short pieces of text referencing other pieces of text, graphical, audio or video data. Their purpose is to classify an often large number of textual or other data units.

comments Comments are short memos that can be attached to the whole project (useful for describing the project), whole documents (useful for basic information about the document), codes (useful for definitions of codes) and quotations (useful for annotating parts of the text).

cooccurrence explorer A tool to explore which codes cooccur (overlap) with other codes. It also shows which codes were used with each primary document.

copybundle Copybundling turns a project into one compressed file containing all associated files (primary document data sources, etc.). This file can be moved to another computer and unpacked to any location. The copybundle function can be conveniently used to back up projects and to move projects between computers.

documents The data for your project; these can be textual data, audio data, graphics or videos. The software calls all these primary documents (PDs).

embedded objects Objects like Excel tables, images, PowerPoint slides, formulas and audio or video files can be embedded in primary documents, comments and memos. Most objects can be activated and edited within ATLAS.ti without the need for explicitly opening the application that was used to create them.

families Families are a way to form sets of primary documents, codes and memos for easier handling. Families are often used for filtering, and when formulating queries in the query tool in order to restrict the scope of a query to, for example, respondents with particular characteristics.

filter Filtering is a way to restrict your work in a project to just certain documents, codes or memos with certain characteristics.

graphic files More than 20 graphic file formats are accepted by ATLAS.ti as valid data sources for PDs, including BMP, JPEG and TIFF. Scanners often produce TIFF and digital cameras usually create JPEG images.

hermeneutic unit The hermeneutic unit or HU simply means your ATLAS.ti project. It is the container that holds everything relevant to your E-Project (e.g. data, codes, networks, memos, etc.).

HTML ATLAS.ti can convert your project into HTML format. One use is to create a web publication of your project.

HU editor The HU editor is the main window and usually the first thing you see after starting the system. It lets you manage, view and annotate primary documents, which are typically the starting point of your research.

hypertext A hypertext is a network with text (or other media) as nodes. The original text is taken out of its linear form. This is a good way to track reactions to a suggestion in a focus group or highlighting contradictions in an interview. The relevant passages of text are shown in the network view where links such as 'contradicts', 'supports', and so on can be added.

margin area The margin area is next to the primary document and displays the codes, hypertext and memos that are linked to different quotations (passages) in it.

network An ATLAS.ti network is the set of *all* objects and their links inside the hermeneutic unit (HU). It exists independently of any display-oriented characteristics (layout, colour, line width, etc.). It is the *logical structure* of the HU's objects. It exists even before the first network view is created.

network view A network view is typically only a subset of this global structure of nodes and links combined with an individual layout of nodes. It is like viewing the same thing; that is, the network, from different angles and with different pieces visible.

node Nodes are the objects which are displayed in a network view. They can be codes, memos, primary documents, quotations, families and other network views.

object crawler With the object crawler, you can search all the parts of your project within ATLAS.ti that contain text. Searches are not restricted to just textual primary documents: codes, memos, quotations, all families, code-code links, hyperlinks, and the HU can be searched. In addition, the scope of the search can be limited to certain fields.

object managers There are object managers for primary documents, quotations, codes and memos. They allow you to not only access the particular object but also have additional functions – such as including dates when an object was created, where a primary document is located on the computer, and so on. They can also be used to drag and drop an object into a network.

operands Operands refers to code and code families which can be used to construct a query in the query tool.

operators Operators are the tools to combine operands when constructing a query in the query tool. In ATLAS.ti these are boolean, proximity and semantic operators.

PD family table This is a matrix table between primary documents and their families. These can be exported and/or imported from Excel.

primary documents Primary documents refer to your data in ATLAS.ti. This includes multimedia data as well as textual data.

proximity operators Proximity operators are used when constructing queries in order to retrieve data. Proximity describes the spatial relation between quotations. Quotations can be embedded in one another, one may follow another, and so on.

query tool The query tool is used for retrieving quotations using the codes they were associated with during the process of coding. A query is a search expression built from operands (codes and code families) and operators (e.g. NOT, AND; OR, etc.) that define the conditions that a quotation must meet to be retrieved (e.g. all quotations coded with both codes A and B).

quotations A quotation is a segment from a primary document that is interesting or important to the user. In textual documents, they are passages of text; in graphic documents they are a section of the graphic; in video or audio files, they are a segment of the file.

semantic operators Semantic operators are used in the query tool when you want to retrieve data based on relations you created between codes in the network tool.

special paths Absolute paths to documents are exact and inflexible. To overcome this restriction, a more flexible reference type is offered: special paths. This is done through two special path variables, HUPATH and TBPATH. The HUPATH is the folder in which the HU is stored. While there is one HUPATH for every opened HU, there is only one TBPATH, which is explicitly set by the user.

super codes A super code is a saved query expression (a combination of codes) created in the query tool. It automatically updates itself as more coding is done.

super family Super families are created when you combine families using boolean operators.

text search The text search tool is used to search within primary texts for the occurrence of specific text strings that match a designated string or pattern.

XML ATLAS.ti can convert automatically a project as an XML export. This gives you the flexibility to use XML stylesheets to customize outputs from the project.

MAXqda 2007

activation Activation is the process by which you retrieve data from MAXqda. You activate the text(s) from which you wish to retrieve data and you activate the specific code(s) you wish to retrieve from the activated texts.

active codes Codes that have been activated.

active texts Texts that have been activated.

attributes Attributes are variables. Their values are linked to the texts in your project. They are managed as a table.

code matrix browser The matrix provides an overview of how many text segments from each text have been assigned to a specific code (for all the codes).

code relations browser This matrix looks at the cooccurrence of codes. It shows how many text segments any two codes are attached to.

code system The code system is displayed in the code system window. Codes can be organized hierarchically as a catalogue system in a code tree.

code tree The code tree includes codes with all their sub-codes.

codeline The codeline gives a picture of the coding in a piece of text. The X-axis displays the paragraphs of the text and the Y-axis displays the codes. Clicking on a point in the matrix will display the particular paragraph in question.

colour coding Colour coding is a way to mark up the text as you would with a highlighter pen. There are four colours you can use to highlight the text and the text is coded with the name of the colour.

crosstabs Crosstabs is a matrix table between attributes and codes.

document system The document system is the container that holds all the texts in your project.

external links External links are links to web sites or files on your computer from within a text in the text browser. They are displayed like hyperlinks.

hyperlinks Text files with hyperlinks can be imported into MAXqda with the links intact. Hyperlinks can point to any file or web page.

lexical search Lexical searches are the way you can search for words or phrases in your texts or memos.

logbook The logbook is where you write your research journal or diary.

MAXdictio MAXdictio is the quantitative content analysis add-on module.

MAXmaps MAXmaps is the graphics add-on module that allows you to create models in MAXqda.

retrieved segments Retrieved segments are the number of segments (passages of text) that have been assigned to a particular code. When doing searches the retrieved segments are listed in the retrieved segments window.

sets Sets are temporary groups of text that allow you to restrict the scope of a search to a particular group of texts. The texts are not duplicated; the texts in the set are short cuts to the text.

text browser The text browser is your main working area. It is here that you code texts, write memos and insert external links.

text comparison chart The text comparison chart is a matrix table which displays texts in the rows and paragraphs in the columns. This is useful for the analysis of structured texts and allows you to compare coding across the texts.

text links Text links are used to link segments of text within a text or across texts. They are created as hyperlinks.

text preprocessor The text preprocessor allows you to import structured and pre-coded text files. They need to be prepared in a certain way in Word in order for the preprocessor to automatically code them.

text retrieval Text retrieval is the way you retrieve coded text. Simple retrieval is by activating texts and codes. More complex retrievals can be done by using boolean or proximity operators.

TextPortrait TextPortrait is a visual tool that shows the sequence of codes for a selected text. The codes need to be colour coded in order to use this feature.

texts Texts refer to the documents in your project.

weight filter It is possible to apply weights to your codes – from 0–100. You can then filter for coded segments with certain weights.

NVivo 7/8

advanced find Facility used to find project items based on specific criteria. You access advanced find by clicking options on the find bar (at the top of list view).

ancestor node Tree nodes or cases above a selected node.

annotation Text that can be linked to selected content in a source – like scribbled notes in the margin.

attribute A classification or fixed characteristic of a case, such as gender, age or location.

attribute value The values of an attribute. For example, for the attribute of gender – 'male' or 'female' – would be the attribute values.

audio Source materials such as recorded interviews, music, sound effects and other forms of audio that may be relevant to your research. Types of audio files that can be imported into NVivo include *.mp3, *.wma and *.wav. An audio source contains the audio file and a transcript column.

auto code A quick way of coding that uses heading styles or paragraph numbers to create nodes and code at them.

boolean operator The use of AND, OR or NOT to combine search terms.

case A special kind of node – the only kind to which you can attach attributes such as gender or age. You can use cases to gather content about a person, site, institution or other entity involved in your research. Like tree nodes, case nodes can also be organized in hierarchies.

casebook A matrix displaying cases, attributes and attribute values. You can create cases, attributes and values in NVivo or you can import them from a tab-separated text file. To open the casebook, on the tools menu click casebook > open casebook.

child node A node below a parent node.

classification In NVivo, 'classification' refers to relationship types and attributes. Relationship types provide a way of 'classifying' relationships and attributes provide a way of 'classifying' cases.

coding Selecting source content and defining it as belonging to a particular topic or theme. By creating nodes and coding at them, you can catalogue your ideas and gather material by topic.

coding density Areas in a source or node in which most coding occurs. The coding density bar is visible when you display coding stripes. The colour graduations indicate the coding density from light grey (minimal coding) to dark grey (maximum coding).

coding excerpt A passage of text coded at a node. When exploring a node, you can set display options for coding excerpts (view>coding excerpts).

coding reference An occurrence of coding. When you open a node, you can see all the references to source material that are gathered there.

coding stripes Coloured stripes that enable you to see coding in a source or node.

descendent node Tree nodes or cases below a selected node.

detail view The bottom-right pane in NVivo. You explore documents, nodes and models in this view. You can choose to 'undock' detail view if you want to work with sources, nodes or models in a separate window.

document Source material such as field notes, transcripts, interviews, literature reviews or whatever material that is relevant to your project. You can 'code' a document (or any part of it) to categorize the information that it contains. You can import documents or create them in NVivo.

embed To store a media file inside your NVivo project as opposed to linking to a file stored externally.

external Source material that cannot be imported into NVivo. This might include items such as newspaper articles, books, video footage or audio tape. You can use the external to represent the unimportable material and record any notes or summaries that can be coded as required.

folder A place in navigation view for storing your project items. You can create your own folders for organizing sources, queries and models.

free node A free node is a 'standalone' node that has no clear logical connection with other nodes and does not easily fit into a hierarchical structure. You can convert a free node into a tree node by moving it into a tree node folder.

hyperlinks A link from content in a source to a file or URL outside of your NVivo project.

links In NVivo, links refer to memo links, annotations and 'see also' links.

list view The top-right pane in the NVivo window. You view the contents of your NVivo folders in list view.

log entry Comments, descriptions, notes, hyperlinks or ideas entered against the whole or portion of the image in a picture source. A picture source may or may not contain a log entry.

matrix A matrix is a collection of nodes resulting from a matrix coding query.

memo A type of source that you might use to record thoughts and observations. If a memo is related to a particular source or node you can create a 'memo link' and link the two together.

model A visual representation of your project and its contents.

navigation view The panel on the left side of the NVivo window. It contains buttons that enable you to access project items.

node A container for a theme or topic within your data. For example, you can create a node called 'community' and code all community-related data at it. When you open the node you can see all the community-related data gathered in one place. Types of node include free nodes, tree nodes, cases, relationships, matrices and results.

parent node A top tree node or case which is above other nodes in a hierarchy.

picture A type of source that contains an image file and log entries.

query A way of asking questions about your data. You can save a query and run it as your project progresses.

relationship A node that defines the connection between two project items. For example, the relationship between two cases (Anne loves Bill) or between two nodes (poverty impacts health).

relationship type A word or words (usually verbs) which define the relationship between two project items. For example, 'impacts', 'causes', 'employs', 'loves' and so on. Relationship types also have a direction.

results A node or list of project items resulting from a query. You can store a results node in the queries results folder or move to the main node system for coding.

see also link A link from selected content in a source or node to selected content (or entire content) in another source or node.

set A collection of short cuts to specified project items.

shadow coding Indirect coding in an audio or video source – when you code a transcript entry, the corresponding portion of the media is 'shadow coded'.

When you view coding stripes, this 'indirect' coding appears as a shadow on a coding stripe.

sibling node Tree nodes or cases that share the same parent node.

source In NVivo, 'sources' is the collective term for your research materials anything from hand-written diaries to interview transcripts in Microsoft Word format. You store sources in the documents, externals or memos folders.

timespan A timespan is the duration of time for a transcript entry. For example, Jane spoke from the two-minute point to the ten-minute point (00:02:00–00:10:00). When importing transcript entries from a table, you can include a timespan for each row in the table.

transcript Contains audio or video transcriptions against specific timespans. You can also include notes, hyperlinks or comments in the transcript or content column as needed in your research. Transcripts can be coded on their own or as part of a specific timespan.

tree node Nodes that are organized in a hierarchical structure moving from a general category at the top (the parent node) to more specific categories (child nodes). You can use them to organize nodes for easy access, like a library catalogue.

video Source materials such as focus group discussion videos, television ads and other forms of video that may be relevant to your research. Types of video file that can be imported into NVivo include *.mpg, *.mpeg, *.wmv, *.avi and *.mov. A video source contains the video file and a transcript column.

XSight 2.0

analysis frameworks A structure for inputting, analysing and interpreting your research findings. Your thematic framework is in here.

articulations Commentaries representing what the respondent said, expressed in the words of the researcher. Your summaries of what the respondent said.

brand sort An analysis framework that facilitates the division of brands into discrete segments based on shared characteristics/requirements/needs or benefits.

category A term used to group brands as part of a brand sort exercise.

commentaries The data you enter as articulations, verbatims and ideas in an analysis framework.

concept analysis Developing and evolving concepts based on respondent feedback as facilitated in a concept analysis framework.

documents Transcripts, diaries, client proposals, discussion guides or any document that you import into a project.

generic analysis framework A flexible structure for inputting, analysing and interpreting data that can be used for most research projects.

headings A topic or theme used to categorize respondent feedback in a generic or concept analysis framework. In brand sort and picture sort analysis frameworks headings are categories, brands and pictures.

ideas Researcher observations and insights in analysis frameworks or maps.

map A diagram that provides a visual way of organizing ideas and insights.

overall An option you can select in analysis frameworks that enables you to add ideas at a higher level, without selecting a specific sample or heading. For example, click <<overall>> in the samples list, to add an idea to a heading that is not related to a specific sample.

picture sort A projective exercise where respondents are asked to associate a selection of different visual images with a number of brands.

presentation A draft slide presentation that you can create using data from analysis frameworks, queries and maps. Export the presentation to PowerPoint for final formatting.

project artefact A document type that includes client proposals, discussion guides, concept statements and other materials related to the research.

project data A document type that includes transcripts, typed notes, diaries, self-completions and other materials containing your research data.

query A method of extracting project information based on specified criteria. For example, you could use a query to extract all the verbatims for a selected heading. You can save queries and run them as required.

report A draft summary that you can create using data from analysis frameworks, queries and maps. Export the report to Microsoft Word for final formatting.

respondent A group or individual providing feedback in a research project.

sample characteristic Demographic information about a respondent (e.g. gender, ethnicity, income, marital status and age).

segment The category/brand association as defined by respondents in a brand sort analysis framework.

sort The brand/picture association as defined by respondents in a picture sort analysis framework.

source The document from which a commentary was copied.

Subsample A combination of respondents (potentially based on sample characteristics) that can be created for efficient data input and analysis. For example, you could create a subsample consisting of male respondents.

tag A visual symbol used to classify commentaries in analysis frameworks and maps. For example you could add a tag to all the 'great quotes'.

template A skeleton project that can be used as the basis of new projects.

verbatims Commentaries representing direct quotations from a research respondent.

Appendix 5: Resources

Software featured in this book

ATLAS.ti 5
Scientific Software Development GmbH

http://www.atlasti.com

MAXqda 2007
VERBI Software. Consult. Sozialforschung. GmbH

http://www.maxqda.com

QSR NVivo 7/8
QSR XSight 2
QSR International Pty Ltd

http://www.qsrinternational.com

QDAS discussion forums

Each of the developer's web sites above have FAQs on their web sites for their software. In addition, each run their own user discussion forums which you can access through the developer web site (see above).

Qual-software@jiscmail.ac.uk is a general QDAS discussion email list run by the CAQDAS Networking Project at the University of Surrey. To join email: jiscmail@jiscmail.ac.uk

SUBJECT: Leave blank

BODY: Join Qual-Software [your name]

QDAS training and support

SdG Associates and SdG Knowledge Ltd.

Silvana di Gregorio's training and consultancy business based in London, UK and Boston, USA. Workshops and Masterclasses in ATLAS.ti 5 and NVivo 8. On-site training and consulting in ATLAS.ti, NVivo, MAXqda and XSight.

www.sdgassociates.com

Silvana@sdgassociates.com

On-line CAQDAS and Qualitative Data Analysis

University of Huddersfield and University of Surrey, ESRC Research Methods Project

http://onlineqda.hud.ac.uk

CAQDAS Networking Project

University of Surrey
Offers training and consultancy services

http://caqdas.soc.surrey.ac.uk

Qualitative Research Network: University of Massachusetts-Lowell

Online training in NVivo 7 and 8

http://continingued.uml.edu/qualitativeresearch.htm

Judith_Davidson@uml.edu

References

Agar, M. (1991) The right brain strikes back, in N. G. Fielding and R. M. Lee (eds.) *Using Computers in Qualitative Research*. Newbury Park, CA: Sage Publications.

Audit Commission (2005) *The Framework for Comprehensive Performance Assessment of District Councils from 2006: Consultation Document*. London: Audit Commission Publications.

Audit Commission (2006) *The Framework for Comprehensive Performance Assessment of District Councils from 2006: Analysis of Consultation Responses* (Summary Report). London: Audit Commission Publications.

Barone, T. (2001) *Touching Eternity: The Enduring Outcomes of Teaching*. New York: Teachers College Press.

Bazeley, P. (2007) *Qualitative Data Analysis with NVivo*. Thousand Oaks, CA: Sage.

Bazeley, P. and Richards, Lyn (2000) *The NVivo Qualitative Project Book*. Thousand Oaks, CA: Sage Publications.

Blaikie, N. (1993) *Approaches to Social Inquiry*. Cambridge: Polity Press.

Blaikie, N. (2000) *Designing Social Research*. Oxford: Polity Press.

Blumer, H. (1969) *Symbolic Interactionism*. Englewood Cliffs, NJ: Prentice Hall.

Bogdan, R. and Biklen, S. (2007) *Qualitative Research for Education: An Introduction to Theories and Methods*. Boston, MA: Pearson.

Cabinet Office (2007) *Better Regulation Executive* (www.cabinetoffice.gov.uk/regulation/consultation/government: accessed 6 February).

Center for Leadership Studies (1993) *Leadership Effectiveness and Adaptability Description (LEAD) Survey*. Center for Leadership Studies: Escondido, CA (www.situational.com/).

Chadwick, B. A., Bahr, H. M. and Albrecht, S. L. (1984) *Social Science Research Methods*. Englewood Cliffs, NJ: Prentice Hall.

Charmaz, K. (2006) *Constructing Grounded Theory*. Thousand Oaks, CA: Sage.

Clifford, J. and Marcus, G. (eds.) (1986) *Writing Culture: The Poetics and Politics of Ethnography*. Berkeley: University of California Press.

Coia, P. (2006) How a global law firm works with NVivo 7. *Nsight*, Issue 29, June: QSR.

Creswell, J. (2003) *Research Design: Qualitative, Quantitative and Mixed Methods Approaches*. Thousand Oaks, CA: Sage Publications.

Creswell, J. (2007) *Qualitative Inquiry and Research Design: Choosing Among Five Traditions* (2nd ed). Thousand Oaks, CA: Sage.

Davidson, J. (2005a) Genre and qualitative research software: the role of 'the project' in the post-electronic world of qualitative research. Paper presented at the American Educational Research Association Annual Meeting, Montreal, CA, April.

Davidson, J. (2005b) Learning to 'read' NVivo projects: implications for teaching qualitative research. Paper presented at the 2nd Teaching Qualitative Research using QSR Products Conference, University of Wisconsin, Madison, WI, April.

Davidson, J. (2005c) Reading 'the project': qualitative research software and the issue of genre in qualitative research. Paper presented at the 1st International Congress of Qualitative Inquiry, University of Illinois, Champaign-Urbana, IL, April.

Davidson, J. and Olson, M. (2003) School leadership in networked schools: deciphering the impact of large technical systems on education, *International Journal of Leadership in Education*, 6(3): 261–81.

Declercq, A. (2002) Coding: the problem of making choices. *Nsight*, Issue 17: QSR.

Denzin, N. and Lincoln, Y. (eds.) (1994) *Handbook of Qualitative Research*. Thousand Oaks, CA: Sage Publications.

Department of Health (2005) *Research Governance Framework for Health and Social Care* (2nd ed). London: HMSO.

di Gregorio, S. (2000) Using NVIVO for your literature review. Paper presented at the Conference on Strategies in Qualitative Research: Issues and Results from Analysis Using QSR NVivo and NUD*IST, Institute of Education, London, 29–30 September.

di Gregorio, Silvana (2001) Teamwork using QSR N5 software: an example from a large-scale national evaluation project, *NSight Newsletter*, November: QSR.

di Gregorio, S. (2003) Analysis as cycling: shifting between coding and memoing in using qualitative software. Paper presented at the Conference on Strategies in Qualitative Research: Methodological Issues and Practices Using QSR NVivo and NUD*IST, Institute of Education, London, 8–9 May.

di Gregorio, S. (2005a) Software tools to support qualitative analysis and reporting. Paper presented at the Conference on Business Intelligence Group, The New B2B: A Widening Horizon, Chepstow, 11–13 May.

di Gregorio, S. (2005b) Using NVIVO in an iterative way. Paper presented at the 6th International Strategies in Qualitative Research Conference, University of Durham, 21–23 September.

di Gregorio, Silvana (2006a) Research design issues for software users. Paper presented at the 7th International Conference on Strategies in Qualitative Research, University of Durham, 13–15 September.

di Gregorio, S. (2006b) The CMS Cameron McKenna project – how it looks in NVivo 7. *Nsight*, Issue 29, June: QSR.

di Gregorio, S (2007) Software-Instrumente zur Unterstutzung qualitativer Analyse, in R. Buber and H. Holzmuller (eds.) *Qualitative Marktforschung: Konzpete, Methoden, Analysen*. Wiesbaden, Germany: Gabler.

Directive 95/46/EC of the European Parliament and of the Council of 24 October 1995 on the protection of individuals with regard to the processing of personal data and on the free movement of such data. *Official Journal L 281, 23/11/1995 P. 0031–005*.

Disability and Rehabilitation Research Project on Emerging Disability and Systems Change (www.communityinclusion.org/project.php?project_id=5: accessed 19 December 2007).

Eisner, E. (2002) *The Educational Imagination: On the Design and Evaluation of School Programs* (3rd ed). Upper Saddle River, NJ: Merrill Prentice Hall.

Ellis, C. (2004) *The Autoethnographic I: A Methodological Novel about Autoethnography*. Walnut Creek, CA: Alta Mira Press.

Ereaut, G. (2002) *Analysis and Interpretation in Qualitative Market Research*. London: Sage.

Ereaut, G. and di Gregorio, S. (2002) Qualitative data mining. Paper presented at the AQR Conference, London, 6 June.

Ereaut, G. and di Gregorio, S. (2003) Can computers help analyse qualitative data? Paper presented at the AQR Conference, London, 6 June.

Ereaut, G. and Segnit, N. (2006) Warm words: how are we telling the climate story and can we tell it better?, Institute for Public Policy Research, London.

ESRC (2005) *Research Ethics Framework*. Swindon: Economic and Social Research Council.

Fielding, N. and Lee, R. (2007) Honouring the past, scoping the future. Plenary paper presented at CAQDAS 07: Advances in Qualitative Computing Conference, Royal Holloway, University of London, 18–20 April 2007.

Fine, M. (1994) Working the hyphens: reinventing self and other in qualitative research, in N. K. Denzin and Y. S. Lincoln (eds.) *Handbook of Qualitative Research*. Thousand Oaks, CA: Sage Publications.

Flick, U. (1998) *An Introduction to Qualitative Research*. London: Sage Publications.

Frow, J. and Morris, M. (2003) Cultural studies, in N. K. Denzin and Y. S. Lincoln (eds.) *The Landscape of Qualitative Research: Theories and Issues*. Thousand Oaks, CA: Sage.

Geertz, C. (1988) *Works and Lives: The Anthropologist as Author*. Stanford: Stanford University Press.

Gibbs, G. (2002) *Qualitative Data Analysis: Explorations with NVivo*. Buckingham, UK: Open University Press.

Gilbert, L. (1999) Reflections of qualitative researchers on the uses of qualitative data analysis software: an activity theory perspective. PhD thesis, University of Georgia, Athens, GA.

Glesne, C. (2006) *Becoming Qualitative Researchers: An Introduction* (3rd ed). Boston, MA: Pearson.

Goetz, J. and LeCompte, M. (1984) *Ethnography and Qualitative Design in Educational Research.* San Diego, CA: Academic Press, Inc.

Hesse-Biber, S. N. and Leavy, P. (2006) *The Practice of Qualitative Research.* Thousand Oaks, CA: Sage Publications.

Jacobson, D. (1991) *Reading Ethnography.* Albany: State University of New York Press.

Janesick, V. J. (2000) The choreography of qualitative research design, in N. K. Denzin and Y. S. Lincoln (eds.) *Handbook of Qualitative Research.* Thousand Oaks, CA: Sage Publications.

Kouzes, J. and Mico, P. (1979) Domain theory: an introduction to organizational behavior in human service organizations, *Journal of Applied Behavioral Science,* 19, 449–69.

Kuhn, S. and Davidson, J. (2007) Thinking with things, teaching with things: enhancing student learning in qualitative research through reflective use of things. *Qualitative Research Journal, 7*(2), 63–75.

Lawrence-Lightfoot, S. and Davis, J. D. (1997) *The Art and Science of Portraiture.* San Francisco, CA: Jossey-Bass.

Layder, D. (1998) *Sociological Practice: Linking Theory and Social Research.* London: Sage Publications.

Layder, D. (1993) *New Strategies in Social Research.* Cambridge: Polity Press.

Lewins, A. and Silver, C. (2007) *Using Software in Qualitative Research: A Step-by-step Guide.* Thousand Oaks, CA: Sage Publications.

Lofland, J. (1971) *Analyzing Social Settings: A Guide to Qualitative Observation and Analysis.* Belmont, CA: Wadsworth Publishing Company.

Lofland, J. and Lofland, L. (1995) *Analyzing Social Settings: A Guide to Qualitative Observation and Analysis* (3rd ed). Belmont, CA: Wadsworth Publishing Company.

Mandel, L. (2007) Doing what it takes: the impact of organizational issues on Massachusetts School-Based Health Center Success. Heller School for Social Policy and Management, Brandeis University, May, Ann Arbor: ProQuest/UMI Dissertation Publishers, UMI Number: 3259732.

Marshall, C. and Rossman, G. (1989) *Designing Qualitative Research.* London: Sage Publications.

Mason, J. (2002) *Qualitative Researching.* London: Sage Publications.

Maxwell, J. A. (1996) *Qualitative Research Design: An Interactive Approach.* Thousand Oaks, CA: Sage Publications.

Miles, M. and Huberman, A. (1994) *Qualitative Data Analysis* (2nd ed). Thousand Oaks, CA: Sage Publications.

Mills, C. W. (1959) Appendix: on intellectual craftsmanship, in C. W. Mills *The Sociological Imagination.* New York: Oxford University Press.

Mori Social Research Institute (2005) Views of new deals for communities – Focus Group Report, Research Study conducted for the Neighbourhood Renewal Unit, ODPM.

Morse, J. M. and Richards, Lyn (2002) *Readme First for a User's Guide to Qualitative Methods.* Thousand Oaks, CA: Sage Publications.

Nadler, D., Tushman, M. and Nadler, M. (1997) *Mapping the Organizational Terrain [In] Competing by Design: The Power of Organizational Architecture.* New York: Oxford University Press.

Nasukawa, Tetsuya (2006) TAKMI (text analysis and knowledge mining) and sentiment analysis, IBM Research, Tokyo Research Laboratory. Paper presented at Agenda Setting Workshop: Bridging Quantitative and Qualitative Methods for Social Science using Text Mining Techniques, National Centre for e-Social Science, Manchester, 28 April.

Office of Public Sector Information (1998) *Data Protections Act 1998.* London: HMSO.

Penna, S. (2007) Beyond planning a field trip: a case study of the effect a historical site's educational resources have on the practices of four urban eighth grade social studies teacher. Unpublished dissertation, University of Massachusetts Lowell.

Pool, R. (2005) Increasing the accuracy of sexual behaviour and adherence data, in B. Saxena, N. Chandhiok, W. Stones and A. Stone. Workshop on Socio-Behavioural Aspects of Microbicide Trials for HIV Prevention, New Delhi, 5–6 December.

Rettie, R., Robinson, H., Radke, A. and Ye, X. (2007) The use of CAQDAS in the UK market research industry. Paper presented at the CAQDAS 07 Conference: Advances in Qualitative Computing, Royal Holloway, University of London, London, 18–20 April.

Richards, Laura (2005) Conducting a consultation for the Audit Commission. Internal paper.

Richards, Laura (2006) Using NVIVO in the Audit Commission. Presentation at a lunchtime seminar at the Audit Commission.

Richards, Lyn (1999) *Using NVivo in Qualitative Research*. Victoria, Australia: Qualitative Solutions and Research, Pty. Ltd.

Richards, Lyn (2004) Validity and reliability? Yes! Doing it in software. Paper presented at the 5th International Conference on Strategies in Qualitative Research: Using QSR NVivo and NUD*IST, University of Durham, Durham, UK, September.

Richards, Lyn (2005) *Handling Qualitative Data*. Thousand Oaks, CA: Sage Publications.

Richards, Lyn (2006) Farewell to the Lone Ranger? What happened to qualitative = small? Paper presented at the Strategies in Qualitative Research Conference, University of Durham, Durham, UK, 13–15 September.

Richards, T. (2004) Not just a pretty node system: what node hierarchies are really all about. Paper presented at the 5th International Conference on Strategies in Qualitative Research: Using QSR NVivo and NUD*IST, University of Durham, Durham, UK, September.

Ritchie, J. and Lewis, J. (eds.) (2003) *Qualitative Research Practice*. London: Sage Publications.

Rutherford, M. and Gallo-Cruz, S. (2007) Great expectations: the emotional production and consumption of midwife-assisted birth experiences. Unpublished manuscript.

Rutherford, M. and Gallo-Cruz, S. (forthcoming) Selling the ideal birth: rationalization and re-enchantment in the marketing of maternity care, in S. Chambre and M. Goldner (eds.) *Patients, Consumers and Civil Society: Advances in Medical Sociology* (vol. 10). Bingley: Emerald.

Siccama, C. (2006) Work activities of professionals who occupy the role of faculty support staff in online education programs. Doctoral dissertation, University of Massachusetts Lowell.

Sin, C. H. (2006) Using QDAS in the production of policy evidence by non-researchers: Strengths, pitfalls, implications for consumers of research. Paper presented at Strategies in Qualitative Research Conference, University of Durham, Durham, 13–15 September.

Strike, K., Anderson, M., Curren, R., van Geel, T., Pritchard, I. and Robertson, E. (2002) *Ethical standards of the American Educational Research Association: Cases and commentary*. Washington, DC: American Educational Research Association.

Swales, J. (1990) *Genre Analysis: English in Academic and Research Settings*. New York: University of Cambridge Press.

Vince, J. and Sweetman, R. (2006) Managing large scale qualitative research: two case studies. Paper presented at the Conference on Words instead of Numbers: The Status of Software in the Qualitative Research World, Association for Survey Computing, Imperial College London, 29 September.

Walkowski, J. and Nordgren, J. (2007) Qualitative research analysis tools: a shopper's guide. Unpublished transcript of an online bulletin board discussion, QRCA.

Wasser, J. and Bresler, L. (1996) The interpretive zone: conceptualizing collaboration among teams of qualitative researchers. *Educational Researcher*, 26(4), 5–15.

Wasserman, S. and Faust, K. (1999) *Social Network Analysis: Methods and Applications*. New York: Cambridge University Press.

Index

Related books from Open University Press

Purchase from www.openup.co.uk or order through your local bookseller

QUALITATIVE DATA ANALYSIS
EXPLORATIONS WITH NVivo

Graham R. Gibbs

A welcome step in the advance of qualitative methods, this text integrates software at every stage of a thorough introduction to approaches and techniques. With clear examples, each step in NVivo is clearly described and thoughtfully explained in the context of what is being done and how it supports qualitative inquiry.

> Professor Lyn Richards, Director, QSR

...a very detailed, clearly expressed and structured text which will be of immense help to anyone wanting to use NVivo for a research project.

> Professor Colin Robson, author of *Real World Research*

- How can qualitative analysis of textual data be undertaken?
- How can the core procedures of qualitative analysis be followed using computer software such as NVivo?
- How can the extra tools NVivo offers the analyst be used to support and improve qualitative analysis?

Qualitative Data Analysis introduces readers to key approaches in qualitative analysis, demonstrating in each case how to carry them out using NVivo. NVivo is a new, powerful computer package from QSR, the developers of NUD+IST. It provides the researcher with an extensive range of tools and the book shows clearly how each can be used to support standard qualitative analysis techniques such as coding, theory building, theory testing, cross-sectional analysis, modelling and writing. The book demonstrates how different styles of analysis, such as grounded theory and narrative, rhetorical and structured approaches, can be undertaken using NVivo. In most cases, the analysis is illustrated using documents from a single data set. There are copious figures, tables, guides and hints for good practice. The result is an invaluable text for undergraduates and an essential reference for postgraduates and researchers needing to learn both qualitative analysis techniques and the use of software such as NVivo.

Contents

Series editor's foreword – Acknowledgements – List of tables – List of step-by-step guides – Introduction – What is qualitative analysis? – Getting started with NVivo – Data preparation – Coding – Memos and attributes – Searching for text – Developing an analytic scheme – Three analytic styles – Visualizing the data – Communicating – Glossary – References – Index.

2002   224pp
978–0–335–20084–9 (Paperback)

ESSENTIALS OF SOCIAL RESEARCH

Linda Kalof, Amy Dan and Thomas Dietz

Essentials of Social Research is a well-balanced and engaging treatment of the many facets of doing research. Capturing a trend toward the use of multiple methods and perspectives, the authors weave theoretical insights with interesting findings and applications on a variety of topics. Their use of common examples from one chapter to the next is an innovative way of conveying the value of a multi-method approach to inquiry. And, they let us in on a secret shared by many researchers, which is that research is fun and we enjoy doing it. There is something here for students across the spectrum of the social and behavioural sciences.

> Daniel Druckman, George Mason University and the University of Queensland, Australia

Clearly written, well-thought out and logically organized, the book is an ideal text for all undergraduate courses. . . . I particularly like the book's thoughtful discussion of the quantitative/qualitative debate. The authors are even-handed about the strengths and weaknesses of the methods, noting that each is appropriate some of the time, neither is appropriate all of the time and the best empirical research often combines the approaches. . . . Finally, the application problems at the end of each chapter are so well thought out that a faculty member need not spend hours developing the basic homework assignments and can focus on designing appropriate research project for the students.

> Helen Roland, University of California, USA

- What is meant by 'the scientific method'?
- How do I go about collecting data?
- Should I use qualitative methods, quantitative methods, or both?

Essentials of Social Research is an introductory text designed to provide straightforward, clear answers to the key questions students have about research methods. Written for those with no prior background in social research methodology, it covers the fundamentals of social research, including: types of research, reasoning and data, basic logic of quantitative and qualitative inquiry, major data collection strategies, and the assessment of research findings.

In addition, this handy guide:

- Offers ongoing exercises to illustrate the text material
- Covers basic critical thinking skills
- Emphasizes the complementary contributions of quantitative and qualitative methods
- Provides examples of research from published literature

Essentials of Social Research is key reading for all undergraduate social scientists undertaking research.

Contents
List of Figures, Tables and Boxes – Introduction – Foundations – The discourse of science – Basic logic of quantitative inquiry – Basic logic of qualitative inquiry – Collecting the data – Assessing the findings – Exercises using research from the published literature – Glossary – References – Index.

2008   240pp
978–0–335–21782–3 (Paperback)   978–0–335–21783–0 (Hardback)

SOCIAL RESEARCH 3e
ISSUES, METHODS AND PROCESS

Tim May

a welcome third edition of an already well-known and widely used text . . . truly 'user-friendly'

Network

The third edition of this tried and tested book works very well and should be extremely successful . . . its strength is that it covers all the principal areas of research in an accessible and lively style, treating each approach in relation to the philosophical and methodological debates that underpin them. It is logically organised and each chapter is well-structured . . . complex topics are clearly explained for the inexperienced reader, at the same time it contains enough of substance and food for thought for more advanced students.

John Scott, University of Essex

Praise for the previous edition:

This is the finest introduction to social research I have ever read . . . Methods are meticulously worked through from official statistics to comparative research via surveys, interviews, observation and documentary analysis . . . The writing is clear, concise and scholarly with the bibliography a delightful A to Z compendium of the best in sociology.

British Sociological Association Network

The fully revised and updated third edition of this hugely popular text incorporates the latest developments in the interdisciplinary field of social research, while retaining the style and structure that appealed to so many in the first two editions. Tim May successfully bridges the gap between theory and methods in social research, clearly illuminating these essential components for understanding the dynamics of social relations.

The book is divided into two parts, with Part I examining the issues and perspectives in social research and Part II setting out the methods and processes. Revisions and additions have been made to Part I to take account of new ways of thinking about the relationship between theory and research, and values and ethics in the research process. These take on board advances in post-empiricist thinking, as well as the relations between values, objectivity and data collection. Where necessary, recommended readings and references to studies that form the bases of discussions throughout the book have been updated. In Part II, additions have been made to the chapter on questionnaires, and elsewhere new discussions have been introduced, for example, on research on the internet, narratives, case studies and new technologies. The reader will detect many other changes, the intention of which is to aid understanding by staying up-to-date with the latest innovations in social research. The chapters follow a common structure to enable a clear appreciation of the place, process and analysis of each method, and to allow the comparison of their strengths and weaknesses in the context of discussions in Part I.

The clear writing style, chapter summaries, questions for reflection and signposts to further readings continue to make this book the ideal companion to social research for students across the social sciences. In addition, it will be recognised as an invaluable source of reference for those practising and teaching social research who wish to keep abreast of key developments in the field.

Contents

Acknowledgements – Preface to the second edition – Preface to the third edition – Introduction – Part one: Issues in social research – Perspectives on social scientific research – Social theory and social research – Values and ethics in the research process – Part two: Methods of social research – Official statistics: topic and resource – Social surveys: design to analysis – Interviewing: methods and process – Participant observation: perspectives and practice – Documentary research: excavations and evidence – Comparative research: potential and problems – Bibliography – Author index – Subject index.

2001   254pp
978–0–335–20612–4 (Paperback)